The Evolution of the British Party System 1885–1940

Pearson Education

We work with leading authors to develop the
strongest educational materials in history,
bringing cutting-edge thinking and best learning
practice to a global market.

Under a range of well-known imprints, including
Longman, we craft high-quality
print and electronic publications which help
readers to understand and apply their content,
whether studying or at work.

To find out about the complete range of our
publishing please visit us on the World Wide Web at:
www.pearsoneduc.com

The Evolution of the British Party System1885–1940

Robert Self
London Guildhall University

An imprint of **Pearson Education**

Harlow, England · London · New York · Reading, Massachusetts · San Francisco · Toronto · Don Mills, Ontario · Sydney
Tokyo · Singapore · Hong Kong · Seoul · Taipei · Cape Town · Madrid · Mexico City · Amsterdam · Munich · Paris · Milan

Pearson Education Limited
Head Office
Edinburgh Gate
Harlow
Essex CM20 2JE
England

and Associated Companies throughout the world

Visit us on the World Wide Web at:
www.pearsoneduc.com

———————————————

First published 2000

© Pearson Education Limited 2000

The right of Robert Self to be identified as author of
this work has been asserted by him in accordance with
the Copyright, Designs and Patents Act 1988.

ISBN 0 582 38176 2 PPR
ISBN 0 582 38177 0 CSD

British Library Cataloguing in Publication Data
A CIP catalogue record for this book can be obtained from the British Library.

10 9 8 7 6 5 4 3 2 1
05 04 03 02 01 00

Typeset by 7 in 11/12pt Garamond

Transferred to digital printing 2005

Printed and bound by Antony Rowe Ltd, Eastbourne

For Katie – as always

Contents

Contents

Acknowledgements

A large number of debts are incurred in the preparation of a volume of this sort. First, a study of this breadth would never be possible without the specialist monographs and articles of the many historians whose work is, I hope, fully acknowledged in the Notes and References. Secondly, I am extremely grateful to a variety of librarians, archivists and the owners of manuscript collections which I have consulted and which have, whether directly or indirectly, helped shape the judgements in this volume. For access and/or permission to quote from material in privately owned collections I am obliged to Viscount Addison, Earl Baldwin of Bewdley, the Syndics of Cambridge University Library, the Master and Fellows of Churchill College, Cambridge, the Earl of Halifax, Vice-Admiral Sir Ian Hogg, Mrs A. Stacey and the Trustees of the Bridgeman family archive and the Keeper of the Public Records. I have also consulted and quoted from collections held by a number of other libraries and institutions, namely Birmingham University Library, the Birmingham Central Library, the Borthwick Institute of Historical Research, the British Library, the Bodleian Library, Cambridge University Library, the House of Lords Record Office, Newcastle University Library, the Public Record Office and the Scottish Record Office. I apologise to any copyright holder whom I have inadvertently failed to contact or trace. Finally, debts of a more personal kind also exist. I am particularly grateful to Professor Iwan Morgan, Dr Justin Fisher and Robert Walsha for their advice, comments and useful pieces of information. I also owe much to my friend and former colleague Don Minter who so regularly persuaded me that there was a niche for such a book. The usual disclaimers apply about all remaining errors of fact, analysis and interpretation. Above all, however, I am (as always) deeply grateful to Katie without whom this work would never have seen the light of day.

Chapter one

Introduction

'The party tie is the strongest sentiment in this country – stronger than patriotism or even self-interest', Joseph Chamberlain told Lord Randolph Churchill in December 1886.[1] In saying this Chamberlain was not thinking exclusively of the high political world of Westminster. 'No one', he wrote to his son in January 1895, 'who has not worked among the electors can be aware of how strong are old prejudices in connection with party names and colours and badges. A man may be a good Unionist at heart, and yet nothing can persuade him to vote "blue" or give support to a "Tory" candidate.'[2] Party was central to the new mass politics after 1885 because it made electoral choice comprehensible. As Graham Wallas noted in *Human Nature in Politics* in 1908, 'A party is primarily a name, which, like other names, calls up when it is heard or seen, an "image".'[3] Many were undoubtedly disappointed and alarmed by this sort of 'non-rational' basis for electoral behaviour in the emerging new democracy, but few were prepared to deny the intensity of the tribalistic collective passions that such labels and images were capable of arousing. Before the Great War, the novelist Robert Tressell noted in *The Ragged Trousered Philanthropists*, that in Edwardian elections

> people forgot all about unemployment and starvation, and became enthusiastic about 'Grand Old Flags' ... all that mattered was to score off their hated 'enemies' their fellow countrymen the Tories, and carry the grand old flag to victory. The fact that they had carried the flag to victory so often in the past without obtaining any of the spoils, did not seem to dampen their ardour in the least.[4]

In his classic work on *Popular Government* in 1885, Sir Henry Maine attributed this fierce partisanship more to 'a survival of the primitive combativeness of mankind than a consequence of conscious intellectual differences'. Twenty years later, Sidney Lowe also noted in similarly militaristic terms the uncompromising fashion in which party attachments were placed at the centre of British political life.

> The parties ... instead of being two groups of believers endeavouring to propagate their own particular faith, are two armies of active combatants, each desiring above all things to follow its own chosen champion to victory. Not the defeat of a principle, but the defeat of a leader and his 'side' is the really mortifying thing.[5]

The party sentiment which mattered so much to late Victorians and Edwardians continued to dominate British political life for much of the twentieth century. Yet despite Coke's frequently repeated assertion that the British party system has existed 'since time immemorial',[6] the development of parties and the party system in Britain into a recognisably modern form has long been the subject of intense controversy among historians. Unfortunately, the search for origins has been complicated by the difficulty of establishing aspects of continuity and change within the broad contours of an evolving system of political competition. As Frank O'Gorman laments, 'Most historians have detected significant continuities before and after Reform [in 1832]. The historian of party is positively embarrassed with them.'[7] Although some recent studies suggest that electoral politics in Hanoverian England were far more open, independent and participatory than previously assumed, not all revisionist historians are prepared to endorse the far bolder claim that 'the political, religious, and social cleavages that were to become so obvious in later nineteenth-century England were already evident among portions of the populace by the end of the eighteenth-century'.[8] Similarly, at a more general level, some historians have contended that the British party system 'has a continuous history since the reign of Charles II, however tenuous at times, and has its roots in the earlier struggle between Cavaliers and Parliamentarians'. According to such a view, by 1679 the use of the Whig and Tory labels had gained national political currency and corresponded with real party divisions in Parliament, while the elections of 1679–81 were the first to be fought on party lines. Yet as Bulmer-Thomas also warns, it is important 'not to think of the parties of the seventeenth century in modern terms. They were no more than loose groupings of men who found it convenient to work together in Parliament. They had little in the way of organisation ... There were almost as many Tory opinions as there were Tories, and Whig opinions as there were Whigs.'[9] Qualifications such as these have prompted many other historians to contend that the notion of party can really only be traced back to the 1780s and 1790s and that some form of two-party alignment had its roots in the two decades after the Napoleonic Wars.[10]

Yet although it can scarcely be denied that organised parties have a long history, there can be relatively little dispute that the roots of the modern British party system and recognisably modern parties can be traced back to the critical events of the mid-1880s, as a direct response to the challenge of the new mass politics inaugurated by developments in electoral law which took place after 1867 and culminated in the reforms of 1883–5. In many respects, the general election of 1880 represented a significant watershed in this development insofar as 'it was the first general election fought on a national level; it was the last to be disgraced by widespread corrupt practices'.[11] The emergence of a mass electorate and stricter methods of controlling corruption and coercion demanded the adoption of new forms of party structure and novel methods of electoral mobilisation in order to enable party leaders to appeal directly to the people for a mandate founded on popular legitimacy. As discussed in Chapter 3, most of these forms and structures of modern party organisation date from this period rather than before the Second Reform Act in 1867. After 1880, the decline in the number of uncontested seats also meant that for the first time general elections were truly general and national in scope and fought by more cohesive parties unified by labels which had lost the 'softness' of earlier generations.[12] Moreover, an increasingly party-orientated electorate responded to these appeals by casting their votes on the basis of new forms of party identification as local loyalties and confessional alignments were gradually superseded by class voting – albeit that neither the speed nor regional uniformity of this process should be exaggerated.[13] Equally significantly, these electoral and organisational repercussions of mass politics had equally profound implications for the broader constitutional context within which this competition took place, as the prevailing mid-century doctrine of 'parliamentary government' gave way to a distinctly twentieth century concept of 'party government'.[14]

The mid-1880s also inaugurated a new era of party alignments built around redefined doctrinal cleavages. Although academic commentators and practising politicians have traditionally celebrated the essential 'naturalness' of the two-party system as a permanent feature of British political life,[15] it was only after 1885 that the classic conditions for its existence emerged as the two main parties increasingly became aggregative agencies seeking to maximise the breadth of their electoral base by amalgamating as many groups, interests and demands as possible.[16] The Irish Home Rule crisis in 1886 was central to this transformation. Although initially enfeebled by schism and defection, over the next twenty years, a purged and radicalised Liberal party constructed a Progressive Alliance which harnessed Irish Nationalists and the newly established Labour party in order to dominate Edwardian politics. For their Tory opponents, the mid-1880s were a period of equally radical realignment. The death of Disraeli in 1881 and the succession of Lord Salisbury marked a distinct watershed between half a century of political failure and impotence as an irrelevant 'Country party' and the beginning of two decades of remarkable electoral ascendancy. Supported by dissentient Liberal opponents of Home Rule, the new Unionist alliance under Salisbury rapidly emerged as the defender of the social order and all forms of property against Gladstonian Radicals, socialists, confiscatory taxation and the encroachment of the State. In the wings, the 1880s also witnessed an upsurge of rural radicalism, the 'socialist revival' and the growth of a 'New Unionism' more receptive to socialist ideas and leadership. In 1884, both the moderate Fabian Society and the avowedly Marxian Social Democratic Federation were established to campaign for their own particular brands of socialism. Four years later Keir Hardie established the Scottish Labour Party and the Independent Labour Party followed in 1893, at a time when a ferocious employer counter-offensive spurred by economic depression began to convert older craft unions to the cause of independent labour representation. From these modest beginnings the Labour party grew eventually to supersede the Liberals and to form its first government in 1924, less than a quarter of a century after its birth.

These developments coincided with an equally fundamental transformation of the political agenda. After 1880 a new awareness of the problems of poverty caused by the malfunction of the market and the maldistribution of mid-

Victorian prosperity was generated by social investigators like Booth and Rowntree and by the publication of more sensational pamphlets like Andrew Mearn's *The Bitter Cry of Outcast London* (1883). The Third Reform Act had massive implications for the impact of this 'discovery'. As Sidney Webb warned the Royal Commission on the Aged Poor in the early 1890s, the newly enfranchised working man would soon come to adopt a more instrumental view of his voting rights as a means, not to determine the party allegiance of the next Ambassador in Paris or even to decide questions of war and peace, but rather to alter 'the conditions under which they live and work': a hard-headed pragmatism which opened the way for a new style of class politics.[17] 'New Liberal' (and later Labour) responses to these pressures prompted the acceptance of a far broader definition of the role and responsibilities of the collectivist State and signalled a qualitative change in the substance of British politics. Thereafter, a bitterly contested divide over social and fiscal politics separated redistributive collectivist Social Radicals from a Unionist party committed to the defence of wealth, property and versions of individualism. On these foundations, the central defining party cleavage was laid for most of the next century.

Each of these developments has stimulated a vast, complex and often truly intimidating corpus of scholarly research. Over many of the most pivotal issues, such as the emergence of class politics, the rise of Labour, the decline of the Liberals, the impact of war, the franchise factor and ideology, fiercely contested controversies continue to rage unabated. Although students of this period are fortunate in having access to a variety of excellent histories of each of the major parties, the purpose of this slim volume is to provide a broader overview of this crucial period in the evolution of the modern British party system as a whole. In particular, by exploring the dynamic interaction of the various forces of franchise, class consciousness, doctrine and organisation, it attempts to explain the rapidly changing fortunes of the parties as they struggled to address the challenges of collectivism, mass democracy, war and economic uncertainty. Above all, in the limited space available, it seeks to go beyond a simple narrative of events to provide some insight and contribution to the many controversies and debates which surround this truly pivotal period in British political development.

Notes and references ————————————————————————

The place of publication is London unless otherwise stated.

1 G.R. Searle, *Country Before Party: Coalition and the Idea of 'National Government' in Modern Britain, 1885–1987* (1995), p. 1.

2 Peter Fraser, *Joseph Chamberlain* (1966), pp. 166–7.

3 Graham Wallas, *Human Nature in Politics* (1908), p. 84.

4 Tressell quoted P.F. Clarke, *Lancashire and the New Liberalism* (Cambridge, 1971), p. 15.

5 S. Lowe, *The Governance of England* (1904), pp. 116, 128.

6 Alan Beattie, *English Party Politics* 2 vols (1970), I, p. 295.

7 Frank O'Gorman, *The Emergence of the Two-Party System, 1760–1832* (1982),

p. 119. N. Gash, *Politics in the Age of Peel: A Study in the Technique of Parliamentary Representation, 1830–1850* 2nd edn (Hassocks, 1977), pp. x, xviii.

8 John A. Phillips, *Electoral Behaviour in Unreformed England: Plumpers, Splitters and Straights* (Princeton, New Jersey, 1982), p. 310. For a more sceptical view see Frank O'Gorman, *Voters, Patrons and Parties: The Unreformed Electoral System in Hanoverian England, 1734–1832* (Oxford, 1989), p. 390 which claims that 'it is hard to see more than a few distant anticipations of the origins of the social cleavages of the Victorian era within the unreformed system'. For a more general critique see Miles Taylor, 'Interests, parties and the state: the urban electorate in England, *c.*1820–72', in Jon Lawrence and Miles Taylor, eds, *Party, State and Society: Electoral Behaviour in Britain since 1820* (Aldershot, 1997), pp. 50–78.

9 I. Bulmer-Thomas, *The Growth of the British Party System* 2 vols (1967), I, pp. 3–4. Also Sir Ivor Jennings, *Party Politics, vol II The Growth of Parties* (Cambridge, 1961), pp. 1–52.

10 O'Gorman, *The Emergence of the Two-Party System*, pp. 93–101, 121; Brian Hill, *The Early Parties and Politics in Britain, 1688–1832* (1996), p. 235 and his *British Parliamentary Parties, 1742–1832: From the Fall of Walpole to the First Reform Act* (1985); Brian Harrison, *The Transformation of British Politics 1860–1995* (Oxford, 1996), p. 35.

11 Cornelius O'Leary, *The Elimination of Corrupt Practices in British Elections, 1868–1911* (Oxford, 1962), p. 158; Trevor Lloyd, *The General Election of 1880* (1968), p. 133.

12 J.P.D. Dunbabin, 'Parliamentary elections in Great Britain, 1868-1900: a psephological note', *English Historical Review* 81 (1966), p. 85; M. Pugh, *The Making of Modern British Politics, 1867–1939* 2nd edn (Oxford, 1993), pp. 3–4.

13 G.W. Cox, 'The development of a party-orientated electorate in England, 1832–1918', *British Journal of Political Science* 16 (1986), pp. 187–216; Kenneth D. Wald, 'Class and the vote before the First World War', *Journal of Political Science* 8 (1978), pp. 441–57 and *Crosses on the Ballot: Patterns of British Voter Alignment since 1885* (Princeton, New Jersey, 1983); Henry Pelling, *Social Geography of British Elections, 1885–1910* (1967), p. 416.

14 Angus Hawkins, ' "Parliamentary government" and Victorian political parties, *c.*1830–*c.*1880', *English Historical Review* 104 (1989), pp. 638–69 and *British Party Politics, 1852–1886* (1998), ch. 8.

15 Lowe, *The Governance of England*, p. 126; L.S. Amery, *Thoughts on the Constitution* (Oxford, 1947), pp. 16–17; Reginald Bassett, *The Essentials of Parliamentary Democracy* (1935), ch. 2.

16 G. Sartori, *Parties and Party Systems: A Framework for Analysis* (Cambridge, 1976), pp. 185–92.

17 Bentley B. Gilbert, *British Social Policy 1914–1939* (1970), p. 305. See also Peter Clarke, 'Electoral sociology in modern Britain', *History* 57 (1972), p. 49.

Chapter two

Development of the electoral system before 1914

During the nineteenth century, the entire structure of electoral and party politics in Britain experienced an extraordinary process of transformation. Although recent research suggests that electoral politics in Unreformed England were significantly more 'partisan, participatory and popular' than has traditionally been accepted,[1] the fact remains that before 1832 elections were still conducted within the structural confines of an extremely restricted franchise and an outmoded system of constituency representation. The half century after the Great Reform Act, however, witnessed a painfully slow, but incremental, transition towards a far more participatory form of genuinely popular government. Although it is tempting to focus on the three great steps of reform in 1832, 1867 and 1884, such landmarks need to be seen against a far broader background of constituency redistribution and halting efforts to control undue influence, corruption and intimidation. The climax of this process of evolution arrived in 1885 when the principle of male suffrage was more or less established, the worst anomalies in the distribution of seats had been removed and electoral corruption had largely been curbed. Yet for all that, the scale of this 'democratic' transformation should not be exaggerated. On the eve of the Great War, only 29.7 per cent of the total adult population of the United Kingdom had the vote. Even among adult men, the proportion theoretically eligible to vote rose from around 20 per cent in the 1860s, to 36 per cent after 1867, peaking at 63–66 per cent after 1884. Although these developments were crucially important, therefore, the exclusion of all women and some two out of five men suggests that the transition to full democracy was still far from complete by 1914.

2.1 The Franchise and Redistribution Acts, 1884–1885

Although the Great Reform Act of 1832 increased the electorate from 516,000 to 813,000 (within a population of 24,000,000) and took the first steps towards the purification of the system by removing some bogus communities and endowing new centres of population with representation, it scarcely constituted a revolution. Rather, as many contemporaries recognised, its importance lay less in its immediate effects than the ultimate potentialities of its principles for future reform. Yet ironically, for the architects of this measure, the principal objective had been to establish a permanent settlement

6

of the issue in order to save the aristocratic constitution by making it more effective. This inevitably necessitated the amelioration of the legitimate grievances of unrepresented groups by bringing them within a cautiously modified system. Throughout, Lord Grey had sought a settlement which offered 'sure ground for resistance to further innovation'. Lord John Russell, the principal framer of the legislation, had earned the nickname 'Finality Jack' for insisting upon precisely this point.[2] Yet opponents of reform were less confident of such an outcome. As Peel explained his opposition to the Bill, 'I was unwilling to open a door which I saw no prospect of being able to close.'[3] Such scepticism proved to be well founded and by 1848 'Finality Jack' himself had come to the conclusion that his initial position was untenable. After the failure of a Liberal measure in 1866, Disraeli executed a complete volte-face over reform in 1867 with the promise of an immediate Bill which eventually went far beyond anything contemplated by the Liberals.

Whatever Disraeli's motivations, contemporaries were apt to talk in awed tones of the Second Reform Act as something akin to 'shooting Niagara' when it expanded the electorate from 1,400,000 to 2,520,000. This enlargement was most impressive in the boroughs where the franchise was extended to all settled householders and £10 lodgers. In the counties, the qualification was reduced to encompass £12 ratepayers and £5 copyholders and leaseholders. Although this more restrictive franchise meant that nearly all landowners, tenant farmers, middle class householders and even the better class of village tradesmen had the vote, the overall impact of 1867 was to increase still further the traditional inequality between borough and county representation. After 1867, the ratio of electors to population in England and Wales was one in fourteen in the counties but only one in seven in the boroughs. There could be no hope of 'finality' while such a massive discrepancy persisted. By 1877, the Liberals were formally committed to the equalisation of the franchise and in 1884 they finally legislated to redeem their election pledge. The 1867 borough qualification was thus transferred to the counties with no abrogation of existing qualifications. On this basis, the Franchise Bill aroused little controversy and passed in the autumn with only slight modification. Attempts to introduce amendments to exclude town freeholders from voting in the counties, to enfranchise propertied women and to reform university representation, plural voting and ancient qualifications were all swept aside by Gladstone's adamant determination to avoid overloading the Bill with issues which could safely be left until the future. In so doing, a far closer approach to democracy was deferred. Yet despite Gladstone's caution, after 1884 some 5,708,000 adult males were entitled to vote, around two-thirds of the total male population. Although full democracy would have to wait until after the Great War, the Franchise Act of 1884 was truly the culmination of the process begun in 1832. In 1832 the occupation franchise had first emerged in both the counties and boroughs while the standard of value was different. In 1867 the standard of value was effectively abolished in the boroughs and lowered in the counties. In 1884 the franchise in the UK as a whole had been equalised to the occupation of a house.[4]

Far more controversy surrounded the Redistribution Act of 1885 which the Conservatives insisted should accompany the household franchise. By the 1880s the case for some form of redistribution was accepted by both parties. The disparities between counties and boroughs and between the representation of agriculture and industry was always great and in many ways 1867 had aggravated these inequalities. In England and Wales the ratio of MPs to population was one to 73,203 in the counties, but only one to 41,365 in the boroughs; in the industrial county divisions of the North West the ratio was one to 150,000 while in the rural boroughs of the South West only one to 12,000. As a result, by the mid-1880s, a quarter of the electorate were represented by two-thirds of the MPs.[5] Such manifest injustices provided a potent stimulus to those demanding not only the assimilation of franchise qualifications, but also the equalisation of the value of each vote cast. In the event, Gladstone accepted the principle of redistribution (as he had since 1872), but adopted a distinctly conservative posture towards the practice. In contrast, Lord Salisbury, the Conservative leader, emerged as the real radical. Already gravely alarmed by fears of Tory vulnerability within an electorate encompassing village artisans, miners, agricultural labourers and tenant farmers, for Salisbury a bold scheme of redistribution was essential to protect their agricultural county support-base against the burgeoning forces of democracy and the urban voter. Moreover, as the small over-represented boroughs had shown themselves to be less loyal to the Conservative cause than anticipated, Tories had little to lose from their radical redistribution. In a series of meetings at Downing Street between 19 and 27 November 1884, Salisbury employed his considerable statistical skills to achieve a remarkable personal triumph. Having largely dictated the terms of redistribution in a form most favourable to his party, Salisbury helped lay the foundations for Conservative electoral hegemony for the next two decades.[6]

The Redistribution Act of 1885 brought about the effective demise of the double-member constituency. Although the commonest form of representation in England since the thirteenth century, after 1885 only twenty-three remained in existence. In their place, Salisbury established the single-member constituency as the norm; polling districts which were designed to create more socially homogeneous units through boundaries reflecting 'the pursuits of the people'. Having adopted a population benchmark of 50,000 as the basis for redistribution, seventy-two boroughs (returning seventy-nine members) with a population below 15,000 were disenfranchised and absorbed into the counties while thirty-six double-member constituencies with between 15,000 and 50,000 inhabitants lost one of their MPs. Together with those seats disenfranchised for corruption, a few minor mergers and adjustments, and a slight enlargement in the size of the House of Commons, some 182 seats were available for distribution. Of these, 142 were given to England and Wales, 14 to Scotland and 21 to Ireland. Despite the scale of the redistribution and the acceptance of the principle that representation should be directly related to population, this did not create a situation of numerical equality in constituency size or the value of each vote. Nor was it ever intended that it should. Indeed, as the driving force behind redistribution, Salisbury had prevailed in his view that the Burkean notion of 'interests' should have a central role in the identification of socially homogeneous constituencies in order to separate agriculture from industry and middle class Conservative suburbs from working class areas.[7] Thus, many small boroughs like Windsor, Durham, and Salisbury, each with around 3,000 electors, continued to return their own member while at the other end of the spectrum, the Romford division of Essex had 61,000 electors. Rural constituencies also retained their substantial advantage in both county and borough representation. Similarly, despite an unsuccessful Conservative effort to reduce the number of Irish seats in 1905, Ireland remained grossly over-represented with 103 members representing an average of 6,700 electors compared with 13,000 in England.[8] Moreover, in the absence of any machinery for periodic redistribution, these inequalities increased as population swarmed into areas of new industry and suburbia. Thus, while in 1885 no seat in the new dispensation contained over 100,000 inhabitants, in 1901 there were fifty and by 1911 this had risen to a hundred. By this stage, a third of all seats diverged from the average by more than 50 per cent.[9]

Yet for all its deficiencies, it would be wrong to underestimate the impact of 1885. The modern system of plurality (first-past-the-post) voting in single-member constituencies dates from 1884–5, as does the broad principle of numerically equal polling districts, although the machinery to achieve it would not be created until 1944. Redistribution largely destroyed both the double-member seats and the smallest boroughs. While far from perfect, the ratio of seats to population also became far more uniform throughout the county divisions while the bias towards agriculture and the counties of the southern seaboard was substantially reduced. Moreover, while malapportionment remained a significant problem throughout the following century, the largest electorate was now only eight times the size of the smallest rather than the 250 times which had prevailed before 1885.[10] Above all, very few existing constituencies were left undisturbed by redistribution which shifted over a million borough voters into the counties (to join two million new county voters) and 1,200,000 county voters into newly created urban seats.[11] In this new socially more homogeneous middle class suburbia, the forces of 'Villa Toryism' would provide the Conservatives with one of their most secure electoral foundations safely insulated from the prospect of being swamped by urban Radicals. At the same time, the emphasis upon 'the pursuits of the people' in the drawing of new boundaries further assisted the Conservatives by separating agriculture from mining and urban areas to maintain landowner influence. In the longer term, this effort to secure Tory interests by creating socially homogeneous single-member constituencies provided a substantial impetus for the emergence of class voting. Ironically, however, it was the anachronistic survival of a few double-member seats which provided the opportunity for Labour's initial breakthrough before 1914 by allowing Liberals and Labour to run in harness against the Tories, just as Whigs and Radicals had for much of the preceding century.

2.2 The elimination of corruption and intimidation

Although franchise reform was important, equally crucial measures were designed to eliminate the near endemic corruption and intimidation which existed within the electoral system. Far from reducing the level of bribery and the cost of elections as desired, electoral corruption actually increased as a direct result of the 1832 Reform Act. One reason for this phenomenon was quite simply that the increased electorate and reduction in the scope for traditional control through 'rotten' and 'pocket' boroughs, produced more contested elections and hence the need for more illicit money spread over a greater number of importunate electors. Some boroughs like Totnes, St Albans and Sudbury were already notoriously venal before 1832 and old habits persisted. Yet despite some optimism that the new £10 householders would prove to be more stalwart, independent and honest, in reality they soon revealed themselves to be just as venal as their predecessors in their desire to share in the economic spoils which attended the possession of the vote. As Gash notes, 'The franchise was still a financial asset; and even for the non-voter elections meant more trade, free drinks and easy money.'[12]

Corruption was a many-headed hydra and the forms it assumed were limited only by local custom and ingenuity. In county elections, such inducements tended to take the form of traditional 'treating' at a local tavern, but this was regarded more as a customary benevolence and a compensation for the inconvenience of voting than it was offered or accepted as a bribe. In the boroughs, however, the picture was less edifying. Treating at the hands of 'fuddlers' was often on such a scale as to have devastating effects on the moral and physical health of the borough. More flagrant forms of bribery also flourished in a variety of ingenious forms. Direct financial inducements could be offered in rents or loans on favourable terms, or the payment of the rate arrears necessary to qualify as an elector. Payment of travel expenses served the same purpose, as did the widespread use of fraudulent forms of employment on election 'committees' or as canvassers where the only real labour was to drink free ale. Despite the ingenuity of such means, the preferred and most convenient form of corruption for both sides was straightforward bribery. Even in the 1830s it was not abnormal for a borough contest to cost each side between £2,000 and £5,000. Sometimes, such costs could be truly phenomenal, as in Nottingham in the 1841 election where the successful candidate paid out £12,000 and the two unsuccessful candidates expended another £4,000–£5,000 on some 5,000 electors.[13] Indeed, so extensive was corruption that the 1841 election produced the so-called 'Bribery Parliament'; a title it could equally well have shared with those elected in 1847, 1868 and 1880.[14] As one of the most detailed studies of these developments concludes, it is 'almost impossible to overstate the importance or the extent of corrupt practices in England during the generation which succeeded the passing of the Reform Act of 1832'.[15]

Despite the scale of corruption and a genuine preference for purer (and thus cheaper) elections, nothing substantial was done to curb the problem until 1854. Certainly existing legislation had no effect upon the elector's belief that bribes were a traditional right. Nor did the exposure of bribery confer any stigma upon the reputation of the candidate. After minor legislative advances in 1841 and 1842, the Corrupt Practices Prevention Act of 1854 established precise definitions for an astonishingly comprehensive variety of corrupt practices and subjected both giver and recipient to severe new penalties. In order to expose such corruption, the Act also established auditors to scrutinise election expenses, but the effectiveness of this potentially important step was swiftly undermined by the incapacity of auditors and the ingenuity of agents. Nevertheless, for all its deficiencies, in a political climate in which corruption was scarcely considered a crime, the 1854 Act represented a significant advance towards the intended goal, although perhaps its main effect was to encourage the submission of fraudulent accounts and to push corruption beneath the surface rather than to eliminate it altogether.[16]

The battle against intimidation and electoral violence made even less progress during the mid-nineteenth century than the fight against electoral corruption. Like bribery, intimidation probably increased after 1832 and for similar reasons as great landowners and borough patrons were compelled to use force – or more often, the judicious threat of force – to reassert their control over traditional fiefdoms. Like corruption, intimidation took many forms from 'exclusive dealing' with shops of a particular party affiliation at one end of the spectrum, through to evictions, electoral riot, kidnap and the employment of armed gangs of 'bludgeon men' to disrupt meetings and terrorise electors into compliance or abstention. Against this background of potential and actual violence at open hustings and public voting, Gash contends that 'the traditional Eatanswill picture of early Victorian elections is in fact not so much an exaggerated as a pale and euphemistic version of the contemporary scene'.[17] Although legislators had approached the problems of intimidation and corruption from the perspective of more effective methods of discovery and punishment, for half a century Radicals had argued that the solution lay in prevention through the secret ballot. By transforming the exercise of the franchise into an essentially private act, the ballot undermined the value of both bribery and threats as a means of influencing votes. Although initially proposed in 1832, for much of the next forty years few parliamentary issues were debated with such regularity or with so little support. Yet although Gladstone and many leading ministers still preferred open voting in principle, they were compelled to act by revelations of the persistence of disorder, bribery and intimidation at the 1868 election, despite a substantial increase in the size of the electorate. In the event, acceptance of an eight-year trial for the ballot was the price Gladstone paid for Bright's membership of the Cabinet in 1868. After unsuccessful Bills in 1870 and 1871, the Ballot Act finally obtained the support of an indifferent Parliament and an unenthusiastic government in 1872.[18]

By abolishing public nomination and voting, the secret ballot significantly reduced the level of disorder, drunkenness and violence which attended the electoral process. Yet although no petitions for intimidation were lodged after

1872, the ballot did not entirely eradicate the problem. Landowners continued to extract pledges from rural tenants and labourers who were often rightly afraid that the ballot was less secret than it appeared.[19] Nevertheless, on balance, historians generally agree that the 1872 Act dealt 'a severe blow to the exercise of undue influence' and represented the triumph of the 'politics of opinion' over that of influence and bribery.[20] At a more general level, by curbing disorder and rowdiness, the ballot removed the sense of distasteful burden which had previously accompanied the exercise of the vote and conferred some new degree of respectability upon the democratic process. In contrast, the impact of the ballot upon corruption is more debatable. In many of the most notoriously corrupt boroughs it had scarcely any discernible effect at all as secrecy simply enabled voters to accept bribes from both sides, whereas in the old days of public voting men who had been bribed could be relied upon to stay bribed. Elsewhere, however, the secret ballot undoubtedly reduced both the value and need for a bribe because the outcome could not be guaranteed. Anyway, with a larger electorate voting in secret, the use of less direct forms of collective inducement such as giant picnics and entertainments became a more economical form of respectable influence which enabled the new party organisations to mobilise voters without risk of agency.

Although the number of petitions for corruption did fall somewhat after 1868, the period between the Second and Third Reform Acts witnessed the final attack upon corruption. Disraeli's Election Petitions Act of 1868 resolved problems of lax and partisan enforcement by transferring jurisdiction over election petitions from the Commons to the High Court to be tried by a judge without a jury, in the constituency to which the petition related. Although far from perfect, it was hoped that such courts would encourage the electorate to identify breaches of electoral law as crimes rather than customary practices. The Corrupt Practices (Municipal Elections) Act of 1872 went a step further by providing a special tribunal and new penalties. More important, after revelations about widespread corruption in the 1880 election, the Corrupt and Illegal Practices Act of 1883 was far more stringent than its 1854 predecessor. The 1883 Act consisted of three distinct elements: punishment, the definition of new illegal practices and the introduction of strict schedules limiting expenditure. Of the three, the latter provisions were the most important. In borough constituencies with fewer than 2,000 electors the maximum expenditure was set at £350; for those with more than 2,000 electors it was raised to £380 with £30 for each additional 1,000 electors – approximately half the average spend in the elections of 1868 and 1880.[21] In the counties, the amounts were set at £650 and £710 respectively with £60 for every 1,000 additional electors. In Ireland the figures for boroughs and counties were £200/275 and £500/540 respectively. Not only did the Act limit the maximum total expenditure, it also defined precisely the amounts to be spent on specific purposes such as candidates' personal expenses and the employment of polling agents, messengers and clerks. Moreover, to avoid the old practice of buying votes under the pretence of employing canvassers and bandsmen, none of those paid could vote. Similar restrictions were applied to the hire of committee rooms and far more stringent conditions were imposed upon the nominated election agent with regard to the timely submission of election accounts. If the candidate was found guilty, he was excluded permanently from taking his seat and if his agent was convicted then the candidate was excluded for seven years. This could also be accompanied by a year's imprisonment (with or without hard labour) and a maximum fine of £100. Similarly, electors found guilty of corruption were disqualified for seven years from the electoral register and from holding public or judicial office.[22]

Although not universally welcomed, the 1883 Act radically transformed the entire character of campaigning, improved electoral purity and dramatically reduced the expense of elections as the average cost per vote fell from 18/9d in 1880 to 3/8d by December 1910.[23] By 1906, Seymour calculated that £500 was not an unusually low cost for a contested borough and £1,000 was a high figure for a county.[24] The final and arguably most important blow to the politics of money came with the 1885 Redistribution Act which simply disenfranchised the most irredeemably corrupt boroughs. Until 1865, the sixty-four most corrupt constituencies returned no fewer than 113 of the 658 MPs in the House of Commons. In 1885, twenty-five of these constituencies were totally disenfranchised and most of the others were deprived of their second member. Of the thirty-four constituencies (with forty-six seats) which remained, perhaps half continued to be corrupt long after 1883. Certainly, electoral corruption did not come to an end in the mid-1880s. In 1908 Lowell suggested that corruption was still a factor in twenty to twenty-four (mainly southern) constituencies.[25] Although even as late as 1923 Frank Gray could be found guilty of astonishing levels of over-spending in his campaign at Oxford, by then it was an extremely rare case. Despite allegations of electoral irregularities thereafter, no MP was actually charged with submitting false election expenses until after the 1997 general election.[26]

2.3 The franchise in Britain after 1885: 'Democracy tempered by registration'

The arrival of the household franchise in the mid-1880s is often portrayed as a major watershed between the ancient electoral system and something recognisably modern in style, operation and form. Certainly this was how Joseph Chamberlain saw it in July 1885 when he proclaimed in the preface to *The Radical Programme* that under Gladstone's ministry, 'government of the people by the people ... had at last been effectively secured'. Ten years later, the Labour pioneer Keir Hardie was also pleased to acknowledge that the 'battle of the franchise' had been won and that 'today only the details remain to be adjusted'.[27] For many years historians and political scientists tended to follow where contemporaries led in accepting the 1880s as the arrival of 'democracy'. In particular, there was a tendency to argue that the Franchise Act of 1884 'went almost all the way to universal male suffrage'.[28] Yet as Neal Blewett demonstrated in his seminal contribution to this debate, the substantial difficulty with this view is that the electoral system displayed 'some remarkable contrasts with the present electoral dispensation' – not least, the fact that in 1914 only some 63.3 per cent of adult males actually appeared on the electoral register. As this figure was artificially inflated by the existence of at least half a million plural voters, only around 59 per cent of adult males enjoyed the franchise on the eve of the Great War. Far from being in the vanguard of democratic nations, therefore, in 1914 Britain had one of the most restrictive franchises in Europe and stood alone with the Kingdom of Hungary (among the countries purporting to have a representative system) in not possessing manhood suffrage. As Blewett argued, historians have 'tended to over-emphasise the achievements of the reforms of the mid-1880s and to overlook the anomalies remaining. They have magnified the triumphs of principles, minimised the reality of practice.'[29]

In part, this was because last ditch Whig efforts to salvage as much of the old electoral dispensation as possible ensured that the cause of democracy was substantially diluted by the operation of a system that was cumbersome, confused, incomplete and riddled with bizarre anomalies. Another obvious problem stemmed from the complexities created by 450 years of accumulated but uncodified legislative additions to a franchise dating back to 1429. For example, the county franchise in 1832 consisted of no fewer than 400 different kinds of title conferring the copyholder qualification, in addition to the 570 different kinds of freeholder tenure in existence since 1430. Still further additions to the franchise in 1867 and 1884, combined with the failure to abolish or codify ancient qualifications, merely aggravated the problem still further.[30] As a result, Sir Charles Dilke, the acknowledged parliamentary authority on the subject, sifted through a bewildering array of franchises to identify seventeen well-known qualifications in 1909. Three years later, Pease claimed there were eleven with at least nineteen variations. On the other hand, however, despite the proliferation of qualifications to vote, three practical limitations excluded more than two out of three adults and two out of five men from exercising the vote: the absence of a franchise qualification, the specific disqualification of certain groups and the many and various disabilities introduced by the cumbersome and capricious operation of the registration process which translated theoretical qualifications into actual votes.

In the first category, the explicit exclusion of women from the franchise was the most important factor as it accounted for half the adult population. Although spasmodically discussed in Parliament since 1832, the case was not seriously laid before the Commons until 1867 when Mill contended that justice demanded that taxation and representation went hand in hand. A long and largely non-partisan debate on female enfranchisement during 1884 was again founded on the argument that 30,000 female tenants farmed land without a vote while their male labourers possessed such a right.[31] Moreover, under the Married Women's Property Acts of 1870, 1874 and 1882, women were able to own and retain their property on marriage while many women never married at all yet still paid local taxes and managed property. For the Victorians, however, 'women' tended to be equated with married women and it was thus confidently assumed that their interests would be upheld by their enfranchised fathers, brothers and husbands in precisely the same way that agricultural labourers had once enjoyed 'virtual representation' through the vote of their landowning employer. Indeed, given suspicions of the intellectual and temperamental qualities of both groups prior to 1884, confidence in the appropriateness of 'virtual representation' was reinforced by the belief that neither group was really 'fit' to exercise the vote properly. Although the issue lapsed for some time after the 1880s, as the largest anomaly, female enfranchisement inevitably re-emerged to arouse greatest controversy in Edwardian England.[32]

Those men expressly excluded by electoral law were almost always the victims of the established belief that the vote represented a privilege and a near-sacred responsibility. As such, its exercise was intimately associated with Victorian notions of social, economic and personal 'fitness'. Only those fit by reason of their independent means, their material stake in society and educational attainment were to be trusted with the destiny of the Empire. Ultimately, this came down to a definition of 'fitness' rooted in property. Although the three great reform measures of the nineteenth century had extended the size and scope of the electorate, it remained firmly based upon property whether by occupation, ownership or (as in the servant franchise) an economic relationship with the owner of property. Of the seven key franchises, only the university franchise and the vestigial freemen's qualification were not of this sort and together they accounted for less than 1 per cent of the electorate by 1911. Yet the significance of property did not lie exclusively in its economic importance. In a classical exposition of the broader case, a Whig MP argued in September 1831, 'In a country where no public provision was made for the education of the people, it necessarily happened that a certain amount of income was the only general and practical criterion of a required degree of intelligence'. In 1832, Grey had defended the extension of the vote to the wealthy productive middle classes on precisely the grounds that they had made 'wonderful advances in both property and intelligence'.[33] Nothing in 1867 or 1884 loosened this connection between property and the vote.

In practice, the application of this test of fitness excluded a number of groups from the franchise. First, the 1832 Act had specified various categories of those deemed incapable or unworthy such as lunatics, criminals, aliens, paupers and men guilty of electoral corruption. Second, it had established the principle that those otherwise qualified to vote in borough elections should be debarred if recipients of parochial Poor Law relief within the last twelve months – a rule never applied to counties. Whether in the form of direct Poor Law assistance or indirect aid such as school meals after 1905, such reliance upon the State demonstrated a failure to meet the test of economic self-reliance and independence. In 1905 Beveridge upheld this principle on the grounds that they were 'not citizens in fact and should not be so in right' – particularly as the vote would confer electoral control over public relief agencies from which they may benefit.[34] The impact of these exclusions was substantial and accounted for perhaps 800,000 of the five million men excluded. Finally, other groups which failed to conform to any franchise requirement included domestic servants (except in Scotland), bachelor sons living with their parents without exclusive use of their own room, soldiers in barracks and the poorest class of lodgers in rooms with an unfurnished rental of under £10. Excluding sons living at home whose numbers cannot be computed, it has been estimated that these provisions directly and indirectly excluded one and a half million adult males, some 12 per cent of the total in the United Kingdom.

Beyond these exclusions, a further 3,750,000 adult males were disenfranchised by the complex web of registration law and the cumbersome operation of its machinery. The absence of an authentic register of eligible voters contributed substantially to the excessive duration, inordinate expense and violence attending elections in Unreformed England. Although the principle of separating registration from voting was incorporated into the 1832 Reform Act, the system of registration proved to be a major constraint upon the growth of the electorate from the outset. In part, this failure could be attributed to the apathy of prospective voters themselves. After both 1832 and 1867 interest soon waned among some groups of new electors for whom the 'privilege' of voting was not worth the effort. Yet in reality, the registration system itself provided a major cause of the pain and inconvenience which inclined them towards apathy. The worst abuses of the system by party election agents were partially reduced by an 1878 Act which ensured that preliminary lists in the boroughs were far more comprehensive by incorporating a broader range of relevant information: an innovation extended to the counties in 1885. Although none of these changes were fundamental in character, or resolved all of the problems, the system undoubtedly did operate far more smoothly after 1878 and perhaps resulted in a greater extension of voting rights than had actually followed the Second Reform Act of 1867.[35]

Yet the impact of the remaining difficulties and anomalies should not be underestimated. By the turn of the century, registration was still governed by the accumulation of 118 Acts of Parliament, over 650 judicial decisions and 60 different official forms.[36] It was also in the hands of local Poor Law overseers whose laxness had made them a byword for 'inefficiency, ignorance and indifference' by the 1870s.[37] The annual cycle of registration which began in April and ended on 1 January each year was a remarkably complex and inflexible process. As the occupation, household, lodger and service franchises all required possession of the qualification for twelve months prior to registration, the six-month delay between the preparation of the register in July and its coming into effect in January meant that a minimum of eighteen months was necessary to get on to the register. If during the twelve months prior to the July compilation of the list, the voter moved to another constituency or shifted from one type of franchise to another (say, from householder to lodger), the necessary continuity of qualification was lost and the vote was consequently forfeit.[38] Specific groups consistently fell victim to discrimination from this registration cycle. Although the class and party bias was not all in one direction as mobile professions like the clergy, teachers and government officials all suffered from the requirement for continuous occupation,[39] the working class were subject to particular discrimination given not just their higher mobility in order to find work and avoid high public transport costs, but also their greater likelihood of multiple occupation and their continuous uncertainty of employment.[40] In particular, the lodger qualification introduced in 1867, supposedly for the benefit of artisans, proved practically inoperative. Although by 1884 their numbers had swelled to 22,000 in England and Wales, only in Westminster did they approach even 10 per cent of the electorate.[41] Thus, although the Registration Acts made it easier to register lodgers in the boroughs in 1878 and in counties in 1885, the necessity for annual registration proved to be extremely onerous as it involved the sacrifice of a day's wages to uphold the right – an extremely high price to pay for the poorest section of the electorate. Moreover, its value was even more questionable when a move to new lodgings within the same constituency would entail the loss of that vote. Outside Scotland, where the registration system was far more efficient, therefore, Seymour concluded in 1915 that registration conditions ensured 'the lodger franchise is almost entirely an election agent's franchise, since it is hardly possible to bring one's name on the list without the aid of an agent'.[42] Registration obstacles alone were thus annually responsible for the disenfranchisement of a further million electors and discriminated particularly against the working classes. Labourers within London fell special victim to the artificial division of the metropolis into twenty-eight parliamentary boroughs which created a substantial obstacle to long-term occupation, whether as a householder or a lodger.[43]

Finally, in a system almost contrived to exclude as many from the franchise as possible, one further undemocratic element to survive well into the twentieth century was the right of men of property to vote wherever they had a qualification. Perhaps the record in this period was held by one 'reverend pluralist' with twenty-three separate votes, although in January 1910 two brothers allegedly cast 35 votes between them and as early as 1867 one man cast eighteen. Moreover, the significance of this privilege was enhanced substantially by the increasing use of the motor car in an age in which general elections were still held over several weeks. Best estimates suggest that there were between 500,000 and 600,000 plural votes in 1910 – some 7 per cent of the electorate – concentrated largely in the commercial and business seats of the major cities or in those county seats containing rapidly growing suburban extensions. In party terms, one classic contemporary study suggested that 80 per cent of plural voters were Conservatives. Yet Blewett's more recent analysis tends to confirm Seymour's impressionistic conclusion that (outside the university seats), 'the plural vote was distinctly less partisan than is often alleged', with more like a 6:4 or even 7:3 bias to the Conservatives rather than the 4:1 of contemporary estimates – albeit still sufficient to cost the Liberals between twenty-one and thirty seats in December 1910.[44] Although this view has been tentatively challenged on the basis of limited local study,[45] the fact that the Conservative defence of the practice shifted from one of principle to pragmatic resistance, while the Liberals sought unsuccessfully to abolish plural voting in 1906, 1912 and 1913, only to be defeated by the Tory majority in the House of Lords, suggests that contemporaries believed in the existence of a deeply entrenched Tory bias.

When taken together, the combined effects of disenfranchisement and the plural vote meant that the top 11 per cent of the adult male population enjoyed vastly greater electoral power than the bottom 89 per cent, while the middle class as a whole were twice as well represented on the register as they were in the adult male population.[46] On this basis, there is considerable scope for scepticism about the extent of democracy prior to 1918. In 1840, Russell confessed that too many restrictions had been introduced into the registration system in 1832 from the fear that the country would be swamped with new voters.[47] In the event, while his fears were unjustified, the precautions proved far more restrictive and durable than he could ever have anticipated. Yet whether democratic or not, these reforms provided a powerful impetus for the development of recognisably modern party structures seeking to mobilise electoral support in a distinctly twentieth century fashion.

Notes and references

The place of publication is London unless otherwise stated.

1 Frank O'Gorman, *Voters, Patrons and Parties: The Unreformed Electoral System in Hanoverian England, 1734–1832* (Oxford, 1989), pp. 2, 7–9, 368, 384–5, 393; John A. Phillips, *Electoral Behaviour in Unreformed England: Plumpers, Splitters and Straights* (Princeton, New Jersey, 1982), pp. 16, 115–23 and his *The Great Reform Bill in the Boroughs: English Electoral Behaviour, 1818–1841* (Oxford, 1992). Also Nicholas Rogers, *Whigs and Cities: Popular Politics in the Age of Walpole and Pitt* (Oxford, 1989).

2 J.P.D. Dunbabin, 'Electoral reforms and their outcome in the United Kingdom, 1865–1900', in T.R. Gourvish and Alan O'Day, eds, *Later Victorian Britain, 1867–1900* (1988), p. 95.

3 Norman Gash, *Politics in the Age of Peel: A Study in the Technique of Parliamentary Representation, 1830–1850* 2nd edn (Hassocks, 1977), pp. 7–8.

4 Charles Seymour, *Electoral Reform in England and Wales: The Development and Operation of the Parliamentary Franchise, 1832–1885* (New Haven and Oxford, 1915), pp. 287–95, 485–6.

5 Ibid., pp. 490–1.

6 Andrew Jones, *The Politics of Reform, 1884* (Cambridge, 1972), pp. 204–11; Mary Chadwick, 'The role of redistribution in the making of the Third Reform Act', *Historical Journal* 19 (1976).

7 Henry Pelling, *Social Geography of British Elections, 1885–1910* (1967), pp. 6–9.

8 Martin Pugh, *The Making of Modern British Politics, 1867–1939* 2nd edn (Oxford, 1993), pp. 9–10.

9 Neal Blewett, *The Peers, the Parties and the People: The General Elections of 1910* (1972), p. 365.

10 Dunbabin, 'Electoral reforms and their outcome', p. 108.

11 Richard Shannon, *The Age of Salisbury, 1881–1902: Unionism and Empire* (1996), p. 105.

12 Gash, *Politics in the Age of Peel*, pp. x–xi, 112.

13 Ibid., pp. 127–35.

14 Trevor Lloyd, *The General Election of 1880* (1968), pp. 109–33.

15 Seymour, *Electoral Reform*, p. 193.

16 Ibid., pp. 231, 358, 410–12.

17 Gash, *Politics in the Age of Peel*, pp. 137–53.

18 Bruce L. Kinzer, *The Ballot Question in Nineteenth Century English Politics* (New York and London, 1982), pp. 1, 244–5.

19 Lloyd, *General Election of 1880*, p. 131; Blewett, *Peers*, p. 375; P.F. Clarke, *Lancashire and the New Liberalism* (Cambridge, 1971), p. 251.

20 Kinzer, *Ballot Question*, p. 245; T.J. Nossiter, *Influence, Opinion and Political Idioms in Reformed England: Case Studies from the North East, 1832–1874* (Hassocks, 1975), p. 7.

21 H.J. Hanham, *Elections and Party Management: Politics in the Time of Disraeli and Gladstone* 2nd edn (Hassocks, 1978), pp. 251, 268, 274–5.

22 Cornelius O'Leary, *The Elimination of Corrupt Practices in British Elections, 1868–1911* (Oxford, 1962), ch. 6.

23 Ibid., pp. 206–7, 238; W.B. Gwyn, *Democracy and the Cost of Politics in Britain* (1962), p. 55.

24 Seymour, *Electoral Reform*, p. 448.

25 Hanham, *Elections and Party Management*, pp. 281–3; A.L. Lowell, *The Government of England* 2 vols (1908), I, p. 238.

26 *The Times*, 24 April 1998. Fiona Jones, Labour MP for Newark.

27 H.C.G. Matthew, R.I. McKibbin and J.A. Kay, 'The franchise factor in the rise of the Labour Party', *English Historical Review* 91 (1976), pp. 724–5.

28 D.E. Butler, *The Electoral System in Britain 1918–1951* (Oxford, 1953), p. 5.

29 Neal Blewett, 'The franchise in the United Kingdom, 1885–1918', *Past and Present* 32 (1965), pp. 27, 31.

30 Seymour, *Electoral Reform*, pp. 17–18, 24–35, 85–7, 478–9.

31 Ibid., p. 477.

32 See S.S. Holton, *Feminism and Democracy: Women's Suffrage and Reform Politics in Britain, 1900–1918* (Cambridge, 1986); M. Pugh, *Electoral Reform in War and Peace, 1906–18* (1978), chs 3, 10. Although excluded from the parliamentary franchise, the Municipal Corporations (Franchise) Act of 1869 enabled some women to vote in local government elections.

33 Gash, *Politics in the Age of Peel*, pp. 14, 18–19.

34 H.V. Emy, *Liberals, Radicals and Social Politics, 1892–1914* (Cambridge, 1973), pp. 160–1.

35 Seymour, *Electoral Reform*, pp. 379–80. Also J.A. Thomas, 'The system of registration and the development of party organisation, 1832–1870', *History* 25 (1950), pp. 81–98.

36 Peter Marsh, *The Discipline of Popular Government: Lord Salisbury's Domestic Statecraft 1881–1902* (Hassocks, 1978), p. 194.

37 Hanham, *Elections and Party Management*, pp. 399–400.

38 Blewett, 'The franchise', pp. 38–9.

39 D. Tanner, 'The Parliamentary electoral system, the "Fourth" Reform Act and the rise of Labour in England and Wales', *Bulletin of the Institute of Historical Research* 56 (1983), pp. 205–19.

40 Paul Thompson, *Socialists, Liberals and Labour: The Struggle for London, 1885–1914* (1967), pp. 69–70.

41 Seymour, *Electoral Reform*, pp. 283–4, 364.

42 Ibid., p. 381.
43 Blewett, *Peers*, pp. 361–2; Thompson, *Socialists, Liberals and Labour*, pp. 70–1.
44 Blewett, 'The franchise', pp. 44-7 and *Peers*, p. 363; Duncan Tanner, *Political Change and the Labour Party 1900–1918* (Cambridge, 1990), p. 450.
45 G.A. Jones, 'Further thoughts on the franchise 1885–1918', *Past and Present* 34 (1966), p. 136.
46 A.K. Russell, *Liberal Landslide: The General Election of 1906* (Newton Abbot, 1973), pp. 19–20.
47 Seymour, *Electoral Reform*, p. 116.

Chapter three

The rise of modern party organisation

'Organisation and management will beat the strongest party that ventures to rely upon political principle and personal zeal', the authors of *The New Law and Practice of Registration and Elections* assured their readers in 1868.[1] Confidence of this sort proved a major stimulant to the development of party organisation at all levels in late Victorian Britain. The old style of structural improvisation suitable for an era of small electorates and mass corruption had increasingly broken down as the number of voters rose sharply from 2,445,000 in 1868 to 5,708,000 in 1885 and 7,904,000 by 1911. As a direct consequence, parties were obliged to devise cheaper and more effective means of wooing, winning and mobilising voters through new organisational structures and novel forms of propaganda and appeal. Driven by these imperatives, existing organisations were transformed from cadre parties into something akin to mass membership bodies. Or as John Garrard puts it, this period witnessed a transition from informal and sporadically organised 'parties of individual representation' into more permanent 'parties of social integration'. While the former had been galvanised into life at election time and characterised by the control of local notables, the latter sought to move well beyond the political sphere to permeate every aspect of the individual elector's life.[2]

The party organisation that developed during this period tended to be characterised by four distinct features. First, at the constituency level, local mass membership associations emerged to contest elections and sometimes to select candidates. Second, at a national level, the network of constituency clubs and associations coalesced into broader federations which at various times (and with different degrees of success) attempted to use their popular legitimacy to establish a claim to participate in policy formation. Third, these developments stimulated the growth of powerful centralised and centralising party bureaucracies, to control and direct the party in the country and to provide a link between the constituencies and the parliamentary leadership. Finally, as MPs found themselves increasingly dependent upon party labels for electoral success, mid-century backbench independence gave way to far greater levels of cohesion and strict discipline in the division lobbies. Despite considerable regional diversity, therefore, there is much force in the view that household suffrage inaugurated mass politics in Britain as parties were increasingly obliged to project their appeal beyond Westminster.

3.1 Extra-parliamentary organisation

The degree to which developments in local organisation after 1867 merely continued trends established since 1832 has been a source of controversy among historians. Bulmer-Thomas certainly overstated the case in claiming that after 1832

> the need began to be felt for an organisation in each constituency to secure the return of a member of the desired party complexion, and this involved an organisation not only during the actual period of the election campaign to persuade electors to vote the desired way but ... to nurse the constituency.[3]

Others have rightly been more dismissive of any form of continuous extra-parliamentary party organisation in mid-Victorian Britain.[4] Until at least 1867, in the counties, smaller and middling boroughs and even in many towns, local 'associations' were invariably informal and largely ephemeral bodies composed of self-selecting committees of notables who hired a solicitor to conduct the necessary registration and electoral work.[5] Yet in practice, such rudimentary organisation was usually sufficient for the task before 1867, given the fact that electoral preferences and outcomes were often determined more by a combination of 'influence', deference and bribery than by political opinions and rational appeals. Moreover, a twentieth century emphasis upon contest-orientated local organisation obscures the fact that 'general elections were not general' during this period. Indeed, barely half the constituencies typically experienced a contest before the Second Reform Act. Only after 1867 did the numbers of uncontested returns fall rapidly from 210 in 1868 to a norm of 110 by 1880, where it remained for the next forty years.[6] A final factor often overlooked in arguments about the growth of mid-Victorian local organisation is that the general predisposition towards the avoidance of contests meant that elections were often necessitated by a split within one side rather than between formally opposing parties. As a result, any organisation which did exist tended to be essentially personal rather than party in origin and allegiance. By the mid-1880s, however, the combined challenges of a mass franchise, boundary redistribution, more effective limitations upon expenditure and an increasingly aggressive body of activists proved a decisive spur to a more permanent and elaborate organisational structure at constituency level. The outcome transformed the perception of party itself:

> Men came to think of a party, not in terms of individual candidates and party committees, but in terms of a core of party members of all classes in every constituency, united in pursuit of common aims, acting as canvassers in the wards, and meeting together regularly to discuss current political questions, to elect their officers, and to choose parliamentary candidates.[7]

The motive force behind the development of new forms of local organisation was provided initially by the complexities and regularity of a registration process which represented something akin to the remorseless burden of annual elections, and which could only be managed efficiently with more professional permanent structures. Peel had been correct in perceiving that this requirement would transform the nature and role of parties within the political system. Although the period between 1832 and 1847 was one continuous registration battle as the Anti-Corn Law League systematised and perfected the tactics employed by later generations,[8] the registration process provided vast scope for party manipulation right through until the Great War. The principal objective was to exploit the process of claims and objections in order to register as many supporters as possible while excluding the maximum number of opponents. Given the frequency with which seats were won with majorities of below a hundred, the reality was that elections were largely won and lost by the skill and energy of agents and attorneys in the revising courts. In particular, levels of lodger enfranchisement were little more than a map reflecting local party organisation and the marginality of the constituency. A similar picture emerges with regard to mobilisation of the plural vote.[9] Yet although the outcome of such activity could be decisive, there was also a high price to be paid. As Derek Fraser notes, parties were 'committed to a bed of nails, involving mountains of tedious registration minutiae, unwilling to relax for fear of giving ground to their rivals'.[10]

The critical importance of registration, combined with the effects of the Corrupt Practices Act of 1883, had at least three key implications for the development of local constituency organisation in the late nineteenth century. First, it encouraged the trend towards the professionalisation of local party management in the hands of full-time party agents. Until the 1880s, registration had largely been handled by agents drawn from solicitors' firms acting on a commercial part-time basis, but with neither the skill nor interest to promote voluntary effort among party activists. The appointment of professional party agents was thus important because it not only made it possible to dispense with attorneys for registration work, but also replaced them with more highly motivated political organisers fulfilling a broader function. To promote this new professionalism and status, the North of England Conservative Agents' Association was formed in 1872 to discuss registration and electoral law and promote cooperation between con-stituencies. Ten years later its Liberal counterpart was launched, again with a strong northern bias. In 1891, the creation of the National Society of Conservative and Unionist Agents and the Society of Certified Liberal Agents was a significant step towards greater professionalisation within a developing institutional framework and ethos. Like much of the upwardly mobile lower middle class at the time, these bodies were keen to strengthen their pro-fessional status, both by adopting rules and examinations for full membership and through the establishment of minimum salaries and a benevolent fund. In order to brief members on useful tactics, the Conservatives launched an official journal, *The Tory*, in 1892; a venture which was relaunched and revitalised as the *Conservative Agents' Journal* in 1902–4 and more permanently in 1907.[11]

With time, professionalism was accompanied by national standardisation in practice across the country, although the speed and uniformity of the trend between parties and regions should not be exaggerated. The benefits of a specialist agent rather than an attorney had been recognised earliest in the north (especially Lancashire), partly because of the lessons learned from the Anti-Corn Law League with its full-time staff. Although the Liverpool Constitutional Association had a full-time registration agent from 1848, such cases were very rare. Nevertheless, by 1874 Clitheroe was the only Lancashire constituency where the Conservatives retained the services of a solicitor-agent rather than their own full-time professional and by 1906 both parties had a full-time agent in nearly every Lancashire seat. At the other end of the spectrum, however, in Sussex, reliance continued to be placed upon solicitor-agents until well into the twentieth century. Certainly, from a national perspective, it was not until the Edwardian era that the solicitor-agent was superseded altogether by professional party agents – even in the Conservative party where the greatest advances in professionalism and permanence were achieved after 1885.[12] Thus, it was not until after their traumatic defeat in 1906 that the proportion of lawyer-agents fell from two-thirds to under a quarter by 1911.[13] Equally important, the demands of annual registration indicated the need for not just a professional agent, but also some more permanent form of voluntary constituency structure. Organised into a network of ward branches, mass membership thus became a means to convert fellow electors, identify those moving on and off the register for future action in the revising court and, at election times, to provide a pool of volunteer activists capable of canvassing, distributing propaganda, raising finance and mobilising sympathetic voters. In practice, each of these organisational imperatives was substantially reinforced by the Corrupt Practices Act of 1883. Beside its strict penalties which demanded a new breed of professional management to ensure electoral success and avoid disqualification, its equally stringent restrictions upon election expenditure and employment dramatically increased the importance of volunteer activists to fulfil the functions which previously had been purchased.

Alongside the formal structure of constituency associations, from the late 1870s mass membership was complemented by a variety of social clubs and debating societies which in some areas were the only local party structures that existed at all. Central to the appeal of these clubs was an elaborate range of social activities including games, dances, 'glee parties', brass bands and other entertainments, often culminating in an annual fête or summer picnic where party speeches were mingled with jollification to the satisfaction of the thousands who attended. Party-based sickness, burial and cooperative societies represented a further step to permeate party well beyond the political sphere into the fabric of working class life.[14] While large-scale social entertainments offered an opportunity for discreet collective corruption, in many ways, the growth of such clubs reflects the enormous breadth of ambition possessed by their middle class sponsors. For a class and a generation obsessed with the Victorian virtue of 'self-improvement', such clubs represented a vehicle for political education designed to convert newly enfranchised voters and to ensure that they were politically 'fit' for participation in the democratic process. Although for their members the appeal of such clubs was often more social than political, they were undoubtedly popular with a few possessing up to 2,000 members.[15] After concerted efforts to revive the club movement following their 1868 defeat, there were at least 150 Conservative Working Men's Associations spread over fifty-seven boroughs and five counties (predominantly in Lancashire and Yorkshire) by 1874: a growth assisted by the fact that they enjoyed greater freedom to sell alcohol than Liberal clubs. In 1894 an Association of Conservative Clubs was formed to foster political education while enhancing the quality of the social pleasures offered to members. At the same time, all parties developed cycling clubs to exploit a popular sporting craze for political purposes by fostering a sense of partisan comradeship while training a body capable of serving as party despatch riders on election day.[16]

Undoubtedly the most popular and successful of these voluntary organisations was the Primrose League.[17] Founded in November 1883 to honour Disraeli's memory by Lord Randolph Churchill and Sir Henry Drummond Wolff, its objective was the 'promotion of Tory principles – viz the maintenance of religion, of the estates of the realm, and of the Imperial Ascendancy of Great Britain'. By confining its political involvement to general principles and studiously avoiding controversy, the Primrose League helped to give substance to Disraeli's vague desire to turn the Tories into a party of the nation transcending mere class appeal. As Martin Pugh notes, 'by accepting class as a virtue not a matter for apology the League comfortably embraced the Conservative view of social unity'. One obvious manifestation of this aspiration was the organisation of local 'Habitations' into quaintly anachronistic, pseudo-medieval graduations of Kings Companions, Knights Almoners (clergy), Dames, Vavasours and even young Primrose Buds. Although easy to mock the medieval hierarchy of ranks and arcane Masonic rituals inspired by Wolff, the Primrose League exercised enormous appeal and proved an immensely valuable resource for the Conservative Party. Although initially launched as the 'Primrose Tory League', the deletion of the party label enabled it to appeal to a far broader membership attracted by its extensive range of social events and activities. By 1910 there were 2,645 Habitations with a membership exaggeratedly claimed to exceed one million by 1891 and two million by 1910. Although particularly successful in rural and suburban areas, it also thrived in industrial towns and claimed that 90 per cent of its membership was working class and nearly half were women.

Like the political clubs, the success of the Primrose League was built upon its ability to use social attractions to integrate itself into the fabric of the local community and the lives of its members far more effectively than any party could achieve by promoting explicitly political purposes. Covert propagandists actively proselytised for the Tory cause in convenient breaks in the popular entertainment to convert unwary revellers. Although it prohibited direct party electioneering until the 1895 general election, the Primrose League also provided continuity of organisation and commitment between elections to sustain propaganda, fund-raising and registration activity by creating a vast reservoir of unpaid supporters. In so doing, it gave more depth and permanence to local party organisations and helped to sustain the vigour and vitality of grassroots Toryism and the stability of its vote across a broad class base. This was particularly so given its ability to tap the enthusiasm of the unenfranchised. In particular, the admission of women opened the way for their widespread involvement in support of the Tory cause and they swiftly emerged as the party's 'shock troops' in hostile areas. As the historian of the movement notes, 'By the 1890s the sight of the Primrose Dame speeding through villages on her "safety" bicycle or descending *en masse* as the "Primrose Cycling Corps" at by-elections became a painfully familiar sight to radicals.'[18] Yet while a necessary adaptation to the 1883 Corrupt Practices Act, the beauty of the Primrose League was that it enabled the Tories to achieve popular participation within the new electorate in a form far more acceptable to the leadership than that envisaged by activists in the National Union who sought to subject their leaders to the disciplines of something akin to a Liberal 'caucus' (see section 3.2 below).

Where the Conservatives led with their mass membership organisation, the Liberals eventually followed. In part, this process was retarded by Liberal victory in 1868 which encouraged complacency about the organisational implications of the Second Reform Act. Yet a more fundamental difference between the two parties was that while the Conservatives developed their constituency organisation from the local club model of the 1830s using an essentially social appeal, the Liberals enlisted rank-and-file zeal on the basis of 'conviction politics' built around the Dissenting chapel, the trade unions and its many sectionalist reform societies. In particular, the Liberal organisational experience was profoundly influenced by the success of the Anti-Corn Law League. Seeking to emulate its tactics and success, a number of great Nonconformist single-issue pressure groups sprang up during the mid-Victorian period. Among the most prominent, the National Education League campaigned for free undenominational State education, the United Kingdom Alliance championed the cause of temperance and the Liberation Society provided a rallying point for those seeking freedom from State patronage and control of religion.[19] Although the practical value of these groups to the Liberal party can be questioned,[20] the religious passion of Victorian Nonconformism provided it with a potent motive force. Moreover, although each group was formed to redress a specific Nonconformist grievance, cohesion was greater than it often appears given a high level of overlapping membership and regional concentration in the towns of the Midlands and North and throughout the Celtic fringe. Above all, overarching themes and a sense of common purpose were provided by Gladstone's predilection for great moral crusades carried to the faithful by the dramatic growth of a cheap, accessible and strongly Liberal-inclined provincial press after 1855. Ultimately, it was to these great moral pressure groups that mid-Victorian Liberalism looked to provide it with both the structure and the foot-soldiers necessary for constituency and electoral organisation.

Yet the problem was that the Liberal party's reliance on such groups left it vulnerable to a chronic sectionalism which made unity of action difficult to sustain as the various 'fads', 'crotchets' and interests vied to establish priority for their own particularist cause (see section 4.1 below). Any complacent confidence in the existence of a mutually beneficial symbiotic relationship between sections and party was shattered by the experience of Gladstone's first ministry of 1868–74. Although an upsurge of sectionalist frustrations cost the Liberals many votes in 1874, the shock of defeat had a sobering effect upon the pretensions of the faddist pressure groups and forced them to recognise that they needed Liberal success as much as (if not more than) Gladstone needed them.[21] Although during the next thirty years factional squabbles played a major part in enfeebling Liberal credibility and electoral effectiveness, these events represented something of a turning point in the development of more constituency-based Liberal extra-parliamentary organisation. By the early years of the twentieth century the Liberal grassroots were in the process of rapid revival. As Chief Whip, Herbert Gladstone did much to improve constituency organisation, particularly in London and the South, through judicious use of central funds to place agents in key areas, improve the quality of candidates and assert greater central control over cash-starved local associations. This reorganisation scheme often effected 'something like a revolution' in the effectiveness of Liberal registration and propaganda work and laid the foundations for the Liberal landslide of 1906.[22] At the same time, the Liberals copied Conservative forms of extra-parliamentary mass movement. The National League of Young Liberals was established in 1903 as an active propagandist body with 300 branches by 1906 and claiming 120,000 members by 1911. Although never as successful as the Primrose League, Red Rose and Lily Leagues were formed, while to mobilise female supporters the Women's National Liberal Federation and Women's Liberal Federation claimed a joint membership of 100,000. Beyond formal party bodies, opposition to Joseph Chamberlain's crusade for tariff reform after 1903 served to bolster official organisation with a number of ancillary bodies such as the Free Trade Union which contributed activists, organisation and money without being directly included within local election expenses.

Although called the Labour Representation Committee (LRC) until 1906, the Labour party only came into existence in 1900. Unsurprisingly, therefore, its extra-parliamentary organisation before 1914 tended to be rudimentary and makeshift. Yet for all that, its federal nature enabled it to draw freely upon the spontaneous zeal and enthusiasm of the rank-and-file operating within a variety of different constituency bodies ranging from LRC and Independent Labour Party outposts to trades councils and local trade union branches.[23] Although fragmented and piecemeal, this structure was remarkably resilient and often compensated for structural deficiencies with passionate local commitment. Moreover, as its opponents recognised, the explicit association with the unions was a source of considerable potential strength. 'The Labour Party has a ready made organisation of an almost perfect character in the Trade Unions', a Conservative memorandum on electoral organisation noted in 1906.

It deals very largely (apart from its Socialist theories) with everyday facts relevant to the lives of its supporters and easily understood by them. Its real work is done, as the work of political conversion must be done, not on the platform but in the workshop and the home.[24]

Moreover, despite a tiny central staff, lack of experienced agents, primitive organisation and shortage of funds, the strength of Labour's extra-parliamentary organisation was increased by the fact that national figures like MacDonald, Henderson and Hardie devoted much of their energy to establishing their party in the country rather than fighting a hopeless battle within parliament. Like their two established competitors, Labour also created a Women's Labour League in 1906 which played a significant role in building and sustaining local Labour parties, while Blatchford's 7,000 Clarion Scouts (established 1894) spread socialism through cycling.[25] By the end of the nineteenth century, therefore, the structures of popular politics in the constituencies had already taken on a recognisably twentieth century appearance.

3.2 Linking the grassroots to the leaders: the National Union and the Liberal caucus

During the first half of the nineteenth century, insofar as it existed at all, local party organisation had been developed solely as a means to assist parliamentary leaders to win power. With the expansion of the electorate and constituency associations, however, this essentially passive conception came under increasing pressure as a new breed of local activists sought more effective means to influence national policy and leaders. At the same time, with varying degrees of success and enthusiasm, party leaders recognised the benefits of some sort of federation of constituency bodies. Despite the parallel developments in Liberal and Conservative ranks, however, the resulting organisations were markedly different in function, influence and their relationship with respective parliamentary leaders.

As in so many other areas, the Conservatives took the lead in their efforts to consolidate these links with the establishment of the National Union of Conservative and Constitutional Associations in November 1867.[26] As Sir John Gorst informed those assembled to consider its creation, it was 'not a meeting for the discussion of Conservative principles, on which we are all agreed, it is only a meeting to consider by what particular organisation we may make those Conservative principles effective among the masses'. Although the initial intention of young, middle class founders like Henry Cecil Raikes was for the NUCCA to be a propagandist organisation to win over newly enfranchised working men, by 1873 Disraeli's suspicion of any form of single class organisation had ensured that the new body embraced all Conservative associations. The National Union was thenceforth to provide a centre of communication and action between constituencies, to disseminate useful information and literature and to strengthen local associations where they did exist and encourage their formation where they did not. Every association subscribing one guinea was also admitted to the Central Council of the National Union (established 1869). To encourage the participation of local borough leaders, it was also agreed to convene an annual conference. Despite a disappointing start, after 1871 Gorst combined the role of Principal Agent with that of Joint Secretary of the NUCCA, with the result that it became 'an integral part of the Central Office organisation and was used by the party leaders as a mouthpiece and as an organisational front for popular demonstrations'.[27] By 1877 some 791 bodies had affiliated to the National Union – albeit that many were clubs and registration societies rather than constituency associations, and even by 1884 many boroughs and most county associations were not affiliated to the only truly national Conservative organisation.[28]

Despite early indications of the NUCCA's potential value, considerable suspicion existed towards both the concept of the caucus and the popular tone of much of its propaganda. Certainly traditionalists like Salisbury were initially gravely apprehensive that it would acquire pretensions to instruct the leadership on policy. As a result, the purpose of the body was defined explicitly from the outset as essentially consultative. As Raikes warned the seventh annual conference in 1873, the National Union had been created to be 'a handmaid to the party [rather] than to usurp the function of party leadership'.[29] After the Conservative defeat in 1880, however, middle class provincial borough leaders within the National Union became restive with this passive role and more assertive in their desire to make their voices heard; discontents exploited by those like Gorst and Lord Randolph Churchill who hoped to capture the organisation for 'Tory Democracy'. Although always a nebulous concept, during the National Union controversy of the 1880s the problems of defining this 'Great Tory Democracy' are compounded by an evident difference of purpose between its champions. For Gorst and the borough leaders, the intention was less to foist a particular programme upon a reluctant leadership than to promote 'certain methods of organisation' through the associations affiliated to the National Union. On the other hand, Lord Randolph Churchill and the 'Fourth Party' gave the impression of wanting to mobilise the National Union as a caucus on the lines of Chamberlain's National Liberal Federation, in order to wrest control of the party organisation and finance from the unelected Central Committee and pass it to the predominantly elected Central Council of the NUCCA.[30] Ultimately, however, Churchill's dalliance with the National Union was prompted more by personal ambition and opportunism than any instinctive sympathy for the aspirations of Gorst or middle class provincial Conservatives. By 1884, having obtained a deal with Salisbury which admitted him to the party's inner circle, the 'Fourth Party' dissolved and Churchill abandoned Gorst and the NUCCA rebels as abruptly as he had taken them up.

Although in mid-1886 the NUCCA was reformed to address some of the discontents simmering among provincial leaders for a decade, such concessions were a prelude to the NUCCA's resumption of its solid organisational work and subordination to the leadership rather than to a further assertion of grassroots influence. Yet contrary to Lord Blake's assertion that after reorganisation the NUCCA 'went quietly to sleep',[31] even in this later period provincial Toryism still made its voice heard on a variety of issues on which the leadership remained prudently silent. Against leadership advice, the annual conference of 1887 accepted the first of nine protectionist resolutions passed between 1887 and 1903. There were similar demonstrations of independence at the 1890 conference in opposition to free education and in the following year over the creation of a separate Labour ministry. Yet for all this, the party of 'Tory Democracy' knew where to draw the line. Ultimately, this was well short of anything likely to concede control of the party to its activists. Salisbury never forgot the threats of 1883–4 or the risk of Chamberlain using the National Union for even worse insubordination. Hence his insistence that its principal purpose was 'to keep alive & extend Conservative convictions; and so to increase the number of Conservative voters' though clubs and propagandist activity.[32] Similarly, although deeply in debt by the late 1880s, party managers were reluctant to encourage it to become self-supporting for fear that financial security would breed renewed political independence. The right of constituency agents to become delegates to the NUCCA Conference from 1892 further strengthened Central Office control over its activity and agenda.[33] Yet by the same token, activists exercised considerable self-restraint in not presuming to advise their leaders on policy at the risk of damaging party success or unity. Despite the revival of demands for popular representation in the central management of the party in 1905, after 1886 the NUCCA's main function was effectively confined to that of propaganda.

Parallel developments within the Liberal party created a far more difficult relationship between the leadership and the federated voices of constituency leaders determined not to accept the subordinate position assumed by the National Union. To reconstruct their urban associations after defeat in 1874, Liberals looked to the Radical successes of the Birmingham Liberal Association, which under Joseph Chamberlain and Francis Schnadhorst (its Secretary) had become an extremely efficient political machine. The BLA had two distinctive features. First, the entire structure was democratic, representative and based firmly on the town's sixteen wards, which handled their own business and elected officers and representatives to a City Executive Committee plus thirty delegates per ward to a broader deliberative General Committee with oversight over the association's work and the selection of candidates. Together with the 110 members of the Executive Committee, these delegates composed the Birmingham 'Six hundred'. This body in turn elected four of the eleven members of the Committee of Management. The second distinctive feature of the Birmingham caucus was its remorseless politicisation of subordinate institutions like the Council, school board and Poor Law Board of Guardians in order to sustain political activity between parliamentary elections and to provide outlet and reward for the political ambitions of local activists. Although both of these features could trace their origins back to the 1830s, according to Peter Fraser the essential novelty of the

Birmingham ward system was its rigour and permanence: 'Its methodology involved the rationalisation, systemisation and regularisation of earlier developments in order to meet the challenge of a changed political system.'[34]

The Birmingham Liberal Association enjoyed considerable success in 1868 on the basis of its well-disciplined control over its ward organisation and under Joseph Chamberlain and Schnadhorst the Liberals subsequently went on to enjoy a virtual monopoly of municipal and parliamentary representation in the town on a scale hitherto unparalleled in British party history. On this basis it became a model to be emulated by Liberals elsewhere. In May 1877, some ninety-five Liberal Associations responded to Chamberlain's invitation to a conference in Birmingham with the intention of forming a National Liberal Federation. Based in Birmingham and under the control of Chamberlain and Schnadhorst, the NLF became a vehicle to radicalise Liberal policy from below by placing the management of the party firmly in the hands of the people. Although the ostensibly representative structure always concealed a high level of oligarchical control, its claim to democratic legitimacy permitted the NLF to claim the right to control the destiny of the Liberal party – particularly as the number of affiliated associations rose rapidly and included almost all of the larger associations.[35]

The creation of the NLF engendered one of the great controversies of nineteenth century politics, concerning the role and merits of the caucus as a form of party organisation. In particular, Ostragorski launched a damning indictment of its pretensions at popular control over Liberal policy and MPs who were supposedly demoted from their traditional Burkean role as independent 'representatives' to the status of mere 'delegates' controlled by the 'wirepullers' of the caucus. In reality, such claims gravely exaggerated the power of the NLF, which neither dictated policy nor enslaved MPs – far less did it capture the leadership. Instead, when the Liberals took office in 1880 with Chamberlain in the Cabinet, the NLF began a not altogether easy process of absorption as a semi-official organisation supporting the government. When Chamberlain broke with Gladstone in 1886, Schnadhorst and the NLF remained loyal and moved to London. Moreover, in 1888 and 1890 its rules were changed to give the General Committee more control over its agenda, at a time when the participatory element was also clearly waning. Although the faddists enjoyed something of a revival with the 'Newcastle Programme' at the NLF conference in 1891, thereafter it deliberately avoided divisively contentious issues, preferring to act as a vehicle to promote party unity and a consensual version of traditional Liberalism. Like the NUCCA, it also maintained a significant role as a propaganda machine.

3.3 The emergence of a central party bureaucracy

In parallel with the development of popular participation during this period, there was also an increasing professionalisation of the central party machine and the emergence of what amounted to a Principal Agent. The period between the First and Second Reform Acts has been dubbed an era of 'club government'. Although political clubs like the Tory Whites (established 1693) and the Whig Brooks' Club (1764), had long provided a combination of social meeting place and rudimentary centre for party organisation, after 1832 both were displaced. In 1832 the Conservatives opened the Carlton Club as a centre for party management and the Liberals followed four years later with the Reform Club.[36] One of the central characteristics of these political clubs was the pivotal position occupied by the newly emerging general party manager skilled in the arcane arts of electioneering. Despite the success and personal renown of men like Bonham (Conservative) and Coppock (Liberal) in these posts, however, the organisational structures over which they presided remained relatively amateur affairs and within twenty years this form of management had come to an end in both parties.

During the 1850s both parties separated extra-parliamentary management from the task of party discipline in the Commons, although in neither case was the link ever fully severed. In 1853, the Conservatives delegated day-to-day electoral management in the country to Disraeli's solicitor, Philip Rose, who became Principal Agent in reality if not in title. Rose was assisted by Markham Spofforth and together they supervised electoral registration, re-established the network of party agents, oiled local wheels, sounded men of influence and assessed where money and effort could be most productively expended.[37] Similarly, after the sudden death of Coppock in 1857, the Liberals followed the Conservatives in appointing what amounted to a Principal Agent from a leading firm of parliamentary agents to attend to the business of registration and electoral management. This innovation was less successful, however, and soon after the 1865 election the Liberal Chief Whip returned to the older pattern of conducting most of the agent's work himself while delegating the technical and legal work to parliamentary agents;[38] a vast combined burden which represented a major constraint upon organisational effectiveness until 1886. Only with the transfer of the NLF headquarters from Birmingham to London, following the Irish Home Rule schism, did Schnadhorst and Robert Hudson emerge to provide more systematic assistance to the Chief Whip on matters of extra-parliamentary management.

On the other hand, one of the few real Liberal organisational innovations in this period was the creation in 1861 of the Liberal Registration Association. From its inception, the LRA became the most stable element in Liberal organisation and gradually bridged the gulf between the age of 'club government' and the modern era of professional party bureaucracy. Renamed the Liberal Central Association (LCA) in 1877, its main tasks were to promote the formation of local registration societies, to ensure Liberal 'outvoters' were brought to the polls and to provide a link between the local associations and the parliamentary leadership. Under the control of the Chief Whip, its secretary from 1877 was Thomas Roberts who drew on earlier experience as organiser of the Anti-Corn Law League to control all manner of extra-parliamentary electoral management with regard to candidates, agents, speakers and literature. From 1886 the work of the LCA and NLF were coordinated closely within shared premises under Schnadhorst who was

Secretary of both bodies; a position occupied from 1893 by Sir Robert Hudson. Under the LCA's aegis, a Liberal Publications Department was established in 1886 and the *Liberal Yearbook* appeared for the first time in the following year.

It was a measure of its perceived success that their opponents officially launched a Conservative Registration Association in June 1866.[39] Like Schnadhorst, after Spofforth was finally nudged out in 1869, Sir John Gorst and Major Keith-Falconer effectively brought together the leadership and organisational resources of the CRA, the newly formed Conservative Central Office (1871) and the National Union through their role as Joint Secretaries from 1870 to 1876. Yet the relationship between the party bureaucracy and the Conservative leadership was not always easy. Although Gorst worked assiduously at Central Office to strengthen local associations, the National Union and Tory links with the press, his ambition and prickly temperament led to conflict with the new Chief Whip over personality, patronage and interference in Gorst's work.[40] After Gorst's acrimonious departure in 1877, the whips recovered their control until after the 1880 election when the Chief Whip's illness and electoral debacle brought about the disintegration of the entire system. Although Gorst's recall in 1880 prompted a return to the former separation of parliamentary and electoral management, the creation of the Central Committee under W.H. Smith, with responsibility for all questions of extra-parliamentary organisation, revived old demarcation disputes which ended in Gorst's resignation in 1882. His successor, G.C.T. Bartley, was just as prickly and went still further in his pretensions to speak for rank-and-file 'Tory Democracy' when complaining that party leaders failed to consult the Principal Agent on policy. He even presumed to suggest that the National Union should appoint future leaders before eventually resigning in November 1884. As Richard Shannon notes, 'Principal agents had come a long way since Spofforth.'[41]

In the following year Salisbury's appointment of Aretas Akers-Douglas as Chief Whip and 'Captain' R.W.E. Middleton as Principal Agent marked a definite watershed which inaugurated one of the greatest periods of Tory party management. For almost two decades the 'Kentish Gang' of Akers-Douglas and Middleton formed a team of unrivalled efficiency. Both men worked closely together and while Akers-Douglas possessed the social standing, tact and affability to deal with the squirearchy in the parliamentary party and outside it, by background and temperament Middleton was more at ease with the boroughs where he focused his personal efforts heavily upon the need for more effective registration and organisation. From Central Office, 'Middleton stimulated and supervised the development of partisan electoral organisation to a pitch of refinement unmatched before and perhaps since.'[42] Among his other notable achievements were the Association of Conservative Clubs, the creation of Junior Constitutional Clubs aimed at Villa Toryism and a massive increase in the scale and effectiveness of party propaganda, which included the *Constitutional Yearbook* (from 1885) and a *Campaign Guide* (from 1892). More important, under Middleton, Central Office finally achieved some of the status and independence of Gorst's dream as the nerve-centre coordinating local activity and intelligence on electoral moods and then feeding this expertise into central deliberation of policy and tactics. Crucial to this success after 1885 was the fact that Salisbury lent his full support to these developments and his loyal lieutenant. Unable to prevent the democracy he dreaded, Salisbury hoped to mobilise the forces of natural conservatism within middle class Villa Toryism without undermining established power-bases or traditional styles of politics. To do so, he needed to control and educate the new electorate by using the 'wirepullers' he had previously despised. Although Unionist hegemony after 1886 was built upon the robust foundations of the Middleton machine, by the turn of the century his poor health coincided with a rapid deterioration in organisational effectiveness which left it in chaos and tatters by the 1906 general election. Only after two further general election defeats in 1910 were Conservative party structures and organisation subjected to sustained scrutiny and reform. Out of the work of the Unionist Organisation Committee in 1911 emerged the broad pattern of Tory organisation until the Assheton-Woolton reforms of the late 1940s.[43]

3.4 Discipline and control in the parliamentary parties

The final crucial aspect in the development of a recognisably twentieth century party system concerns the emergence of disciplined parliamentary parties under leaders committed to formalised opposition. According to Ostragorski, the period between the First and Second Reform Acts represented 'the golden age of the backbencher'. During these years, the House of Commons enjoyed a remarkable degree of independence and influence unimaginable to strictly disciplined backbenchers a century later. Without effective parliamentary discipline, legislation was made and revised on the floor of the Commons, individual ministers were harried and eight of the nine governments formed between 1835 and 1868 were dismissed after defeat in the lobbies.[44] Yet while backbench indiscipline continued to give parliamentary leaders problems until the 1890s, the decline in dissent occurred relatively swiftly. In the 1850s governments regularly suffered ten to fifteen defeats a year. By 1900 this indignity had been reduced to an average of only once per session. During the last two decades of the nineteenth century there was a particularly marked increase in levels of party voting cohesion in the House of Commons – initially among the Conservatives, who by 1890 were almost monolithic in the lobbies, while the Liberals remained divided and querulous until a decade later.[45]

This decline in backbench independence was the outcome of a process which progressively squeezed MPs between an extended electorate which increasingly came to make and unmake governments on one hand, and an executive which equally decisively tightened its grip upon the policy and legislative process on the other. The advent of mass democracy undoubtedly changed the relationship between the MP and his constituents as both sides came to acknowledge the pivotal importance of party labels. Having voted primarily for a party label rather than a particular candidate, the new mass electorate expected their MPs loyally to support their party leadership in the Commons. Precisely when electors began to vote for parties rather than candidates has been the subject of considerable debate. Professor Vincent suggests the removal of the Stamp Tax in 1856 and the massive growth of the provincial press had a marked effect upon the growth of party loyalties in the 1860s. Similarly, Cox, Feuchtwanger and Mackintosh suggest that it had become 'a permanent feature of English politics from 1868 onwards',[46] while Wald and Beattie follow Hanham in suggesting that the change did not occur until the 1880s.[47] Yet whatever the precise date, there can be little doubt that an extended electorate magnified the importance of party labels and consequently acted as a significant constraint upon the independence of MPs.

These pressures were reinforced by an equally radical transformation in the relationship between Cabinet, majority party and parliament, brought about by the increasing polarisation and partisanship which separated government from opposition after 1886. In the past, governments had regularly carried essentially consensual cross-bench policies with the support of party leaders on the other side of the Commons, against opposition from a wing of their own party. With the rising political temperature after the Home Rule split, however, the proportion of divisions in which the leaders of both parties voted in the same lobby plummeted dramatically from 46 per cent in 1883 to a mere 8 per cent by 1903.[48] This intensification of party warfare had a sobering effect upon potential rebels, for while Radicals may have differed from Gladstone over a variety of issues they were not prepared to put the Conservatives into office in protest. Thus, as backbenchers confronted an effective choice between the retention or loss of power, the influence of the whips inexorably grew. Moreover, although John Mackintosh rightly argues that this would not have been possible without the willingness of a new generation of MPs to acknowledge their duty to both the electorate and their leaders, it was equally true that the sheer volume of public legislation by the end of the century meant that parliamentary leaders regarded backbench obstructionism as so vexatious that they had simply reformed Commons procedures in order to curtail it.[49]

These changes in the operation of the political system signalled a more fundamental constitutional transformation from nineteenth century 'parliamentary government' into modern forms of 'party government'. After 1832, the eighteenth century notion of 'mixed government' based on the need to maintain a balance between King, Lords and Commons to prevent the tyranny of any, gave way to a constitutional focus on the struggle between government and opposition in the House of Commons as the essential conditions of 'parliamentary government'. By the end of the century, however, a combination of developments in response to a mass electorate had inaugurated a new constitutional category, that of 'party government'. This doctrine, which lies at the heart of the modern two-party system, shifted the focus of the constitution from Parliament to a wider arena characterised by a dialogue between two wholly cohesive parties competing for the votes of a mass electorate In order to obtain and legitimise their power. Thus MP's represent, via a vote for the party, the plebiscitory verdict of the electorate on the performance of the current executive.[50]

By the turn of the century, such circumstances had become accepted as a normal, perhaps even the defining, characteristic of British political life.

3.5 The rise of national campaigning, manifestos and programmatic politics

As the number of uncontested seats declined and elections became truly 'general', a new style of political campaigning emerged in Britain. Traditionally, elections had usually been fought around one great issue and it was the duty of party leaders to identify that rallying cry. Gladstone was the master of this type of politics. Theological in outlook and evangelical in his use of the language of sin and conscience, Gladstone believed that politics involved the mobilisation of Christian faith against the evils of the world. His genius lay in his ability to detect a great national evil and to rouse 'virtuous passion' against it. He had exploited this 'politics of moral populism'[51] in support of Italian nationalism in 1859; over the Disestablishment of the Church in Ireland in 1868; over Irish Home Rule in 1886; and almost against the House of Lords in 1894. Yet undoubtedly the greatest of Gladstone's moral crusades was that against Turkish atrocities towards Bulgarian Christians which by 1879–80 had been broadened into a general assault on the cynical evils of 'Beaconsfieldism'. Although there was nothing new about charismatic leadership, Gladstone's greatest innovation was his ability to harness this 'virtuous passion' to a new type of populist politics and electioneering. In support of Disestablishment in Ireland, Gladstone had first 'stumped the country' (or at least, South West Lancashire) in 1865 and again in October 1868. Over the 'Bulgarian atrocities', in November 1879 he set off on the first of his two famous Midlothian campaigns. During this two-week whistle-stop tour he delivered thirty speeches plus many short addresses to enthusiastic crowds besieging his train. In many respects, such tactics were recognisably modern in style, tone and content.[52] First, unlike his counterparts who confined their speeches to Parliament and their own constituents, Gladstone was appealing direct to the people as the ultimate source of legitimacy over the heads of nominal Liberal leaders like Granville and Hartington. Second, there was the sheer scale of his audience. By his own estimates, Gladstone addressed 86,930 people during the first Midlothian campaign. Beyond them stood millions in the country exposed to verbatim reports in the press. Finally the quasi-presidential style of the campaign helped to foster and reinforce something akin to a cult of personality which found ultimate expression in mass-produced busts, portraits and commemorative mugs of the 'Grand Old Man'.

Such tactics did not generate universal approval. It is debatable whether Gladstone's Midlothian campaign actually represented the 'degradation of

British politics' as Selborne believed, but he was correct in believing that it reflected a significant change in 'removing the centre of gravity from Parliament to the platform'.[53] As Lord Kimberley dismally noted in 1883, outdoor meetings were now 'one of the duties in public life', and 'in this country "going on the stump" has become a recognised part of the business of politics and will become more and more indispensable, every year, as democracy gains in strength'.[54] Where Gladstone led, the Conservatives were compelled to follow, particularly when sweeping Liberal gains in 1880 appeared to vindicate these tactics. In 1880 even aloof patricians like Lord Salisbury felt it necessary to overcome personal distaste and 'stump the country' with a Scottish speaking tour to educate public opinion. By 1885 Salisbury shattered the convention that peers should not intervene personally in election campaigns with another provincial speaking tour, while in 1886 Gladstone incurred Royal displeasure with his own breach of the convention against speaking in other people's constituencies.[55] Even after the retirement of Gladstone, enthusiasm for great 'concentrating' issues remained. Rosebery tried vainly to create one out of House of Lords obstructionism in 1894–5 and after 1903 the defence of free trade acquired a moral passion of almost Gladstonian proportions. In 1909 the wickedness of the Lords again rallied the Liberal alliance in a great battle upon what Lloyd George described as the 'one great dominant question capable of absorbing all others'.[56]

Yet at the same time, Joseph Chamberlain had emerged as the champion of a very different style of 'programme' politics – a term coined by its creator to denote a collection of policy proposals capable of aggregating support across a broad spectrum of sectional interests. His *Radical Programme* in 1885 was designed to be just such a comprehensive foundation for an attack on privilege which offered something for almost everyone within the broader Liberal alliance. Although Gladstone was appalled by Chamberlain's language of 'ransom' and the class-based content of his programme, this approach to electoral mobilisation eventually prevailed. By 1889 Harcourt was not alone, either in lamenting that Gladstone's Irish obsession had turned the Liberals into an anachronistic single-issue movement, or in believing that only a broader policy programme offered salvation. Although the NLF's famous Newcastle Programme of October 1891 contained little novel in policy content, its programmatic style of 'omnibus' resolution prompted Ostragorski presciently to declare that henceforth 'The *omnibus* was to take the place of the *old umbrella*.'[57] From these foundations the modern manifesto developed during the 1890s to reinforce the importance of national parties and national styles of campaigning. Although Peel had issued his famous Tamworth manifesto in 1834 on the eve of a general election as a statement of 'the general principles upon which the government proposed to act',[58] no comparable document appeared until Gladstone's address to his constituents at Greenwich in 1874. Caught off balance by the sudden election and Gladstone's manifesto, Disraeli issued something similar to his Buckingham-shire constituents on behalf of the whole Conservative party although without time to consult anyone. Not until 1892 did a Conservative leader issue a message to the electorate as a whole, and even then such declarations were still essentially personal appeals rather than statements of future policy binding the party as a whole.[59] Not until after the First World War did the modern detailed manifesto emerge as the authoritative statement of a party's position.

Notes and references

The place of publication is London unless otherwise stated.

1 E.W. Cox and J.G. Grady, *The New Law and Practice of Registration and Elections* 10th edn (1868), quoted in its entirety in H.J. Hanham's introduction to Charles R. Dod, *Electoral Facts from 1832 to 1853 Impartially Stated* 2nd edn 1853 (Harvester Reprint, 1972), pp. xlv–lxviii.

2 John Garrard, 'Parties, members and voters after 1867', in T.R. Gourvish and A. O'Day, eds, *Later Victorian Britain, 1867–1900* (1988), pp. 127–8.

3 Ivor Bulmer-Thomas, *The Growth of the British Party System* 2 vols 2nd edn (1967), I, p. 76.

4 John Vincent, *The Formation of the British Liberal Party 1857–1868* 2nd edn (Brighton, 1976), p. 71.

5 H.J. Hanham, *Elections and Party Management: Politics in the Time of Disraeli and Gladstone* 2nd edn (Hassocks, 1978), pp. 17, 92; Derek Fraser, *Urban Politics in Victorian England: The Structure of Politics in Victorian Cities* (1979), pp. 115–24.

6 Hanham, *Elections and Party Management*, pp. 191, 197; T.O. Lloyd, 'Uncontested seats in British general elections, 1852–1910', *Historical Journal* 8 (1965), pp. 260–5.

7 Hanham, *Elections and Party Management*, p. 93.

8 John Prest, *Politics in the Age of Cobden* (1977), p. 133.

9 Neal Blewett, 'The franchise in the United Kingdom, 1885–1918', *Past and Present* 32 (1965), pp. 41–2; G.A. Jones, 'Further thoughts on the franchise 1885–1918', *Past and Present* 34 (1966), p. 137.

10 Fraser, *Urban Politics*, p. 187.

11 Richard Shannon, *The Age of Salisbury, 1881–1902: Unionism and Empire* (1996), p. 442; John Ramsden, *The Age of Balfour and Baldwin, 1902–1940* (1978), pp. 51–2.

12 Hanham, *Elections and Party Management*, pp. 233, 240–2; Jones, 'Further thoughts', pp. 34–5.

13 Ramsden, *The Age of Balfour and Baldwin*, p. 52.

14 Garrard, 'Parties, members and voters', pp. 127–50.

15 Hanham, *Elections and Party Management*, pp. 102–6.

16 Peter Marsh, *The Discipline of Popular Government: Lord Salisbury's Domestic Statecraft 1881–1902* (Hassocks, 1978), pp. 204–5.

17 See Martin Pugh, *The Tories and the People 1880–1935* (1985) and *The Making of Modern British Politics 1867–1939* 2nd edn (Oxford, 1993), pp. 54–7.

18 Pugh, *Making of Modern British Politics*, pp. 55–7.

19 D.A. Hamer, *The Politics of Electoral Pressure* (Brighton, 1977).

20 Hanham, *Elections and Party Management*, pp. 119–22.

21 Ibid., pp. 118–21.

22 A.K. Russell, 'Laying the charges for the landslide: the revival of Liberal Party organisation 1902–1905', in A.J.A. Morris, ed., *Edwardian Radicalism 1900–1914* (1974), pp. 62–73.

23 Frank Bealey and Henry Pelling, *Labour and Politics 1900–1906: A History of the Labour Representation Committee* (Westport, CT, 1982 edn), pp. 235–8; Ross McKibbin, *The Evolution of the Labour Party 1910–1924* (Oxford, 1974), pp. 4–43.

24 Ramsden, *The Age of Balfour and Baldwin*, p. 55.

25 Henry Pelling, *The Origins of the Labour Party 1880–1900* 2nd edn (Oxford, 1965), p. 162; C. Collette, *For Labour and For Women: The Women's Labour League 1906–18* (Manchester, 1989). Labour's unequivocal support for female enfranchisement also won it the support of the National Union of Women's Societies which provided £35,000 to support Labour candidates where no pro-suffrage candidate stood. See David Morgan, *Suffragists and Liberals* (Oxford, 1975), p. 125.

26 E.J. Feuchtwanger, *Disraeli, Democracy and the Tory Party: Conservative Leadership and Organisation after the Second Reform Bill* (Oxford, 1968), ch. v; R. Shannon, *The Age of Disraeli 1868–1881: The Rise of Tory Democracy* (1992), pp. 15–17, 21–3.

27 Feuchtwanger, *Disraeli, Democracy and the Tory Party*, p. 130.

28 J.P. Cornford, 'The transformation of Conservatism in the late-nineteenth century', *Victorian Studies* 7 (1963), p. 50.

29 Bulmer-Thomas, *Growth of the British Party System*, I, p. 112.

30 Cornford, 'Transformation', pp. 47–8.

31 Robert Blake, *The Conservative Party from Peel to Thatcher* (Fontana edn, 1985), p. 156.

32 Marsh, *Discipline of Popular Government*, pp. 189, 199–203.

33 Shannon, *Age of Salisbury*, pp. 310–11.

34 Fraser, *Urban Politics*, pp. 192–4.

35 Hanham, *Elections and Party Management*, ch. 7. Also F.H. Herrick, 'The origins of the National Liberal Federation', *Journal of Modern History* 17 (1945), pp. 116–29.

36 Norman Gash, *Politics in the Age of Peel* 2nd edn (Hassocks, 1977), ch. 15.

37 Robert Stewart, *The Foundation of the Conservative Party 1830–1867* (1978), pp. 279–81, 328, 348.

38 A.F. Thompson, 'Gladstone's Whips and the General Election of 1868', *English Historical Review* 63 (1948), pp. 189–200.

39 Stewart, *Foundation of the Conservative Party*, p. 337.

40 Shannon, *Age of Disraeli*, ch. 5.

41 Feuchtwanger, *Disraeli, Democracy and the Tory Party*, pp. 160–5; Shannon, *Age of Salisbury*, pp. 67–8, 84–5, 125–7.

42 Marsh, *Discipline of Popular Statecraft*, p. 189 and ch. 6.

43 Ramsden, *The Age of Balfour and Baldwin*, ch. 3.

44 J.P. Mackintosh, *The British Cabinet* 2nd edn (1968), pp. 179–81.

45 Hugh Berrington, 'Partisanship and dissidence in the nineteenth-century House of Commons', *Parliamentary Affairs* 21 (1967–8), pp. 352–5.

46 Vincent, *Formation of the Liberal Party*, p. 82; G.W. Cox, 'The development of a party-orientated electorate in England, 1832–1918', *British Journal of Political Science* 16 (1986), p. 188; Feuchtwanger, *Disraeli, Democracy and the Tory Party*, p. 218; Mackintosh, *British Cabinet*, p. 162.

47 Hanham, *Elections and Party Management*, p. 209; K.D. Wald, *Crosses on the Ballot: Patterns of British Voter Alignment since 1885* (Princeton, New Jersey, 1983), pp. 6–7; A. Beattie, ed., *English Party Politics* 2 vols (1970), I, p. 145.

48 Berrington, 'Partisanship and dissidence', p. 366.
49 Mackintosh, *British Cabinet*, pp. 201–3.
50 Angus Hawkins, ' "Parliamentary government" and Victorian political parties, *c*.1830–*c*.1880', *English Historical Review* 104 (1989), p. 643; Beattie, *English Party Politics*, I, pp. 136–7.
51 Peter Clarke, *A Question of Leadership: From Gladstone to Thatcher* (Penguin edn, Harmondsworth, 1992), p. 11.
52 R. Kelly, 'Midlothian: a Study in Politics and Ideas', *Victorian Studies* 4 (1960).
53 Mackintosh, *British Cabinet*, p. 178.
54 Angus Hawkins, *British Party Politics 1852–1886* (1998), pp. 279–80.
55 Marsh, *Discipline of Popular Government*, pp. 42, 177, 187; J.P.D. Dunbabin, 'Electoral reforms and their outcome in the United Kingdom, 1865–1900', in T.R. Gourvish and A. O'Day, eds, *Later Victorian Britain 1867–1900* (1988), pp. 118–19.
56 D.A. Hamer, *Liberal Politics in the Age of Gladstone and Rosebery* (Oxford, 1972), p. 325.
57 Ibid., pp. 164–6, 174.
58 Bulmer-Thomas, *Growth of the British Party System*, I, pp. 82–3.
59 Hanham, *Elections and Party Management*, p. 200.

Chapter four

Party realignment and Unionist ascendancy, 1885–1905

4.1 Gladstonian Liberalism and the schism of 1886

The mid-1880s were as important in shaping the nature of party alignments as they were for the development of electoral and party structures. The fact that every general election between 1867 and 1900 produced a change of government led Lord Salisbury to talk of the 'swing of the pendulum' as 'the law of English politics'.[1] Yet in reality, this was no more a regular occurrence after the Second Reform Act than in the two centuries before it. Although in the first thirty years of the nineteenth century the Tories had been the natural party of government, in the period 1830–1885 they had won only two of thirteen general elections and only in 1874 did they form a government which endured. The mid-Victorian era was thus one of Whig–Liberal ascendancy during which they held office for forty-two of these fifty-five years. The events of 1885–6 brought this dominance to a dramatic end. The Liberal split over Irish Home Rule led directly to a fundamental and enduring realignment which resolved itself into the confrontation of two great alliances which ranged Conservative and Liberal defenders of the Union with Ireland against what became a Progressive Alliance encompassing a radicalised Liberal party, the Irish Nationalists and the emergent forces of Labour. In electoral terms, the events of 1885–6 also ushered in a Unionist hegemony of Conservatives and Liberal Unionists. In the twenty years between 1885 and 1905, the Liberals won only one more general election and held office for three unproductive years of minority government.

The fact that this Liberal electoral ascendancy was accompanied by the more profound triumph of liberal values has tempted some historians to talk of a 'mid-Victorian consensus'. In constitutional terms, the franchise and political system had been opened with three major Reform Acts. Legal freedoms of speech, association and press were all assured and religious discrimination was removed against Nonconformists in 1828, Catholics in 1829 and Jews in 1858. Economic liberalism was equally triumphant. After the repeal of the Corn Laws in 1846, free trade assumed the status of a religious dogma to be revered as the source both of Victorian prosperity and of international peace. The commitment to the non-interventionist minimal state, balanced budgets, retrenchment and 'sound' money was equally dominant, although such beliefs did not preclude government action – particularly in public health, the relief of poverty and the limitation of child labour. At the same time, Gladstonian foreign policy rejected cynical *Realpolitik* in favour of high moral purpose and a profound mistrust of imperial expansion, aggressive secret diplomacy and large armaments. By applying the same code of righteousness to external relations as domestic politics, the Liberals thus emerged as the champions of international justice, the rights of small nations and the self-determination of oppressed peoples.

Despite the general clarity and coherence of liberal beliefs, the Liberals were less an ideologically homogenous party than a loose assemblage of factions, sectional interests, 'fads and crotchets'. This heterogeneity of composition and doctrine reflected the circumstances of the party's birth. At a high political level, the most obvious divide existed between predominantly aristocratic, Anglican Whigs and middle class, Nonconformist Radicals. The persistence of these socio-doctrinal cleavages ensured that every Whig–Liberal ministry between 1830 and 1859 ended in internal division in the Commons.[2] Beyond Westminster, Dissenting religion was a major factor in shaping Liberal electoral loyalties. The battles of militant Nonconformism against legal disabilities and the privileged position of the established Anglican Church was a central theme of nineteenth century Liberal politics. Compulsory payment of Church rates ended in 1868; the Church was disestablished in Ireland in 1870; the Test Acts excluding non-Anglicans from Oxford, Cambridge and Durham Universities were abolished in 1871 and Dissenters were finally permitted to be buried in consecrated ground near their chapels in 1880. With the progressive removal of these unifying disabilities, however, Nonconformity ceased to speak with a single voice as it turned towards a proliferation of pressure groups to champion a broader range of confessional causes. Beyond the great forces of the Liberation Society, the National Education League and the United Kingdom Alliance lay a multitude of disparate groups crusading for everything from international peace and women's suffrage to the repeal of the Contagious Diseases Act. This sectionalism was a mixed blessing. Its most positive contribution came from the moral passion which gave Victorian Liberalism its distinctive tone of crusading zeal. Yet there was a high price to be paid for enthusiasm. At various points in the late nineteenth century, Liberal sectionalism threatened to shatter the fragile unity of the broader coalition and the bonds which linked parliamentary leadership to rank-and-file. Above all, by engendering an unwillingness to accept the pragmatic compromises necessary for the conduct of parliamentary politics, obsessive 'faddism' made it difficult both for national leaders to aggregate support and for Liberal governments to construct a legislative programme capable of reaching the Statute Book.

Historians are divided over the degree to which the Liberal party ever enjoyed true doctrinal unity. For some, it was never much more than an alliance of disparate dissident groups pursuing incompatible sectional interests through the agency of a party which otherwise possessed few common ideological bonds.[3] Others contend that an exaggerated focus on factional strife obscures the existence of a common Liberal doctrine which unified and accommodated specific sectionalist differences.[4] There is less dispute that the cement binding this loose alliance was provided by the charismatic leadership and messianic oratory of William Ewart Gladstone. By elevating political discourse and Liberal faith beyond the vulgar materialistic world to a higher moral plane, Gladstone became the voice of the 'Nonconformist conscience'. Invoking the language of religion to mobilise a brand of moral populism as no other contemporary politician could, he turned his party into a political umbrella under which diverse sections found common cause. Yet there were limits to the extent to which the Victorian Liberal party was capable of being led as a cohesive force – even by Gladstone. Both his first and greatest ministry of 1868–74 and his second government of 1880–5 ended in internal disarray and division.[5] On the right, the Whigs appeared increasingly to be a besieged and beleaguered minority fighting for its very existence.[6] At the same time, Radical discontents found new forms of expression through the activities of Joseph Chamberlain and the NLF. Chamberlain's search for 'a new departure in constructive radicalism'[7] led him to embrace a particular brand of materialistic, class-based, populist demagogy against aristocracy and the 'land monopoly' which was designed to transcend divisive faddism and woo the new working class electorate with a programme of 'construction'. *The Radical Programme* gave substance to such hopes with its promise to 'sound the death-knell of the *laissez-faire* system' through 'the intervention of the state on behalf of the weak against the strong, in the interests of labour against capital, of want and suffering against luxury and ease'.[8] In a party which purported to transcend 'class' in the interests of 'community', Chamberlain's programme aroused strong emotions. While Gladstone and his more traditional supporters were appalled by its materialistic class appeal and 'constructive' content, both the Whigs and moderate Liberals in the universities, the press and the City were alienated by its attack on economic rectitude and the rights of property. In such circumstances, a government defeat in June 1885 was seized as a merciful release from further suffering, internal division and possible disintegration.

In the event, the fragmentation which took place in Liberal ranks was more fundamental, more complex and more enduring than anyone anticipated. After the general election of December 1885, the 86 Irish Home Rulers held the balance of power between 335 Liberals and 249 Conservatives. In order to regain the political initiative, Gladstone sought a new 'concentrating' theme in an increasingly fluid political situation. By offering a heavily qualified form of self-government to Ireland, he intended not just to conciliate Parnell but also to preserve the Liberal party from Chamberlainite pretensions to dictate policy.[9] The formation of Gladstone's third ministry set the scene for the final schism. Eighteen Whigs voted against the motion which brought down the Tory 'caretaker' government, while Hartington set an example for his Whig followers by refusing to join Gladstone's government. Chamberlain was persuaded to join on the explicit understanding that the ministry was committed only to examine Home Rule and on the implicit assumption that Gladstone's advanced age and failing health would soon prompt his retirement after failing to carry the scheme. When the details of Home Rule became clear in March, however, Chamberlain resigned from the Cabinet and on 7 June the Bill was defeated on Second Reading by 341 to 313, after 93 Liberals (nearly a third of the parliamentary party) voted with the Conservatives. The Radical Chamberlain and Whig Hartington had been brought together in an unlikely alliance by a combination of Gladstone's determination to reassert his control and Salisbury's insistence that Liberal supporters of the Union should be forced into open schism. The eventual outcome of the crisis both at Westminster and in the provinces, however, was determined more along lines of personal loyalty than ideological conviction about the merits of the issue itself. As a policy, Home Rule had relatively little to commend it to the average Liberal given Parnellite parliamentary obstructionism during the 1880–5 Liberal ministry and their recommendation that Irish voters should support the Conservatives at the ensuing election. For many Nonconformist Radicals, Bright's slogan that 'Home Rule means Rome Rule' also struck a deeply responsive anti-Catholic chord. Nevertheless, the majority of Liberals supported Gladstone because of a deep personal loyalty based on moral empathy, broader ideological affinity and an established hero-worship for a man now synonymous with Liberalism. In contrast, despite Chamberlain's shrewd pandering to materialistic desires, he simply did not command the sort of spiritual and moral force necessary to wrest control from the 'Grand Old Man' – particularly as the taint of opportunism throughout the crisis left him isolated even in his Birmingham heartland.[10]

In the ensuing election of 1886, the Liberal rift was confirmed when the dissentients stood as Liberal Unionists supported by an electoral pact with the Tories. Contrary to Gladstone's expectations, the Conservatives obtained an overall majority of 118, as 316 Tories (plus 79 Liberal Unionists) confronted 190 Liberals and 85 Parnellites. This rout brought to an end half a century of Liberal dominance. Although Chamberlain expected separation to be a temporary prelude to his own triumphant return to the leadership, deep animosity among activists, Gladstone's continued commitment to Home Rule and the calculated personal snub to reunion hopes at the Round Table Conference in 1887 precluded such a possibility. With few other options open to them, Chamberlain's Radical Unionists and Hartington's Liberal Unionists merged in 1889 and moved still closer to their Tory allies within the Unionist alliance. When Salisbury formed his third ministry in 1895 both Chamberlain and Hartington were in the Cabinet. By 1912 the two party organisations were formally fused into the Conservative and Unionist Party.

4.2 Liberal malaise, 1886–1902

Although the schism of 1886 shattered the Liberal alliance, there were some modest compensations. Above all, the party achieved a new sense of common purpose and unity which it had so conspicuously lacked during the discord of 1880–5. During the previous year, Gladstone had concluded that such a split might actually be a beneficial purgative experience from which a more unified and effective Liberal party might emerge.[11] The purging of the Whigs, which began in the early 1880s with the departures of Argyll, Bedford and Lansdowne, was now largely complete. After 1886 only five great Whig families still retained their allegiance to Gladstonian Liberalism. On the Radical wing, Joseph Chamberlain had been ejected but he took few supporters with him. Of the seventy-three Liberal Unionists who survived the 1886 election, only twenty were Radicals and only eleven of these remained by 1892. At the same time, the proportion of Radicals in Liberal parliamentary ranks rose from one-third between 1874 and 1885 to over 70 per cent between 1886 and 1895.[12] More than ever before, therefore, the Liberals were a cohesive Radical force well aligned with the popular Liberalism in the constituencies. Above all, it was a truly Gladstonian party after 1886 insofar as it consisted of men who consciously chose to follow him on an issue which he had elevated into the acid test of Liberal loyalty.

In the constituencies the split was initially even less damaging. Although the Liberals suffered their largest ever net loss of seats in 1886, in straight fights between Gladstonians and Conservatives the loss of votes was often slight and in several cases in the Midlands and North they actually improved their vote to recapture six seats.[13] Thus while Liberal Unionists were able to defeat sitting Liberal MPs in only six seats, Liberals defeated twelve sitting Liberal Unionists. Despite its Birmingham headquarters and Chamberlainite inspiration, the NLF also remained solidly loyal to Gladstone and although no local Liberal Association withdrew from the NLF over Home Rule, some fifty affiliated for the first time after 1886. Symbolic of its shift in loyalties, the NLF moved its headquarters to London offices next to the Liberal Central Association with whom it shared the services of Francis Schnadhorst as Joint Secretary. By the same token, one study suggests that perhaps only 5–10 per cent of party activists were sufficiently hostile to Gladstone's policy to desert the party over Home Rule.[14] Thus, although smaller after 1886, at all levels the Liberal party enjoyed a far stronger sense of collective identity as supporters of Gladstone.

Yet the benefits of greater doctrinal and social uniformity were acquired at an extremely high price. Home Rule accelerated the existing drift of middle class voters and the Liberal intelligentsia towards the Tories, while the 1886 election established a new pattern of Liberal electoral strength confined largely to the Celtic fringe, the West Riding and the North East. The defection of the Whigs made Liberalism more coherent only by depriving it of its wealthiest supporters and their traditional influence in the counties. Their departure also devastated Liberal strength in the House of Lords. Before 1886, the Conservatives had a majority of around 60 in the Upper Chamber. Between 1886 and 1893, it has been calculated that there were 365 Tories and 115 Liberal Unionists confronting a mere 84 Liberals, of whom barely half could be considered loyalists. Moreover, although Liberal Unionist peers often sided with the Liberals on non-Irish issues, their opposition to the Newcastle Programme in 1891 brought even this to an end.[15] Doctrinal homogeneity also implied that the party leadership was now even more dependent upon a network of Nonconformist sectional groups for its support. As the NLF's Newcastle Programme demonstrated, the need to accommodate such a diverse range of interests actually impaired the effectiveness of the party by committing it to a ragbag of fads and crotchets which offered maximum satisfaction to the various constituent groups but deprived the party of any clear priorities or sense of purpose. In fairness, the Newcastle Programme was a coherent statement of the evolving Liberalism of the preceding twenty years, founded upon the commitment to religious and political freedoms, greater powers for community self-government, the assault upon privilege and new interests in social reform.[16] As a purported legislative agenda for a future Liberal government, however, the prioritisation and reconciliation of these goals created substantial practical problems.

By depriving the Radicals of their most dynamic potential successor to Gladstone, the 1886 schism also provoked a long-term crisis of Liberal leadership and doctrine. Although Gladstone was 77 in 1886, he remained Liberal leader for another eight years. While still a focus for personal loyalty, his advanced age, failing health, increasing intellectual rigidity and obsession with Ireland, made him a dubious asset in rapidly changing circumstances. After the schism he did little either to lead the party or to develop policy beyond Ireland and stifled front bench discussion among those who tried to fill this void.[17] Moreover, although the Conservatives' use of the repressive Crimes Act to coerce Ireland after 1887 enabled Gladstone to resume the moral high ground, many of those who supported him were often less than totally committed to Home Rule; reservations reinforced in 1890 when the Nationalist leader was cited as co-respondent in the O'Shea divorce case, thereby splitting Irish nationalism and outraging the Nonconformist conscience against both Parnell and the priority upon Irish affairs. Conversely, for those Liberals increasingly concerned by the 'social problem', Home Rule provided an unwelcome diversion from the promulgation of a more forward-looking and constructive creed which merely reinforced doubts about Gladstone's ability to throw off the shibboleths of traditional Liberal individualism to embrace new notions of 'construction'. Although Gladstone talked of an 'Irish obstruction' to all other legislative progress, therefore, it is more appropriate to see his leadership as the real obstacle to the development of Liberal policy and thought during this critical period of transition. Despite widespread party frustrations, however, while Gladstone remained leader the 'Irish obstruction' did effectively block the legislative road for all other policies. The return in 1892 of a minority Gladstone ministry dependent on the support of 81 Irish Nationalists thus condemned the Liberals to the demoralising futility of a second Home Rule Bill before the measure went down to the largest ever defeat recorded in the Lords by a margin of 419 votes to 41 in September 1893.

Although Gladstone's resignation in March 1894 permitted Ireland to be relegated from the Liberal agenda, it severely intensified the party's problem with leadership. After 1894 the Liberal party appeared to be incapable of containing the disintegrative forces of its own intrinsic sectionalism. Moreover, the bitter personal and political contest for the leadership between Rosebery and Harcourt set the pattern for chronic internecine warfare and personal vendetta which inhibited Liberal efforts to escape from their doctrinal cul-de-sac for another decade. Neither man was well suited to lead the post-Gladstonian Liberal party. Both lacked Gladstone's ability to mobilise the crusading spirit to transcend sectional division. Worse still, both were prepared to fuel such frictions to advance their own position, irrespective of the cost to the party they led. Despite a constructive social record as the first leader of the newly created London County Council (LCC) in 1889–90, Rosebery loathed politics and had little in common with the middle class Nonconformity and Radicalism of his supporters. Rosebery's vision of leadership involved purging the party of its Gladstonian legacy and its unpopular faddism by opportunistically aligning the Liberals with majority opinion in the country rather than with the wishes of the crotcheteers within his own ranks. Yet for all that, his government of 1894–5 struggled vainly to enact the Newcastle Programme in hopeless conditions, given the absence of a Commons majority and the revival of a Lords veto which the Tories used with calculated skill to maximise the damage while avoiding a democratic crusade against aristocratic privilege.[18] Besides the electorally popular Parish Councils Act, the government's only significant success was Harcourt's 1894 Budget which introduced a new system of death duties calculated on the capital value of landed estates and taxed at death on a graduated scale rising to 8 per cent on estates over £1,000,000. Although a severe blow to the inheritors of landed estates, Salisbury did nothing to impede the Finance Bill on the grounds that it would offer the Liberals an opportunity to launch a genuinely popular class campaign against privilege in the Lords.[19] Yet, ironically, although Harcourt's death duties were a major achievement which introduced a new principle of progressive taxation related directly to the ability to pay, Rosebery opposed it as an attack on property likely to leave the Liberals still more dependent on the votes of the propertyless. After his failure to amend the measure, he did not speak to his Chancellor of the Exchequer for six months. At the same time, Harcourt's dislike of the expansionist drift of Rosebery's foreign policy led him to declare in September that he was 'not a supporter of the present government'.[20] Little wonder that by June 1895 a demoralised and chronically divided government seized a minor Commons defeat as a pretext to extricate itself from the misery of office.

This depressing record of high political discord was reinforced by the Liberal ministry's unerring ability to alienate its core supporters. Relations cooled markedly with the NLF when its faddism was blamed for the government's legislative problems. Failure to deliver expected reforms for Scotland and Wales angered Radical support in the Celtic fringe, while working class voters nurtured similar grievances over frustrated hopes of legislation on behalf of organised labour. Beyond specific discontents of this sort, for voters generally, Liberal impotence to overcome the Lords' veto made the government appear weak and ineffectual. Symptomatic of government division was that during the 1895 election Rosebery fought on Lords reform, Harcourt on temperance and Morley on Home Rule, while the bulk of the Liberal party campaigned on Welsh Disestablishment. Devoid of moral fervour, legislative success or electoral credibility, the Liberals suffered a disastrous rout. Too demoralised and impoverished to contest 130 seats (89 more than 1892) and with many other candidates placed too late to be effective, the Liberals obtained only 177 seats compared with 341 Conservatives and 70 Liberal Unionists. In opposition during the next decade, Liberal fortunes declined to their nadir. Fragmented and enervated by internecine warfare, personal feuding increased without the notional bond of office. In November 1896, Rosebery resigned the leadership convinced that the party was unleadable and then retreated into a more congenial position of maverick independence from which to wage war on rank-and-file faddists and senior rivals alike. Although Harcourt succeeded him as Leader in the Commons (with Lord Kimberley in the Lords), he fared little better. Harcourt's genuine aptitude for purely negative oppositional politics made him a more effective parliamentary adversary, but an impossible colleague and a poor leader of a demoralised party of factions sorely in need of a clearer sense of its own doctrinal identity. He resigned in December 1898 blaming Rosebery and his supporters for his failure.

Sir Henry Campbell-Bannerman inherited the leadership in February 1899 in difficult circumstances. Although popular and determined to restore Liberal unity, the outbreak of the South African War in 1899 forced apart the growing fissures between a 'pro-Boer' group denouncing an immoral war waged in the interests of greedy plutocrats and Rosebery's Liberal Imperialist wing which continued to defend the war long after the rest of the party fell in behind Campbell-Bannerman's condemnation of British 'methods of barbarism' in response to Boer guerrilla tactics.[21] Between these two factions, Campbell-Bannerman attempted to rally the centre of the party by focusing on the iniquities of government policy leading up to the war while patriotically supporting the war effort itself. Although neither extreme faction attracted much mass support in parliament or the country, the breadth of division cost the Liberals dearly at the 1900 general election held in the immediate aftermath of what appeared to be victory in South Africa. Deeply divided and without any common programme, the Liberals had little response to a government enjoying renewed popularity on the basis of patriotism, relief at victory and the return of economic prosperity. Unable to contest 163 seats (33 more than 1895), the Liberals won only 184 seats to the 402 achieved by the Unionist alliance.

Electoral humiliation did not reinforce the party's instinct for self-preservation. For the Liberal Imperialists, the party (like the nation) needed to be 'modernised'. Their targets were the faddists within the NLF who chained Liberalism to an outworn Gladstonian heritage as a protest movement of moral indignation.[22] Confident that old party issues and divisions were irrelevant, they anticipated new alignments. Although part of a far broader movement embracing Fabians and collectivist Tories like Milner, the Liberal Imperialist quest for 'national efficiency' was intended to provide the party with a constructive non-socialist creed capable of resolving the 'social problem' while enabling Britain to nuture the 'imperial race' needed to maintain its ascendancy in an increasingly competitive world.[23] In his first major speech for five years, at Chesterfield in December 1902, Rosebery condemned 'the men who sit still with the fly-blown phylacteries' of obsolete Gladstonian individualism in order to assert the link between social reform and imperial security. Implicitly repudiating the Newcastle Programme, he called upon the party to 'wipe its slate clean' and start again with a new more relevant creed. Yet ironically, when Rosebery and Asquith attempted to inscribe their new creed upon this clean slate, they presented little that was truly new or distinctive about either their brand of Liberal Imperialism or their commitment to 'national efficiency'.[24]

It is easy to overestimate the significance of the Liberal Imperialists. In reality, they were always a narrow parliamentary clique cut off from rank-and-file sentiment by their own elitist mentality. Yet by appearing a divisive force seeking to jettison the Gladstonian creed, the Liberal Imperialists reinforced Campbell-Bannerman's authority by permitting him to pose as the custodian of those values which most Liberals still held dear. At the same time, his leadership was strengthened by the tide of electoral support rapidly ebbing away from a Unionist government which stumbled from one crisis to another over issues which reunited Liberals of all shades while equally decisively dividing the Unionist alliance. With militant Nonconformist and Liberal opinion united in a manner not witnessed since Gladstone's Bulgarian agitation of the 1870s, the embarrassing Liberal dilemma over Irish Home Rule was discreetly shelved. Although a vote loser in many areas, Liberal principle and electoral necessity prevented its complete abandonment – particularly given the Chief Whip's calculation in 1905 that some 124 mainland seats contained a significant Irish vote. As the Liberals won 96 of these in 1892 when committed to Home Rule but only 52 in 1900, the lessons were clear. In the event, the problem was neatly relegated to the background by adopting a 'step-by-step' approach in which the newly elected Irish county councils should be allowed to do their work before Home Rule was revived. On this basis, it was possible to exclude Home Rule from the legislative agenda of the next Liberal government while still enabling the party to win 114 of the 124 seats identified by the Chief Whip at the 1906 election.[25] By this stage, however, the Liberal Imperialist challenge had simply fizzled out. In September 1905, Asquith, Haldane and Grey plotted to force Campbell-Bannerman to go to the Lords while leaving Asquith as Chancellor and Leader in the Commons, but this came to nothing when Campbell-Bannerman refused to go and so they accepted generous offers of Cabinet places on his terms three months later. By then, however, Gladstone and Harcourt were dead, Rosebery marginalised, the Liberal party reunited and the 'Irish obstruction' skilfully pushed aside. It was less easy to dispose of demands for independent working class representation, although in the short term even here the Liberals appeared to enjoy some success.

4.3 Liberals, Labour and the birth of the Progressive Alliance

Alongside Nonconformity, labour provided the other great block of support upon which the Gladstonian alliance had been constructed. Although 'Lib–Labism' was intended to denote a specific perspective and a special quasi-autonomous relationship with the Liberal party on questions affecting working men, it was thoroughly integrated into the Liberal alliance, sectionalism was weak and Lib–Labs lacked any specific political creed distinguishable from Gladstonianism. Indeed, while on Home Rule their sympathy actually predated Gladstone's conversion, on all other issues their Liberal faith was built upon the usual combination of Nonconformity, temperance and traditional Radicalism which bound most supporters to the party. Above all, by conceptualising political struggle as a battle of the 'industrious classes' against parasitic landlords, Lib–Labs were often positively hostile to the sort of overtly class demands likely to be corrosive of their identification with Liberalism.[26]

The accommodation of labour within the fabric of the Victorian political and industrial system had gathered pace from the 1870s. Trade Union Acts of 1871 and 1876 allowed the unions to register as friendly societies, protected their funds and safeguarded their legal status. The election of Thomas Burt and Alexander Macdonald as Lib–Labs in 1874 substantially reinforced the links with Liberalism and by 1885 their number had increased to eleven, six of whom were miners. In 1886 Henry Broadhurst became the first working man to hold office in a British government and by 1906 John Burns was the first to ascend to Cabinet rank. Yet despite this progress, by the 1890s the labour interest was beginning to turn its attention towards demands for independent working class representation. The reasons for this change in direction have divided historians. For some, it stemmed from frustrations with the Liberal party as a vehicle for working class candidates and policy aspirations rather than any fundamental differences in doctrine or values. Others, like E.P. Thompson, attribute it to the 'socialist revival' of the 1880s and the formation of new socialist societies and the so-called 'New Unionism'.[27] A third school of thought emphasises the pivotal role of trade union insecurity prompted by industrial depression, hostile labour laws and an aggressive employers' counter-offensive.[28]

Discontent with the Liberal party as a vehicle for working class interests had both an industrial and a political dimension. Although a Liberal government passed the 1871 Trade Union Act, its Criminal Law Amendment Act effectively made picketing illegal, while it also failed to redress other union grievances over the Master and Servant Laws which made breach of contract a criminal offence and resulted in the imprisonment of Beckton gasworkers in 1872. Although the 1892–5 Liberal government introduced significant advances in labour policy,[29] its involvement in the policing of industrial disputes also forced it into repressive confrontations with organised labour which in 1893 culminated in two miners being shot dead by troops at Featherstone during a six-month coal stoppage.[30] At the same time, the struggles of New Unionism highlighted the party's domination by employers who either subscribed to individualistic economic doctrines or left their liberalism at the factory gates. Significantly, the formation of the Independent Labour Party at Bradford in 1893 followed the famous defeat of weavers at Manningham Mills at the hands of a local Liberal employer using the full power of the State to cut wages and defeat union power.[31]

Beyond these industrial grievances, there were broader political and doctrinal causes for labour frustration with Liberalism. First, although the party began to promote social and labour reforms towards the end of the century, such concerns were never a central priority for the majority of Nonconformist or Liberal sectionalists who remained firmly wedded to a more traditional version of Liberalism. Second, for a party convinced that it represented the entire community, Liberals were ambivalent about the question of class support and retained a traditional principled objection to class legislation at the expense of the community. In seeking 'balance' between capital and labour and between propertied and propertyless, the Liberals thus only alienated a working class upon whom they increasingly depended for votes. In the longer term, the very neutrality of Liberalism in rejecting class sectionalism thus made the party appear to be an obstacle to the type of change that Labour and the unions demanded in the years before 1914.[32] Finally these disappointments were reinforced by the frustration of working class electoral aspirations. While miners' MPs had the financial muscle and geographical concentration to exercise leverage over local associations, elsewhere Liberal activists rarely had the resources or the inclination to support poorly educated working class candidates unable to finance their own campaign and constituency organisation – even where they depended on working class votes.[33] Among the future Labour leaders rejected by local Liberals at this time were Keir Hardie, Ramsay MacDonald and Arthur Henderson. For this coming generation of leaders, independent labour representation was the only means of overcoming an uncomprehending middle class prejudice.

A second set of forces conducive to independent labour representation were associated with the so-called 'socialist revival' of the 1880s. These influences were many and varied and not all were overtly socialist in inspiration. Henry George's best-selling *Progress and Poverty* (1880) rapidly caught the public imagination with calls for a single tax on parasitic landlords who otherwise appropriated wealth created by the community for their own ends. The emergence of the 'New Unionism' in the late 1880s among unskilled and casual labour also played a part in this process. Although many would now argue there was little fundamentally 'new' about the movement, it scored some spectacular victories for groups of workers previously denied union protection such as the Bryant & May matchgirls (1888), Will Thorne's Gasworkers' Union and the London dockers in 1889. Although there were probably never more than 2,000 socialists at any point in the 1880s, these battles brought their leaders like Mann, Burns, Thorne and Champion to the attention of a wider public.[34] The proliferation of new socialist societies, movements and campaigns further contributed to this changing mood, often drawing heavily upon the traditional language and moral fervour of Nonconformity to turn a political campaign for the promised socialist heaven on earth into a quasi-religious experience. As the Liberal journalist J.L. Garvin noted after his first encounter with socialists for many years, 'I am amazed. It is not a new party. It is a new religion.' Typical of this spirit was Robert Blatchford's *Clarion*, which won souls for the new religion of socialism with an essentially ethical and moral creed, while his *Merrie England* (1894) sold three-quarters of a million copies. Blatchford also assisted the Unitarian minister, John Trevor, to found the Labour Churches movement in 1891 which at its peak in 1894 had around fifty churches (mostly in Lancashire and Yorkshire), preaching the new fellowship of socialist evangelism.[35]

Three new socialist bodies were particularly prominent during these formative years. First, in 1884 the ex-Tory Henry Mayers Hyndman launched the Social Democratic Federation as Britain's first formally Marxist party.[36] Throughout its existence the SDF was handicapped by its creator's massive ego and his idiosyncratic mix of Marxism, imperialism, anti-Semitism and hostility to both the trade unions and 'palliative' measures which distracted from violent revolution and class war. As a result, this profoundly sectarian body was subject to chronic fragmentation over doctrine, policy and person-alities. Yet for all its weaknesses, the strength of the SDF in London enabled it to exploit unemployment to terrify government with mass demonstrations and riots in 1886–7; tactics it repeated in 1905. Second, at the other end of the spectrum, the solidly middle class elitist reformers of the Fabian Society (also established 1884) believed their own brand of bureaucratic 'Gas-and-water-socialism' would arrive not through class war, but through a gradualist strategy of 'permeation' in which men of influence in all parties were persuaded of the justice of socialist collectivism in order to overcome the deficiencies of the existing system.[37] Third, perhaps the most important of the socialist societies was the Independent Labour Party. Launched in 1893 at Bradford, the ILP was notable for its northern working class origins and membership, its explicitly socialist doctrine and its strategic commitment to political inde-pendence from Liberalism.[38] Although overtly socialist in its programme of collective ownership, the eight-hour day, free education, extended welfare provision and 'taxation to extinction of unearned income', it was not revolutionary. Nor was it hostile to trade unionism and omitted all reference to 'socialism' in its title to avoid alienating organised labour whose support it deemed essential. Yet it was an overtly class-based movement convinced of the need for independence because of the existence of separate working class interests which were unlikely to be realised through a Liberal party composed of men who had so recently repressed strikers and rejected the miners' eight-hour day. Although rather stagnating by the end of the 1890s, the ILP played a leading role in the formation of the Labour Representation Committee in 1900.

The scale and significance of this 'socialist revival' should not be exaggerated. Although the socialists often made much of the noise, a school of

'Labour' historians argue that the growth of independent working class representation had less to do with ideological impulses than with trade union anxieties about the security of their politico-industrial position. By 1898, both 'Old' and 'New' Unionism were in full retreat before a determined and concerted employer counter-offensive, as severe depression intensified efforts to restore profitability at the expense of wages.[39] This counter-offensive took a variety of forms. The creation of the successful Shipping Federation in 1890 and Engineering Employers' Federation in 1894 established a defensive model which other employers soon followed. In 1893 the launch of the National Free Labour Association introduced a form of systematised black-legging intended to undermine unions and the strike weapon.[40] Worse still, a protracted engineering lockout in 1897–8 was a traumatic landmark defeat which did much to convert craft unionism to independent labour representation. In the courts, the trade unions were also forced back onto the defensive by a succession of hostile judgements such as *Lyons v. Wilkins* in 1896 and 1899 which undermined not just their legal position but also their confidence in both the Liberal party and the benign neutrality of the State.

Seemingly assailed from all directions, in 1899 the TUC resolved by a narrow majority to call a joint conference with socialist and cooperative societies to discuss independent labour representation. On 27 February 1900 at Memorial Hall in London, some 129 delegates representing almost 570,000 members agreed to establish 'a distinct Labour group in Parliament' prepared to cooperate with any party to promote legislation favourable to their interest. The creation of the Labour Representation Committee did not guarantee eventual success for an independent Labour movement. The motives of its founding delegates encompassed a broad spectrum, from SDF hopes that the new body would champion class war, through more moderate union and ILP expectations of a separate party, to those like John Burns, now a Liberal MP, who hoped to 'bury the attempt in good-humoured tolerance'.[41] Unlike many Continental socialist parties, the LRC was neither explicitly socialist nor a party, but rather a loose confederation of autonomous unions and socialist societies. Although talk of 'socialism' was carefully avoided to reassure union leaders that the objective was the defence of labour interests rather than the promotion of social transformation, many unions declined either to attend or to join until some time later – most notably the miners who held out until 1909. The Liberal-orientated Cooperative movement also refused to join until 1906 (except in Scotland). Indeed, by their second annual conference in February 1901 the number of affiliated unions had actually declined from forty-one to thirty-four, representing some 353,000 members. The fortunes of the nascent LRC were radically transformed, however, by a House of Lords ruling on the Taff Vale dispute in July 1901. Although the strike was settled in August 1900, the Taff Vale Railway Company sued the union for recovery of its £20,000 losses and the Law Lords unanimously upheld their case. The subsequent imposition of £23,000 in damages upon the railway union (and total costs of £42,000) was a massive blow to both the corporate status of the entire trade union movement and the effectiveness of the strike as an industrial weapon. Yet it correspondingly increased the leverage of those who argued that the unions needed a political wing in Parliament where laws were made because a parliamentary election could be fought at less cost than a case in the courts. Thereafter, LRC membership increased steadily from 455,450 members in 1902 to 1,572,391 by 1914. As the New Liberal L.T. Hobhouse observed, 'that which no Socialist writer or platform orator could achieve was effected by judges'.[42]

Despite its modest beginnings and uncertain future, the Liberals chose to incorporate the LRC into a 'Progressive Alliance' against Unionism rather than to destroy it as a potential challenger.[43] In part, this was because the LRC did not initially represent a threat to the Liberal claim to be the party of radicalism. Despite socialist murmurings in the provinces, the LRC was dominated by unions committed essentially to a defensive 'labourist' doctrine designed to advance the interests of organised labour and redress its immediate grievances. Even self-proclaimed socialists within the LRC were of the reformist rather than revolutionary variety and often had a history of collaboration with advanced Liberals in bodies like the Rainbow Circle. While lamenting the LRC's explicitly class position, therefore, common Gladstonian roots permitted close cooperation in opposition to the Unionist government between 1900 and 1905. Electoral calculations were equally important in prompting the Liberal strategy of incorporation rather than confrontation. In 1901, the N.E. Lanark by-election had first indicated the dangers of splitting the progressive vote when a three-corner contest enabled a Conservative to slip between Liberal and LRC candidates to victory. The victory of David Shackleton at Clitheroe (August 1902) and Will Crook at Woolwich (March 1903), in straight fights with Unionists, demonstrated that the LRC could win in its own right, while in July Arthur Henderson won Barnard Castle in a three-cornered contest. These pressures prompted a secret electoral pact between Ramsay MacDonald (LRC Secretary) and Herbert Gladstone (Liberal Chief Whip) in September 1903 which gave the LRC a free run in a limited number of seats in return for their efforts to encourage working class support for Liberal candidates elsewhere.[44]

Despite rank-and-file discontent, this secret pact offered enormous advantages for the LRC leadership by enabling the party to establish a significant foothold in Parliament for the first time. Perhaps unsurprisingly, many Liberals were alarmed by precisely this possibility from an upstart challenger often aggressively hostile to Liberalism in the constituencies. As the Chairman of the Northern Liberal Federation warned as early as July 1903, they were 'nursing into life a serpent which will sting their party to death'.[45] Given the fortunes of the two partners over the next twenty years, some historians endorse the view that the pact was a major Liberal error of judgement – particularly given their landslide victory in 1906. Yet retrospective wisdom should not obscure the advantageous nature of the arrangement for the Liberals, at least as perceived by those who conducted these negotiations. First, Gladstone did not believe that any fundamental issues actually divided mainstream representatives of the LRC from Liberalism and that they were better regarded as a radical wing of the Liberal party than a dogmatic socialist alternative to it. Second, although the electoral tide turned with astonishing rapidity after 1902, the demoralising recent history of Liberal electoral disaster encouraged the leadership to remove all possible impediments to victory next time – particularly given the exaggerated perception that the LRC might influence the votes of nearly a million men. Third, the creation of an LRC fighting fund of £100,000 promised to save up to £15,000 for a party with chronic financial problems of its own.[46] Finally, in any cost-benefit analysis of the pact it is also important not to exaggerate the scale of Liberal generosity. In return for LRC endorsement of Liberal candidates everywhere else, the junior partner was given a free run in thirty-two of the fifty seats it contested in England and Wales at the 1906 election. Yet although extremely valuable to the LRC, Liberals only genuinely 'stood down' in areas where they were already weak – as in the North West which provided thirteen of the LRC's twenty-nine victories. Conversely, in areas of Liberal strength like Scotland, Wales, the North East, West Riding and mining areas, there was little or no concession.[47] In this context, the MacDonald–Gladstone pact had much to commend it as a mutually advantageous arrangement in which the Liberals maximised the effectiveness of the anti-Tory vote at relatively minimal cost to their own parliamentary representation. As with the selection of Liberal Imperialist candidates for middle class Tory areas to recover seats which an official Gladstonian could not,[48] Liberal leaders hoped that LRC candidates could capture working class Tory votes (and up to ten seats) for the Progressive Alliance on the same basis.[49] Moreover, given the fact that in 1906 only three LRC seats were won against an official Liberal candidate, while ten were won in double-member seats in harness with a Liberal, Liberal leaders had some reason for satisfaction at having contained the electoral threat from the newly renamed Labour party.

4.4 Lord Salisbury and the Unionist alliance

For the Conservatives, the mid-1880s brought a happy release from a long period of electoral failure and political impotence. Despite the fact that censuses in 1851 had shown that for the first time more Englishmen lived in towns than in the country and were Nonconformist rather than Anglican, in electoral terms the Tories remained solidly a 'Country party' and defender of the Established Church, dependent upon a perilously narrow base in the English counties and small boroughs. In 1882 Lord Salisbury believed the death of Disraeli in the previous year meant 'the passing away of an epoch' and foresaw himself as 'the last of the Conservatives'.[50] The further extension of the franchise in 1884 inevitably increased these doubts about the viability of a party of privilege and property in a world in which the propertyless were for the first time a major force. Yet under Salisbury's leadership, after 1885 the tide of history appeared to be reversed. During the next twenty years, the Conservatives achieved three impressive general election victories in 1886, 1895 and 1900 and with only a brief interlude of weak minority Liberal government, the Conservatives held office for seventeen of these twenty years. To some degree, Conservative hegemony in these years was built on the foundations of chronic Liberal weakness and division. Yet after 1885 the Tories also became a different party, as they expanded beyond their traditional role as a representative of landed society, to embrace the new propertied wealth of the urban and suburban middle classes.[51]

Central to Salisbury's strategy was the proposition that the Liberals could not be trusted with the defence of property. The Ground Game Act (1880), the Irish Land Act (1881) and Chamberlain's 'Unauthorised' programme, thus merely confirmed the assertion that the Liberals were a party of loot and spoliation intent upon a general assault upon property. On this basis, traditional landed support was consolidated and extended to embrace urban elites and all other forms of property within a Conservative party undergoing a rapid process of *embourgeoisement* both in Parliament and in the country.[52] In 1885 the Conservatives won a majority in the metropolis for the first time, capturing all but two of the eighteen predominantly middle class seats in London and every one of those in the conurbation outside the LCC boundaries: a voting pattern based on class cleavages which were equally apparent in other provincial cities.[53] Even middle class Nonconformists were integrated into the Unionist alliance – particularly in the South East – as advancing secularisation and the removal of religious grievances increased the potency of class affiliations in defence of property against Radicalism, socialism, labour militancy and 'Rome Rule'.[54] The 'Lords of the suburban villas, the owners of pineries and vineries', as Lord Randolph Churchill had sneeringly dubbed the urban middle class, thus found a new home for themselves within the Unionist alliance: a force which became a formidable electoral bedrock after 1885 with the creation of socially homogeneous suburban single-member constituencies. At the same time, the Conservatives also shook off the narrow sectionalist image of the past in order to reassert the Disraelian claim to be a 'party of the nation' seeking to transcend class politics through an active defence of the Union with Ireland, popular patriotism, Empire and the imperial vision: a platform crucial to their appeal to many working class Tories well into the twentieth century.

As leader of the Conservative party from 1885, Lord Salisbury certainly deserves some credit for this new ascendancy. Yet as Peter Marsh contends, the key to Salisbury's politics was primal fear.[55] A devoutly religious man, afflicted with a highly-strung nature which made him subject to recurrent 'nerve storms', Salisbury adopted a grimly fatalistic view of human nature, the secular world and the ameliorative value of political action. Convinced that human nature was dominated by self-interest, Salisbury accepted class conflict between the 'haves' and the 'have nots' as a natural condition of society. He resigned from Disraeli's ministry in 1867 over the Reform Bill, in despair that popular government would ineluctably provoke such rapacious demands from an ill-educated propertyless class as to destroy the very fabric of political stability and social unity he wished to preserve. Thereafter, his profoundly pessimistic cast of mind made him constant prey to apocalyptic fears about class war, confiscatory taxation and national 'disintegration'. 'We are in a state of bloodless civil war', Salisbury noted in February 1889. 'To loot somebody or something is the common object under a thick varnish of pious phrases.' [56]

Salisbury believed it his duty to set limits to the democratic despoliation of the established order. Rejecting the strategy of Disraeli and Churchill on the grounds that seeking to outbid the Liberals with an adaptive brand of progressive 'Tory Democracy' would lead to disaster, Salisbury sought salvation by remaining true to core principles and rallying like-minded forces to defend the interests and institutions he held dear. As he told the Queen in May 1886, the objective was to turn the Conservatives into a 'party of resistance'. Too much of a realist to believe the tide of popular government could be halted, Salisbury attempted to delay the inevitable in the hope of at least disciplining the forces he could not prevent. His confidence was increased by the belief that 'those who wish to preserve greatly outweigh those who wish to destroy'.[57] As Gladstone's radicalised Liberals progressively abandoned the middle ground with their menacing interference with property and rising taxation, Salisbury appealed to the defensive instincts of the threatened middle class posing as the natural ally of the 'lords of the suburban villas'. Hopes were also entertained of the Conservative working man. While in areas like Liverpool, the strength of working class Conservatism was rooted firmly in anti-Catholic and anti-Irish sentiment, elsewhere Salisbury was convinced that the working class could be won over through an appeal to the national instincts of popular patriotism they shared with all other classes, rather than by playing the dangerous game of opportunist bribery which served only to accelerate the descent into class politics and 'disintegration'.

Although Salisbury's use of defiant tactics was initially unsuccessful, during the mid-1880s he achieved two notable triumphs. First, his skilful leadership over the Redistribution Bill in 1884–5 brought substantial electoral benefits for Conservatism (see section 2.1 above). Secondly, in 1886 he seized the opportunity provided by Gladstone's preoccupation with Ireland to realign party and electoral support along a new cleavage far more favourable to the Tories. Although Gladstone's policy split the Liberals down the centre, it was Salisbury who ensured that the Tories maximised the benefits of schism. Between February and June 1886, he made a series of robust speeches in defence of the Union. By provocatively mobilising the language of Irish racial inferiority and the desirability of coercion, Salisbury deliberately polarised the debate in such a way as to maximise the Liberal rift by precluding any hope of compromise.[58] The outcome of the 1886 general election consolidated the alliance between the Conservatives and those Liberal Unionists who had rebelled over the Bill. In part, this was because Conservative party managers successfully delivered their promise of a free run for all except three Liberal Unionists. More important, the alliance was reinforced by the outcome of the election which left the Conservatives twenty seats short of an absolute majority and thus dependent upon the parliamentary support of seventy-nine Liberal Unionists.

The process of Unionist accommodation and realignment was neither immediate nor entirely harmonious. Personal obstacles played an important role in retarding the process of convergence. From the Conservative perspective, Joseph Chamberlain was an unwelcome and dangerous ally given his unabashed Radicalism, his opportunistic demagoguery, his doctrine of 'ransom' to be demanded from property and recent attacks on Salisbury as a representative of an unproductive class which neither toiled nor spun. Many years would pass before Tory hatred and mistrust abated towards this supposedly unprincipled Radical Jacobin.[59] In 1886-7, Salisbury was also rightly alarmed by the possibility of a maverick alliance between Chamberlain and Lord Randolph Churchill to promote 'Tory Democracy' and an advanced programme of domestic reform.[60] Salisbury's strong moral convictions were appalled in rather different ways by Hartington's lifestyle and liaison with the Duchess of Manchester. On the other side, neither the Hartington nor Chamberlain sections of Liberal Unionism were prepared to abandon their separate identity and heritage as Liberals simply to merge with the Conservatives. Although in July 1886 (and again in January 1887) Hartington preferred to support a Salisbury ministry from outside rather than take office himself, the problem was how far they could vote with Salisbury's government without completely jeopardising their independent identity.[61] Nor was the maintenance of a certain distance between alliance partners merely a matter of positional high politics, prejudice and habit. Real ideological differences also persisted. Chamberlain's Radical Unionists remained advanced Liberals with powerfully reformist instincts on domestic policy and many found little pleasure in cooperation either with Whigs or Tories. The Nonconformist conscience was regularly tested when Salisbury's High Church faith led him to assist the Established Church and its ailing 'voluntary' schools. In Scotland, the continued commitment of Liberal Unionism to Disestablishment, temperance and land reform created further tensions with the Tories.[62] Conversely, protectionist clamour from the Fair Trade League and the National Union threatened to upset the free trade sensibilities of the Liberal Unionists. The relationship was also periodically bedevilled by organisational tensions. Although the electoral pact of 1886 was extended in 1889, and in the following year the party prefix was abandoned altogether in favour of the generic label of 'Unionist', the overall trend of Liberal Unionist parliamentary strength was one of steady decline and there was limited scope for expansion. In these circumstances, tensions over the allocation of seats and the interpretation of agreements persisted until the 1895 election.[63]

Yet despite these pressures and tensions, the Unionist alliance remained intact for a variety of compelling reasons. The recognition of mutual need played an important role. The failure of the Round Table Conference on Liberal reunification in 1887 due to Gladstonian hostility towards Chamberlain, and the breakdown of his relationship with Lord Randolph Churchill later in the same year, convinced 'Radical Joe' that his future lay with Salisbury. Conversely, Conservatives were forced to recognise that Liberal Unionist strength in Chamberlain's West Midland fiefdom and in Scotland delivered important electoral benefits given the pervasive belief (correct in

1886 but mistaken in 1895) that they could not win a majority in Parliament without the alliance. Common agreement on the preservation of the Union with Ireland also provided the cement to sustain the alliance during years when Gladstone single-handedly kept the issue at the top of the political agenda. Moreover, as time went on, this issue permitted the gradual elaboration of related general themes concerning the defence of property rights, resistance to disorder, imperial unity and the integrity of the Kingdom. Ironically, Salisbury's leadership also proved an unexpectedly unifying force behind the alliance. His experience, authority and success in the management of foreign and imperial policy undoubtedly drew the alliance together. Yet he proved equally flexible in his careful management of the competing claims of the two wings of Unionism, as he demonstrated through his generosity with patronage and honours and his legislative concessions over uncontentious questions like allotments for agricultural labourers in 1887 and smallholdings in 1892. More important, although there was no consultation with Chamberlain over the Local Government Bill which democratised county government, this long overdue reconstruction exemplifies Salisbury's quest for balance insofar as the measure was democratic enough to satisfy the Liberal Unionists, while the retention of a power of nomination sweetened the pill for the Tory gentry whose control in the counties was being severely curtailed.[64]

Just as important as what Salisbury actually did, was his careful avoidance of issues capable of dividing the alliance. This was not always so with regard to Church matters. Despite Tory indifference and the prevailing Nonconformity of Chamberlain's Radical Unionists, Salisbury's devout Anglicanism led him to introduce ecclesiastical legislation in every year between 1886 and 1892. Although on the peculiarly controversial question of denominational education, Salisbury prudently recognised that rate-aid to Church schools was 'too strong for the stomachs of our Liberal-Unionist contingent',[65] in 1891 he embraced the radical solution of free elementary education funded from national tax revenues in order to secure the future of predominantly Anglican 'voluntary' schools, despite strong objections from the Education Department, the Conservative party, middle class taxpayers, Liberal Unionists and Nonconformists. Where Salisbury possessed less powerful convictions, however, his desire to avoid destabilising the alliance was more obvious. This was particularly so on social and labour reform. In part, the failure to act stemmed from Salisbury's own preference for self-help rooted in a sceptical pessimism about the ability of legislation to increase human happiness. He was equally opposed to any government interference with the market or the sanctity of property rights and hostile to increased centralisation, public expenditure and direct taxation. Yet the failure to produce more social legislation also reflected the general atrophy of the Disraelian social reform tradition in a defensive party of property, at a time when Gladstonian preoccupations with Ireland removed the danger that elections would become auctions for working class support. Moreover, while Tory party managers were anxious not to antagonise working class voters, they equally well recognised that there was far more to be lost by alienating their business supporters than could be gained in the other direction.[66] Thus, although they implemented the Conciliation Act (1896) to create publicly funded arbitration machinery and Chamberlain's Workmen's Compensation Act (1897), the Conservatives were increasingly sensitive to the anxieties of their business supporters with regard to trade union immunities, eight-hour day legislation and efforts to tighten child labour laws in 1891.

Chamberlain's continued commitment to reform might have threatened the stability of this alliance. Yet in response to Chamberlain's social reform programme in 1892, Salisbury privately conceded his willingness to 'use phrases which will please Joe', but endorsed only those items like smallholdings calculated not to damage the unity of the alliance. In November 1894 Chamberlain proposed another programme of social reform, 'as an antidote to the Gladstonian policy of destruction', but this bold initiative went much the same way.[67]

Ultimately, Chamberlain's surprise acceptance of the Colonial Office in 1895, rather than a domestic portfolio, was a recognition of the limitations of his influence when it conflicted with Salisbury's desire to preserve the stability of the Unionist alliance and the contentment of his own core supporters. The dynamics of Unionist policy-making during this period thus demonstrated the degree to which Salisbury and Chamberlain existed within a carefully regulated symbiotic relationship. For both wings, the alliance was rendered more palatable by the role of two leaders capable of assuring their supporters that cooperation with former enemies did not demand the abandonment of established principles. Yet at the same time, each used the demands of the other to oil the wheels of alliance. Salisbury used the Liberal Unionists as a convenient weapon with which to coerce his own followers into accepting necessary reform – as over democratised county councils, allotments, free education and Irish land purchase. At the same time, Chamberlain continued to press for domestic reform and took every opportunity to exaggerate his success (often to the disquiet of Tory party managers), in order to justify the alliance. Yet, in private, he was enough of a realist to recognise that Salisbury would not give way to his more radical aspirations. As such, Chamberlain came to accept the constraints as well as the benefits of Unionism.

The growing convergence of the Unionist alliance was formalised by the construction of Salisbury's Cabinet in 1895. Although neither Hartington nor Chamberlain joined the Cabinet in 1886, when Churchill rashly overplayed his hand and resigned the Exchequer in January 1887, Hartington encouraged Goschen to become the first Liberal Unionist to join the government. By 1892, Chamberlain was talking about full coalition under the banner of a new 'National party', but electoral defeat saved Salisbury from this disquieting prospect. Nevertheless, the assumption that the Conservatives would always need the electoral and parliamentary support of their Liberal Unionist allies ensured that coalition could not be permanently deferred – despite an eruption of anti-Chamberlain Tory sentiment in the spring of 1895. In constructing the Unionist Cabinet shortly before the 1895 election, Hartington (now Duke of Devonshire) became Lord President, Chamberlain opted for the

Colonial Office, Lansdowne took the War (later Foreign) Office and Goschen went to the Admiralty, with a variety of non-Cabinet offices for other Liberal Unionists. In the event, the Conservatives won an overall majority of their own, but by then it was too late to go back. After 1895, the lines of demarcation between Conservatives and Liberal Unionists became progressively less clearly defined. Despite talks on possible fusion in 1892, however, it was another twenty years before this became an organisational reality. By that stage, however, Salisbury was dead, Balfour displaced, Chamberlain devastated by a stroke, the House of Lords emasculated, landed property assailed and the Unionist alliance faced with the very real prospect of long-term electoral marginalisation.

4.5 Unionist decline and Liberal revival, 1900–1906

The Unionists achieved a landslide victory at the 1895 general election greater than any since 1832. With 340 Conservatives and 71 Liberal Unionists to only 177 Liberals and 82 Irish Nationalists, Salisbury's fears of 'disintegration' and popular government were finally stilled. Comparing the victory to that of the Younger Pitt in 1784, Salisbury looked forward to 'an epoch of continuous rule'.[68] Yet like almost all elections, it was essentially a verdict against a demoralised Liberal government rather than a positive vote for the Unionist opposition. Having acquired a crushing Commons majority of 152, the final years of Salisbury's premiership revealed both the visionless sterility of his brand of Conservatism and the shallowness of its electoral base. As the threat from Home Rule receded after 1894, the absence of a constructive domestic policy was starkly exposed by Salisbury's preference for defensive quietism. His deteriorating health, almost complete preoccupation with foreign affairs and disinclination to provide a domestic lead served only to increase the sense of directionless void at the centre. The vigour, enthusiasm and sense of purpose of the new government thus rapidly ebbed away as it fell back upon a mechanical policy of honouring the fourteen specific commitments given during the general election. Although some significant measures reached the Statute Book, the resulting legislative record has rightly been described as one of 'colourless, deflating compromise'.[69]

Despite the paucity of solid achievement at home, the government derived more support for its foreign and imperial endeavours. The Diamond Jubilee in 1897 became a triumphal celebration of imperial greatness, reinforced the next year when Kitchener defeated the Mahdi and then saw off the French at Fashoda. In October 1899, imperial enthusiasm reached a peak with the outbreak of the second Boer War; an event which unexpectedly proved to be a godsend for the government by reversing the swing of electoral opinion which had deprived them of fourteen by-election seats since 1895. Despite early military disasters, administrative confusion and political incompetence, Mafeking was relieved in May to widespread public rejoicing. In June, Johannesburg and Pretoria were captured. The last pitched battle of the war took place at Bergendal on 27 August, opening the way for the annexation of the Transvaal. At this juncture, the Unionists resolved to exploit the favourable national mood to seize another election victory, despite the fact that Parliament still had two years left to run. The so-called 'Khaki election' was a remarkably boring affair, not least because of the predictability of its result. Despite Chamberlain's vitriolic attacks on the Liberal 'pro-Boers', the extent of popular jingoism during the campaign should not be exaggerated. Most Unionist candidates and Central Office did not fight explicitly jingoistic campaigns and some of those who did were defeated. Conversely, over fifty 'pro-Boers' were returned and of the fourteen defeated most were in seats otherwise vulnerable to Conservative attack.[70] Yet whether the product of aggressive jingoism or simply relief at victory and the return of peace and prosperity, the Unionists obtained 402 MPs to only 184 Liberals. For the first time since 1867, the 'swing of the pendulum' had not displaced an incumbent government.

Despite the impressive scale of victory, Salisbury was rightly apprehensive about the omens and implications of a majority built on such shallow foundations. Disillusion set in almost immediately, as the end of the first phase of the conflict led not to peace, but to a more ferocious guerrilla war which lasted a further seventeen months. Exhilaration and relief at supposed victory thus rapidly gave way, first to resentment at being duped, and then uneasiness as Britain resorted (in Campbell-Bannerman's phrase), to 'methods of barbarism' to crush Boer resistance. Yet although these tactics cost the government some support, the far greater divisions within Liberal ranks prevented this disillusion being reflected at the polls. In by-elections between 1900 and Salisbury's resignation in July 1902, the Conservatives retained nine, gained one and lost one in exceptional circumstances. Yet the Unionist hegemony barely survived Salisbury's leadership. Within two weeks of his departure, the Unionist stronghold of North Leeds was unexpectedly lost on a 13 per cent swing. Four months later, the majority at Sevenoaks was slashed and in November, Orkney and Shetland was lost. During the next three years the Conservatives lost twenty-one seats at by-elections and made no gains. Significantly, the trend was universal across rural and urban seats, and middle class as well as working class areas, as vast numbers of previous Liberal abstainers were attracted to the polls in remarkably high turnouts.[71] This rapid haemorrhaging of Unionist support after May 1902 was largely the consequence of self-inflicted injuries. The succession of Salisbury's nephew, Arthur Balfour, provided the party with brains but not charismatic nor decisive leadership. Like his uncle, he was also perhaps too detached to fully appreciate the partisan implications of policy. Over education, free trade and licensing, government action served simultaneously to undermine the Unionist alliance while unifying Liberal sectionalism in defence of their collective faith. By the same token, the secret pact between MacDonald and Gladstone in 1903, 'Chinese slavery', defence of free trade and the Taff Vale judgement cost the Unionists heavily in industrial constituencies and especially in working class Lancashire and London.

The collapse began with the Education Act of 1902. Although administrative rationalisation and reform were urgently needed to address the chronic plight of impoverished voluntary schools and to rectify the anomalous position of secondary education after the judicial Cockerton judgment (1899–1902), by settling the most contentious sectarian issues in favour of the Anglicans the legislation outraged Nonconformist opinion. Besides provoking a wave of illegal rate-strikes and Dissenting defiance in the country, the Act had the effect of almost immediately reinvigorating grassroots Liberalism in the greatest wave of militant Nonconformist agitation since the 1870s. Liberal revival was dramatically reinforced by the launch of Joseph Chamberlain's great crusade for tariff reform and imperial preference in May 1903. Although in many ways a distinctively Tory response to the intellectual crisis created by the sterility of Salisbury's brand of quietist Conservatism, the effect was to shatter the unity and confidence of the Unionist coalition as 'Whole Hogger' protectionists battled with Unionist Free Traders for the soul of the party, while moderate Balfourites looked on helplessly.[72] Equally important, the assault on free trade united the Liberal alliance as nothing else could in defence of one of the great Victorian certainties. In this mortal struggle the Liberals finally found a great transcendent unifying crusade of almost Gladstonian proportions.

By clinging to office without authority or common purpose, Balfour and the Unionists jettisoned much of their remaining credibility, while accumulating still more grievances among their enemies. The importation into South African mines of cheap Chinese labour, indentured under harsh contracts and kept in appalling conditions, raised the emotional cry of 'Chinese slavery' to unite humanitarians and organised labour. In 1904, temperance passions were aroused by a Licensing Bill which rallied even the more conservative Wesleyan branch of Nonconformity to the Liberals. The heavy costs of military engagements in South Africa and China, combined with naval demands, forced a further rise in income tax and tea duty in 1904, thereby allowing the Liberals to reclaim the Gladstonian mantle of retrenchment while indicting Tory extravagance. Then, in February 1905, Wyndham was forced to resign as Irish Chief Secretary by outraged Ulster Unionists after revelations which called into question the government's commitment to the Irish Union. At the same time, political disasters were compounded by organisational collapse, as the robust superiority of Middleton's party machine rapidly decayed under less competent successors at a time when the Tariff Reform League was intent largely upon internecine warfare to seize control of the local associations, the NUCCA and Central Office.[73]

Confronted by the almost total disintegration of government unity and credibility, in December 1905 Balfour played his last tactical card by resigning rather than dissolving Parliament. By passing the responsibility to form a government to the Liberal opposition rather than the electorate, Balfour hoped Campbell-Bannerman would fail, either because of Rosebery's opposition to official policy on Ireland or because senior Liberal Imperialists would refuse to join such a ministry. In the event, this last gamble also failed. The general election which followed in January–February 1906 produced a landslide victory greater than any since 1832. On an unprecedented swing of 10.6 per cent, the Liberals returned with 400 MPs (216 more than 1900), compared with a combined Unionist strength of 157. Balfour and all but four Cabinet colleagues in the Commons were defeated. Alongside overwhelming victories in Scotland and Wales, the Liberals won a majority of seats in England for the first (and last) time since 1885. On a remarkably uniform swing, the Liberal resurgence was universal across all classes and all major groups.[74] Although the Conservative share of the national vote had fallen by 7.4 per cent since 1900, after allowance is made for a variety of statistical complications, the real decline was more like 10 or even 15 per cent.[75] The election exposed the shallow foundations of Unionist electoral hegemony, built since 1886 by a once superb but now declining party organisation, against a hopelessly divided, poorly funded and ill-organised Liberal party afflicted by chronic abstention among equally demoralised supporters.[76] These negative foundations for the Unionist hegemony always made it vulnerable to a Liberal revival of the sort which occurred after 1902.

Yet while Unionist defeat was predictable given their difficulties since 1900, 1906 was still a classic case of a government losing an election rather than an opposition winning it. The Liberals won the election on a largely negative reactive campaign in defence of traditional Liberal values. The key issues mentioned in over three-quarters of Liberal election addresses were those of free trade, the Education Act, reform of Irish government but not Home Rule, licensing and 'Chinese slavery'.[77] These issues had rallied militant Non-conformity in its greatest crusade against manifest evil since the 1870s. Yet, as for Gladstone after 1868, 1880 and 1892, outrage at Tory wickedness could provide a parliamentary majority without furnishing any positive indication of how it should be employed. This inevitably tended to anchor Campbell-Bannerman's government in a Gladstonian past, rather than propelling it forward to address new issues or embrace novel policy prescriptions. It also increased the fissure within the Progressive Alliance. While the years between 1906 and 1914 saw the re-christened Labour party struggling to assert its distinctive identity as something more than a radical wing of the Liberal party, the existence of fundamental underlying distinctions was clearly already evident in their 1906 election addresses, where the priority was on a very different agenda of working class representation, reversal of Taff Vale, unemployment, old age pensions, the socialisation of property, shorter hours and graduated taxation.[78] These were differences, not of nuance, but of fundamental perspective about working class problems and their resolution; a divergence which neither a return to traditional Gladstonian Liberalism nor a departure into the 'untrodden fields' of social reform and the New Liberalism would necessarily resolve.

Notes and references

The place of publication is London unless otherwise stated.
 1 Sidney Lowe, *The Governance of England* (1904), pp. 129–30, 132.

2 For these events and the origins of the Liberal party see Alan Sykes, *The Rise and Fall of British Liberalism 1776–1988* (1997), chs 1–2.

3 D.A. Hamer, *Liberal Politics in the Age of Gladstone and Rosebery: A Study in Leadership and Policy* (Oxford, 1972), pp. xi, 189–90; Peter Stansky, *Ambitions and Strategies: The Struggle for the Leadership of the Liberal Party in the 1890s* (Oxford, 1964).

4 George L. Bernstein, *Liberalism and Liberal Politics in Edwardian England* (1986), p. 3; Brian Harrison, 'State intervention and moral reform in nineteenth century England', in P. Hollis, ed., *Pressure from Without in Early-Victorian England* (1974), pp. 289–322.

5 Sykes, *Rise and Fall*, pp. 75–87, 100–28.

6 See T.A. Jenkins, *Gladstone, Whiggery and the Liberal Party 1874–1886* (Oxford, 1988); Donald Southgate, *The Passing of the Whigs 1832–1886* (1962).

7 Richard Jay, *Joseph Chamberlain: A Political Study* (Oxford, 1988), p. 71.

8 Hamer, *Liberal Politics*, pp. 99–102.

9 For the high politics of the crisis see A.B. Cooke and J. Vincent, *The Governing Passion: Cabinet Government and Party Politics in Britain 1885–86* (Hassocks, 1974).

10 Graham D. Goodlad, 'Gladstone and his rivals: popular Liberal perceptions of the party leadership in the political crisis of 1885–6', in E.F. Biagini and A.J. Reid, eds, *Currents of Radicalism: Popular Radicalism, Organised Labour and Party Politics in Britain, 1850–1914* (Cambridge, 1991); P.T. Marsh, 'Tearing the bonds: Chamberlain's separation from the Gladstonian Liberals, 1885–6', in B.L. Kinzer, ed., *The Gladstonian Turn of Mind* (Toronto, 1985).

11 Hamer, *Liberal Politics*, p. 122.

12 Bernstein, *Liberalism and Liberal Politics*, p. 9.

13 Michael Kinnear, *The British Voter: An Atlas and Survey since 1885* 2nd edn (1981), pp. 17, 22.

14 P.C. Griffiths, 'The Caucus and the Liberal Party in 1886', *History* 61 (1976), p. 192.

15 G.R. Searle, *The Liberal Party: Triumph and Disintegration, 1886–1929* (1992), p. 38; G.D. Phillips, 'The Whig Lords and Liberalism, 1886–1893', *Historical Journal* 24 (1981), pp. 168–73.

16 Bernstein, *Liberalism and Liberal Politics*, pp. 10, 24–6.

17 Hamer, *Liberal Politics*, pp. 154–6.

18 Stansky, *Ambitions and Strategies*, ch. 3.

19 Peter Marsh, *The Discipline of Popular Government: Lord Salisbury's Domestic Statecraft 1881–1902* (Hassocks, 1978), p. 234.

20 Sykes, *Rise and Fall*, p. 136.

21 Stephen Koss, ed., *The Pro-Boers: The Anatomy of an Antiwar Movement* (Chicago, 1973); H.C.G. Matthew, *The Liberal Imperialists: The Ideas and Politics of a post-Gladstonian Elite* (Oxford, 1973).

22 Matthew, *Liberal Imperialists*, pp. 127–35.

23 Bernard Semmell, *Imperialism and Social Reform: English Social-Imperial Thought 1874–1914* (1960), pp. 62–3; G.R. Searle, *The Quest for National Efficiency: A Study in Politics and Political Thought, 1899–1914* 2nd edn (1990).

24 Matthew, *Liberal Imperialists*, pp. 137, 242–57.

25 Bernstein, *Liberalism and Liberal Politics*, pp. 35, 38.

26 Hamer, *Liberal Politics*, pp. 11–12; John Shepherd, 'Labour and parliament: the Lib–Labs as the first working class MPs, 1885–1906', in Biagini and Reid, eds,

Currents of Radicalism, pp. 197–201.

27 E.P. Thompson, 'Homage to Tom Maguire', in A. Briggs and J. Saville, eds, *Essays in Labour History* (1960).

28 For a critique of these schools of thought see Biagini and Reid, *Currents of Radicalism*, pp. 12–19.

29 David Powell, 'The Liberal ministries and Labour, 1892–95', *History* 68 (1983), pp. 408–26.

30 Roger Geary, *Policing Industrial Disputes, 1893 to 1985* (Cambridge, 1985), pp. 6–24.

31 Keith Laybourn and Jack Reynolds, *Liberalism and the Rise of Labour, 1890–1914* (Beckenham, 1984), pp. 141–2.

32 David Powell, 'The New Liberalism and the rise of Labour, 1886-1906', *Historical Journal* 29 (1986), pp. 381–4, 393.

33 Michael Barker, *Gladstone and Radicalism: The Reconstruction of Liberal Policy in Britain 1885–94* (Hassocks, 1975), pp. 180–8; P.F. Clarke, *Lancashire and the New Liberalism* (Cambridge, 1971), pp. 198–9, 220–1.

34 Henry Pelling, *The Origins of the Labour Party 1880–1900* 2nd edn (Oxford, 1965), ch. 5.

35 Garvin to Edward Goulding, 5 December 1909, in E.H.H. Green, *The Crisis of Conservatism: The Politics, Economics and Ideology of the British Conservative Party, 1880–1914* (1995), p. 205; Pelling, *Origins*, pp. 96–8, 160–3; John Callaghan, *Socialism in Britain since 1884* (Oxford, 1990), pp. 56–9. See also S. Yeo, 'A new life: the religion of socialism in Britain, 1883–96', *History Workshop Journal* 4 (1977).

36 Pelling, *Origins*, chs 2–3; C. Tsuzuki, *H.M. Hyndman and British Socialism* (Oxford, 1961).

37 A.M. McBriar, *Fabian Socialism and English Politics, 1884–1918* (Cambridge, 1962), pp. 95–7.

38 D. Howell, *British Workers and the ILP, 1886–1906* (Manchester, 1983); R.E. Dowse, *Left in the Centre: The Independent Labour Party 1893–1940* (Evanston, 1966), pp. 1–13.

39 Pelling, *Origins*, ch. 10.

40 J. Saville, 'Trade unions and Free Labour: the background to the Taff Vale Decision', in Briggs and Saville, eds, *Essays in Labour History*.

41 Frank Bealey and Henry Pelling, *Labour and Politics 1900–1906: A History of the Labour Representation Committee* (Westport, CT, 1982 edn), p. 31.

42 Peter Clarke, *Liberals and Social Democrats* (Cambridge, 1978), p. 139.

43 See P.F. Clarke, 'The Progressive Movement in England', *Transactions of the Royal Historical Society* 24 (1974), pp. 159–81.

44 Bealey and Pelling, *Labour and Politics*, ch. 6.

45 Roy Douglas, *History of the Liberal Party, 1895–1970* (1971), p. 73.

46 Bealey and Pelling, *Labour and Politics*, ch. 5.

47 Ibid., pp. 245–55.

48 Bernstein, *Liberalism and Liberal Politics*, pp. 40–1.

49 Kinnear, *The British Voter*, p. 30; Duncan Tanner, *Political Change and the Labour Party 1900–1918* (Cambridge, 1990), pp. 165–96.

50 Robert Taylor, *Lord Salisbury* (1975), p. 73.

51 J.P. Cornford, 'The transformation of Conservatism in the late-19th century', *Victorian Studies* 7 (1963–4), pp. 55–7; E.J. Feuchtwanger, *Disraeli, Democracy and the Tory Party: Conservative Leadership and Organisation after the Second Reform Bill* (Oxford, 1968), pp. 80–3; J.P.D. Dunbabin, 'Parliamentary elections in Great

Britain, 1868-1900: a psephological note', *English Historical Review* 81 (1966), pp. 88–90; Peter Clarke, 'Electoral sociology in modern Britain', *History* 57 (1972), pp. 47–9.

52 Green, *The Crisis of Conservatism*, pp. 88–117; J.P. Cornford, 'The parliamentary foundations of the Hotel Cecil', in Robert Robson, ed., *Ideas and Institutions in Victorian Britain* (1967), pp. 268–311.

53 Henry Pelling, *Social Geography of British Elections 1885–1910* (1967), chs 2–3.

54 D.W. Bebbington, 'Nonconformity and electoral sociology, 1867–1918', *Historical Journal* 27 (1984), pp. 633–56.

55 Marsh, *The Discipline of Popular Government*, p. 10. For two recent biographical studies of Salisbury after years of neglect see David Steele, *Lord Salisbury: A Political Life* (1999) and Andrew Roberts, *Salisbury: Victorian Titan* (1999).

56 Alan Sykes, *Tariff Reform in British Politics 1903–1913* (Oxford, 1979), p. 12. For an excellent account of Salisbury's thought see Paul Smith, ed., *Lord Salisbury on Politics: A Selection from his Articles in the Quarterly Review 1860–1883* (Cambridge, 1972), pp. 1–110. Also Michael Pinto-Duschinsky, *The Political Thought of Lord Salisbury 1854–68* (1967).

57 Marsh, *The Discipline of Popular Government*, pp. 106–8.

58 Ibid., pp. 84, 86, 91–2.

59 David Dutton, 'The Unionist Party and social policy, 1906–1914', *Historical Journal* 24 (1981), p. 875.

60 G.R. Searle, *Country Before Party: Coalition and the Idea of 'National Government' in Modern Britain, 1885–1987* (1995), pp. 34–5.

61 Richard Shannon, *The Age of Salisbury, 1881–1902: Unionism and Empire* (1996), pp. 209–11; P. Davis, 'The Liberal Unionist Party and the Irish policy of Lord Salisbury's government 1886–1892', *Historical Journal* 18 (1975), pp. 86–7.

62 I.G.C. Hutchinson, *A Political History of Scotland 1832–1924* (Edinburgh, 1986), pp. 207–12.

63 Shannon, *Age of Salisbury*, pp. 256, 264–7, 398–9.

64 Marsh, *The Discipline of Popular Government*, pp. 127–8, 162–3. J.P.D. Dunbabin, 'The politics of the establishment of County Councils', *Historical Journal* 6 (1963), pp. 226–52.

65 Shannon, *Age of Salisbury*, p. 260.

66 Taylor, *Lord Salisbury*, p. 152.

67 Ibid., p. 151.

68 Ibid., p. 154.

69 Marsh, *The Discipline of Popular Government*, p. 268.

70 Richard Price, *An Imperial War and the British Working Class: Working-Class Attitudes and Reactions to the Boer War 1899–1902* (1972), pp. 97–131. For a different view see M.D. Blanch, 'British society and the war', in P. Warwick, ed., *The South African War* (1980).

71 Neal Blewett, *The Peers, the Parties and the People: The General Elections of 1910* (1972), p. 24.

72 See Alan Sykes, *Tariff Reform in British Politics, 1903–13* (Oxford, 1979); R.A. Rempel, *Unionists Divided: Arthur Balfour, Joseph Chamberlain and the Unionist Free Traders* (Newton Abbot, 1972).

73 John Ramsden, *The Age of Balfour and Baldwin 1902–40* (1978), pp. 45–8; A.K. Russell, *Liberal Landslide: The General Election of 1906* (Newton Abbot, 1973), ch. 2.

74 Russell, *Liberal Landslide*, pp. 145–72; Blewett, *Peers, Parties and People*, pp. 37–41.
75 Kinnear, *The British Voter*, p. 38.
76 Blewett, *Peers, Parties and People*, pp. 21–3.
77 Russell, *Liberal Landslide*, p. 65.
78 Ibid., p. 79.

Chapter five

The challenge of New Liberalism, 1906–1914

'I think the Gladstonian period is slowly coming to an end', Joseph Chamberlain noted in December 1888. 'It will leave great confusion behind it, but its central idea is doomed.'[1] Chamberlain's verdict was prescient, but somewhat premature. Gladstone remained Liberal leader for another five years and his departure did not immediately inaugurate a new style of Liberal politics. The forces which placed poverty and social policy at the top of the political agenda during the last two decades of the nineteenth century were many and diverse. The spur of religious and humanitarian altruism, middle class philanthropy, anxiety about the military security of the British Empire, alarm at lost industrial competitiveness, fear of revolution and a recognition of the power of the newly enfranchised working class all played their part. Yet whatever the reasons, the emergence of a reforming interventionist 'New Liberalism' as a direct response to such concerns signalled a qualitative change in the substance of British politics. Central to this ideological transformation was a fundamental theoretical debate about the rights and duties of the individual and their relationship with society, economy and the State. As the Chairman of the Poor Law Commission later encapsulated this new mood: 'The object and incitement of the nineteenth century was to accumulate wealth, whilst the duty of the twentieth century is the far more difficult task of securing its better distribution.'[2] Doctrinal and policy responses to this challenge created a bitterly contested divide between redistributive collectivist 'Social Radicals' and the majority of Unionists committed to the defence of wealth, property and versions of individualism. Within a few years, this battle extended well beyond questions of social reform to encompass more ferocious struggles over budgetary politics and the sources and structure of taxation. On these foundations, the central defining cleavage between Conservatism and the forces of progressivism were laid for much of the next century, at a time when electoral allegiances were in the process of rapid transition from a confessional to a class alignment.

5.1 The reformulation of Liberalism

Nineteenth century Liberalism has always been intimately associated with the doctrine of 'individualism' and the attendant Victorian virtues of personal responsibility, thrift and self-help. The 'good society' was one which sought to provide the greatest measure of individual freedom compatible with the common good. Although never strictly synonymous with *laissez-faire*, mid-Victorian Liberalism had commenced from the assumption that State intervention in the operation of the market mechanism and contractual obligations was both morally wrong and practically misguided. From such a premise, Bright and the 'Manchester School' had vehemently opposed the Factory Acts as an unwarranted interference in entrepreneurial freedom and the sanctity of the market, while Radicals like Labouchere and Bradlaugh had opposed social legislation as 'immoral' because it 'would strike a blow at the self-reliance of the individual'.3 In reality, of course, Liberal practice had not adhered rigidly to these austere principles. During the nineteenth century much had been done in the interests of those, like women and children, deemed either unable to defend their own interests or incapable of entering into binding contracts. Moreover, the utilitarianism principle of the 'greatest happiness of the greatest number' had provided a permissive foundation for some paternalistic intervention – particularly in municipal health and sanitation. Such departures from principle had not gone entirely uncontested. The popularity of Darwinian science had revived traditional opposition to all forms of artificial activity obstructing the free play of evolutionary forces and competitive individualism. Such themes were prominent in Herbert Spencer's *The Man versus the State* (1884) and Thomas Mackay's collection, *A Plea for Liberty* (1891).4 Yet even at the height of their popularity, the ideas of Spencer and Mackay did not represent the dominant strand of Liberal thought. Increasingly a complex mixture of traditional Liberalism and utilitarianism was combined with the fashionable influences of idealist philosophy and evolutionary theories to lay the foundations for what became the 'New Liberalism'.5

T.H. Green, Professor of Moral Philosophy at Oxford, played a crucial role in this transformation by redefining the nature of the freedom which lies at the heart of Liberal philosophy and action. Rejecting the traditional negative concept of liberty as the absence of restraint, Green advanced a positive notion of freedom as the ability of all individuals to realise their true potential. As this objective could not be achieved in isolation from all other men seeking to do the same, Green stressed interdependence and the notion of a 'common good' which was inextricably associated with the collective fulfilment of individual progress. As the modern State was the means to obtain this 'common good', State action was thus transformed from its traditional role as a constraint upon individual responsibility and freedom into a new positive agency to secure the greatest happiness of the greatest number by removing obstacles to individual self-improvement.6 Henceforth, the scope for legitimate State action would thus depend on how widely such obstacles to individual development were perceived to exist. Certainly, in the hands of J.A. Hobson and L.T. Hobhouse, the idea of liberty as the presence of opportunity rather than the mere absence of restraint, opened the way for a very substantial regulatory and facilitating role for the State.

The 'two Hobs' were undoubtedly the key figures to build on the foundations laid by Green. Although they accepted that in the past the principal barriers to individual freedom had been constitutional and legal and that their removal had demanded the restraint of State power, they argued that the precepts of Cobdenite Liberalism represented an outmoded philosophical approach to the novel challenges of a new century. In particular, the traditional Liberal idea of freedom was meaningless when individuals were victims of an untrammelled free enterprise which deprived able-bodied men of any control over their security of employment or freedom from poverty. As Hobhouse put it in a much-quoted passage in *Liberalism* (1911), 'Liberty without equality is a name of noble sound and squalid result.' As massive disparities of wealth and income produced inequality of opportunity for self-development, they were thus presented as a form of coercion which the community had a collective duty to overcome. By using State power to attack these forms of social and economic coercion, New Liberals thus argued that far from being an evil, government intervention positively increased rather than diminished liberty. Anyway, as all social life involved coercion, Hobhouse contended this merely substituted one form of coercion exercised by individuals for that of the benevolent State. As such, it was 'a question not of increasing or diminishing, but of reorganising, restraint'.[7] Or as John Simon noted in 1897, alongside 'the idea of individuality as secure *from* legislative interference, there has grown up, in apparent contradiction, the idea of individuality as secured *by* legislative interference'.[8] In practice this meant endowing the State with extensive powers with respect to property, public ownership of utilities and key industries, the introduction of a living wage, graduated taxation and a substantial redistributive function alongside public provision of pensions, housing, education, insurance schemes, legal aid and credit facilities for all. Thus, although the attitude of the 'two Hobs' towards the State was not without its ambiguities, on such foundations government clearly now possessed vast scope to intervene in areas previously the preserve of immutable economic laws or personal responsibility. The outcome was a new kind of politics and a 'New Liberalism' which, in Peter Clarke's view, represented a kind of 'social democracy'.[9]

5.2 The conversion of the Liberal party

New Liberal philosophical ideas were disseminated to a wider audience through the universities (particularly Green's Oxford), through progressive non-party organisations like the Rainbow Circle (established 1893) and through the pages of an influential national and provincial Liberal press. Yet despite growing awareness of poverty and gradual shifts in the intellectual thought world of Liberalism, during the 1890s the Liberal party was slow to react to such stimuli. Despite the efforts of some historians to challenge the view of Gladstone as an 'Old Liberal' opponent of State intervention and social reform,[10] as Prime Minister from 1892 to 1894 the 82 year old Liberal leader continued to express alarm at the perils of 'socialistic legislation'. Moreover, Gladstone was not alone in these doubts and divisions within the

Cabinet over the priority to be accorded to social and labour reforms reflected a more fundamental division within the party as a whole. Even within its Radical wing, Hugh Emy points out a crucial distinction between 'traditional Radicals' who retained an enthusiasm for Gladstonian prescriptions and 'Social Radicals' whose advanced opinions on these questions often meant that their programmes in the 1890s were not markedly different from those of the Labour movement.[11] In this context, electoral defeat in 1895 and 1900 retarded rather than promoted a rethinking of Liberal policy. By forcing the party back into its heartlands of Yorkshire, the North East and the Celtic fringe, these elections took a heavy toll among New Liberal MPs while reinforcing the relative strength of more traditional ideas and interests.[12] Nor did the Liberal landslide of 1906 radically transform this situation, although the influx of a significant body of influential Social Radicals to the Liberal benches did marginally change the doctrinal balance within the parliamentary party. In policy terms, however, the election was won on the basis of old issues rather than new ones (see section 4.5 above). Hamer thus suggests that 1906 was less the beginning of a new age than a reversion to 1880 when the Liberals had been swept to power almost entirely on a tide of reaction against Conservatism after a deliberately negative campaign.[13] As a result, in office after 1906, the Liberal Cabinet vainly devoted much early exertion to reforms of a distinctly nineteenth century variety, as debts were paid to sectional interests such as Welsh and Scottish farmers, temperance enthusiasts, Nonconformists and the trade unions – albeit that with the exception of organised labour which obtained the reversal of Taff Vale in the Trades Disputes Act and another Workmen's Compensation Act (both 1906), the other sectional interests had actually achieved very little of substance by 1908.[14]

A variety of forces combined to frustrate both Old and New Liberals after 1906. The veto power of the House of Lords represented a substantial external check upon Liberal freedom of manoeuvre and this was exercised regularly, whenever electoral unpopularity or indifference permitted, to the intense disappointment of Nonconformist 'faddists'. Yet an equally important constraint upon the success of the New Liberal agenda was the relative lack of influence and appeal of their ideas in the Cabinet, the Commons and the constituencies. Certainly since becoming leader Campbell-Bannerman had consistently demonstrated his disinclination to revise his faith in a more traditional conception of Liberalism.[15] 'The policy upon which the Government has taken office … is the policy of retrenchment', he declared in ringing Gladstonian tones in March 1906.[16] Thus, although soon after becoming Prime Minister he had talked of 'a course of strenuous legislation and administration, to secure those social and economic reforms which have been too long delayed', he confined commitment strictly to the level of rhetoric.[17] Moreover, Cabinet composition militated against radical departures. The inclusion of Radicals like Lloyd George should thus not obscure the still overwhelming preponderance of old Gladstonians like Loreburn, Morley, Bryce, Ripon and Burns who regarded New Liberalism with suspicion.[18] New Liberal weakness in Cabinet was reflected elsewhere. In the parliamentary party after 1906 there were only between 50 and 60 Social Radicals, with a core of 25–30, among the 400 Liberal MPs. Moreover, given the absence of any organised institutional strength in the Commons, the NLF or the constituencies, the prospects for further recruitment were relatively limited. Even within their own constituencies, their hold upon the loyalties of their electors was relatively vulnerable and Liberal activists invariably remained tenaciously wedded to the priorities of the Old Liberalism as embodied in the 1891 Newcastle Programme.[19]

Yet despite this inertia, from the spring of 1908 social reform became an increasingly pressing priority for the Liberal government. With his health in rapid decline, Campbell-Bannerman resigned in April 1908 to be succeeded by Asquith. Together with Lloyd George at the Treasury and Churchill at the Board of Trade, this towering triumvirate provided the dynamic driving force behind the triumph of New Liberalism.[20] Between 1908 and 1911 the New Liberalism enjoyed its legislative golden age. In 1908, a nearly universal scheme of State-funded old age pensions was introduced without any taint of pauperism or disability attached to it. The following year, labour exchanges were created to coordinate and improve the operation of the jobs market and the Trade Boards Act established a mechanism to set minimum wages and conditions for four notorious 'sweated' trades (extended in 1913 to cover five more). In 1911 Lloyd George's National Insurance Act represented the high point of the social reform programme. Unlike State-funded pensions, financial imperatives ensured this was funded by the more regressive principle of National Insurance in which worker, employer and State each contributed, although Lloyd George expected eventually to replace this with a wholly State-financed system. Part II of the Act covered a third of the industrial workforce with compulsory unemployment insurance administered by the labour exchanges. Part I dealt with the more complex and controversial question of health insurance for a far broader range of workers and offered free medical care along with sickness, disability and maternity benefits.[21] In addition to these social reforms, after 1908 the government also introduced important measures dealing with the labour market. The Development Commission envisaged in the 1909 Budget was intended to generate employment when trade was slack, while the National Insurance Act was a first step towards protection from the poverty caused by unemployment. To promote industrial harmony, Lloyd George actively extended the practice of industrial conciliation and the number of arbitration boards rose from 162 in 1905 to 325 by 1913. Despite a persistent ambivalence about the statutory regulation of hours within the party leadership, in 1908 a Coal Mines (Eight Hours) Act was passed, to be followed by a Shops Act (1911) which reduced hours in the retail trades. In 1912 a Coal Mines (Minimum Wages) Act brought another protracted campaign to a successful conclusion, although many Liberals opposed the extension of the principle more widely. Moreover, while after 1911 the dynamism and momentum of the New Liberalism did slacken as social reform was increasingly pushed aside by traditional preoccupations with education, Welsh Disestablishment and Irish Home Rule, this should not be overstated. Besides the extension of trade boards in 1913, the launch of the Land Campaign in 1913–14 and Lloyd George's audacious Budget of 1914 all clearly indicated that the reform offensive was intended to continue with higher direct taxation funding maternity and child-care clinics, a housing programme and minimum wages in agriculture. Ultimately, however, it was less over the substance of social reform than the method by which it was to be financed that the most determined battles of these years would be waged.

5.3 Liberals and the politics of taxation

Changing attitudes towards taxation were pivotal to the transformation which occurred in the ideological cleavage between the parties during the Edwardian period. Hobson was correct in asserting that Lloyd George's 1909 'People's Budget' was the product of 'no continuous theory of taxation but sheer political necessity', given the existence of an almost £16,000,000 budget deficit for 1909–10 and grandiose future plans for labour exchanges and National Insurance. Yet it would be wrong to regard this Budget simply as either a pragmatic effort to raise money for social reform (and naval building), or as a backward-looking manifestation of a traditional Radical antipathy towards aristocratic privilege, landed power and the drink trade. Rather it was part of a far broader trend in Liberal thought and policy which exposed the fundamental divergence between the parties over the purpose, sources and nature of taxation and government revenue.

The nineteenth century orthodoxy on the purposes of taxation suggested that the prime objective was to balance the budget at a level consistent with the minimum of expenditure and the maximum respect for private property. On this basis, there existed a broad cross-party consensus that the chief responsibility of government was to maintain the conditions for financial stability in which private individuals could flourish and make their own decisions. Moreover, taxation should be levied in accordance with the principle of 'equality of sacrifice', without differentiation between the source or size of income for fear of rewarding one class at the expense of another – an offence both on economic grounds as well as of justice, because differentials in wealth reflected rewards for initiative, enterprise and hard work. To do otherwise, it was argued, would threaten the very basis of production, capital accumulation and investment. This fiscal consensus on the principles of taxation, established by Peel and refined by Gladstone, had already been breached from necessity rather than ideological conviction during the nineteenth century. Between 1870 and 1895, public expenditure as a percentage of GNP rose dramatically from 1 to 19 per cent before continuing on an even more alarming upward trend. Although the South African War exacerbated the difficulties, the underlying problem was rising ordinary planned expenditure to fund costly Conservative measures like free education, housing reform and workmen's compensation. This fiscal crisis of the late Victorian State compelled politicians of all parties to consider the sources of government income more closely. Unionist Chancellors like Goschen considered a revenue tariff in 1889 before turning to Estate Duty, while Sir Michael Hicks Beach increased income tax and introduced a registration duty on imported corn. Conversely, in the 1894 Budget, the Liberals had reformed death duties into a single graduated estate tax which embodied a modestly progressive structure based on the ability to pay and a recognition that the State had a claim to socially created wealth. As such it tentatively raised new Liberal themes while effectively widening the gulf with the Conservatives. More important, following the popular success of Henry George's 'single tax' tours of Britain in the 1880s, New Liberal thinkers increasingly argued that as much wealth was the consequence of community development rather than individual enterprise, it was possible to differentiate between earned and unearned income. From this position, it was but a short step to the view that this unearned income represented the unjust desserts of capitalists which the State had a positive duty to tax – if only to ensure that the wealth created by society should be appropriated for social ends.[22]

Changes in Liberal attitudes towards the sources of taxation were accompanied by an even more radical transformation in perceptions of its purposes. Between 1895 and 1905 the New Liberal case for the State's redistributive role was based less on arguments about social justice than Hobson's under-consumptionist economics, which argued that mass poverty hampered prosperity for the community as a whole by restricting economic growth and productive capacity.[23] After 1906, however, two factors transformed this emphasis. First, the massive cost of social reform led to a recognition that direct taxation offered the only efficient and equitable means of financing it: a notion of 'fair shares' which led easily to the principled defence of taxation based on the ability to pay. Secondly, Liberals needed to refute Conservative claims that tariff reform offered the only viable means of financing social reform because, as Asquith later claimed, 'if it could not be proved that social reform (not socialism) can be financed on free trade lines then a return to protection is a mortal certainty'.[24] By the Edwardian period, therefore, taxation sharply divided the parties by highlighting profound conflicts between private rights and public good. As such, the New Liberals were advancing a positive constructive role for fiscal policy which went well beyond merely balancing the budget.

Asquith's 1907 Budget represented a major watershed in two fundamental respects. First, he introduced the principle of income differentiation in the form of a lower rate of tax on earned than unearned incomes. This was accompanied by the novel principle of financial continuity, by which governments should plan for rising expenditure for years ahead rather than treating each year's finances as if it were self-contained: an innovation defended on the grounds that the commitment to social reform had become 'a permanent and integral part of the financial system'.[25] Two years later, Lloyd George's 'People's Budget' of April 1909 extended these principles and tapped new sources of revenue.[26] Four of its seven new taxes were on land or site values and included a tax on the 'unearned increment'. Although together these land taxes raised relatively little, they were symbolically gratifying to Liberal (and Labour) backbenchers as a blow to the evils of landlordism. More important financially, however, were the increases in existing taxes, including higher duties on alcohol, tobacco and death, direct tax increases on earned incomes over £2,000 p.a. and on all unearned incomes, along with a new super-tax on those receiving over £5,000 p.a. The significance of the 1909 Budget was twofold. First, this new revenue was obtained without infringing free trade, thereby rebutting Conservative claims that social reform demanded tariff reform. Second, by imposing three-quarters of the tax increases on one-tenth of the population and by emphasising the redistributive fairness of direct taxation based on the ability to pay, the class bias of the Budget was unmistakable. Lloyd George's 'War Budget ... to wage implacable warfare against poverty and squalidness' was thus to be funded by soaking the rich while deliberately leaving the middle and working classes alone.

The Budget was not designed to provoke the Tory-dominated House of Lords into a final cataclysmic confrontation, but this was the result. Either way, the Liberals gained. Unable to resist the provocation of the People's Budget, less because of what it contained than what its land valuation provisions threatened for their future security, Balfour urged the Lords to abandon the constitutional convention and reject the Finance Bill in November 1909. The January 1910 election completely eliminated the Liberal majority, leaving it dependent on the support of 82 Irish Nationalists and 40 Labour MPs. To break the stalemate, Asquith demanded a mass creation of Liberal peers to coerce the Lords into accepting a restriction on their power of veto, but the King declined to operate the 1832 precedent without a second general election. Before it could be held, however, the King died in May. After an inter-party conference struggled unsuccessfully for five months to find a compromise solution, Asquith finally obtained the desired Royal pledge and a second election was fought in December 1910 over the powers of the Lords. Although the result was almost exactly the same as in January, the prospect of being swamped by the promised mass influx of new Liberal peers persuaded the Lords grudgingly to pass the Parliament Act in August 1911; a measure which abolished their veto over financial Bills while reducing it to a two-year delaying power over all other legislation.[27]

Equally indicative of the radicalisation of Liberal ideas in this sphere was the growing emphasis upon a land policy in 1913–14 – both as a partial response to the problems of industrial society and as a source of revenue with which to fund further social reform.[28] At both a principled and a pragmatic level, the value of the Land Campaign was enormous in providing support for the collectivist initiatives of the New Liberalism. Above all, land offered the most obvious example of socially generated income and the easiest target for taxation of the unearned increment – particularly in urban areas where municipal development rapidly increased land values without any corresponding degree of individual enterprise. Even from a purely tactical perspective, the land issue offered a variety of attractions. First, it reinforced claims that extensive social reform could be funded without tariff reform, while offering a panacea for various industrial and urban problems. Second, by attacking traditional enemies like privilege and 'feudalism', the Land Campaign offered scope for a unifying crusade capable of embracing traditional Radicals and New Liberals. Third, all this could be achieved while leaving the Labour leadership stymied because, as they conceded privately, land was 'the economic bedrock of reform' but they could not identify themselves with the campaign too closely 'for fear of losing their independent position and bringing grist to the Liberal mill'.[29] Fourth, by providing a new source of revenue, the Land Campaign offered a means of relieving the rate burden and thereby restoring electoral support among the middle classes whose grievances at higher local taxation had given the Conservatives some municipal successes. Finally, in rural areas it enabled Liberals to rally support among farmers and agricultural labourers in Conservative marginals while driving a wedge between farmers and landlords: a not entirely unrealistic hope given the sheer scale of the rural campaign at its peak in May–June 1914. Certainly the perceived importance of the Land Campaign can be judged by the state of near panic that the 'Land Robbery' issue induced in Conservative ranks between 1912 and 1914.

5.4 Unionist crisis and the politics of taxation, 1906–1910

Despite Unionist ascendancy since 1886, the Edwardian era is rightly described as 'a period which Conservatives would prefer to forget'.[30] In the aftermath of their worst electoral rout between 1832 and 1997, Sir John Gorst predicted in 1906 that 'the old Conservative party has gone forever and ... hereafter the Liberal and Labour parties will divide the supremacy in the state'.[31] Having fallen back on hopes that the swing of the pendulum would return them to office, the two general elections of 1910 removed the Liberal majority, but left the Unionists apparently stranded as a permanent opposition unable to make a decisive breakthrough against a solid anti-Conservative Progressive Alliance. Thereafter, the Unionists remained in opposition until the war finally came to revive their fortunes. Although the equivocating Balfour was driven from the leadership in November 1911 and his successor, Andrew Bonar Law, introduced an aggressive 'new style' of bloody-minded negative resistance to rally party unity, fear of permanent political marginalisation engendered a spirit of near panic in Conservative ranks which eventually led it down some dangerous paths – particularly over Irish Home Rule where they came close to subverting the constitution in their avowed support for armed resistance in Ulster during 1913–14. With the House of Lords emasculated and unable to make an electoral breakthrough, the future looked bleak. Despite a substantial recovery at by-elections after December 1910, the likelihood of another general election defeat in 1915 may even have jeopardised the Conservative party's credibility as an integrative vehicle for the political right in Britain.[32]

Against this background, historians have increasingly tended to characterise the period immediately before the Great War as a potentially near-terminal 'crisis of Conservatism' (see section 5.6 below). Too easily dismissed simply as the culmination of a series of policy and political difficulties concerned with tariff reform, the constitutional crisis and Balfour's weak indecisive leadership, in reality this crisis had its roots in a far more fundamental failure to establish a Conservative *raison d'être* capable of consolidating its natural constituency while extending its electoral base. Moreover, the apparent vitality of New Liberalism and the perceived electoral popularity of social reform served further to intensify this crisis of identity, while imparting a new sense of urgency to their search for a distinctively Conservative response.

Unionist reactions towards the New Liberalism were complex, deliberately ambiguous and often ambivalent. Despite the Disraelian rhetoric of Tory social reform, during the 1890s advocates of a positive social policy designed to woo the working class had confronted massive obstacles in persuading the party of its merits. As Green notes, Salisbury 'seemed to have provided the Conservatives with a quite sizeable bird in the hand, and they were reluctant to relinquish this no matter how many were seen lurking in the bush by the advocates of a more positive appeal'.[33] This was particularly so as they feared that any such departure meant sacrificing core interests in an attempt to outbid New Liberals moving rapidly to the left.[34] Moreover, beyond their alarm at the assault upon property, Conservatives were equally dismayed by the damaging effects these reforms had upon traditional bonds of hierarchy, social obligation and political order. Social reform was thus blamed for promoting industrial unrest after 1911 because Conservatives alleged that it encouraged belief in the 'ever-progressive transference of wealth from those who have worked and saved to those who, whether from misfortune or from fault, have no claim but their poverty to the charity of the State'. The New Liberalism was thus to be resisted as the high road to 'moral corruption' and ultimately to naked class conflict and revolution.[35]

Yet despite these attitudes and their own reluctance to legislate while in office, after 1906 the Unionists often accepted, even commended, some Liberal social reforms. Although in part this was to avoid the electoral unpopularity likely to result from opposition (as over the Trades Disputes Act), it was also true that many Liberal proposals had established antecedents in Conservative discourse.[36] Old age pensions were greeted enthusiastically, as was Part II of the National Insurance Bill dealing with unemployment. Legislation on school meals and medical inspections, labour exchanges and trade boards was treated as non-controversial, while over State-sponsored smallholdings there was some degree of cross-party consensus.[37] Even with regard to industrial intervention, Steel-Maitland conceded in March 1910 that Conservatives now accepted that 'the old theory that the State should no longer interfere in any way in industry ... has been relegated to the rubbish basket'.[38]

In reality, Conservatives were less appalled by the substance of reform than the means by which it was funded. On this basis, they attacked these reforms as 'socialistic' because the State promoted the interests of the propertyless at the direct expense of the propertied. Salisbury had warned as early as 1867 that the new democracy would soon employ taxation as 'an instrument of plunder', and in Edwardian England his nightmare appeared to become a reality.[39] For Conservatives, the ideal form of taxation was indirect rather than direct and founded upon as broad a base as possible so that a large number of taxes each individually rested lightly upon the population. It should also be 'proportionate', insofar as it involved equal contribution without reference to the Liberal notion of ability to pay. Such a doctrine provided ample scope for Conservative resistance to New Liberal budgetary departures. In this context, Lloyd George's so-called 'People's Budget' in 1909 was perceived to be a potentially revolutionary effort to rewrite the rules of the political game by benefiting one class to the detriment of Conservative supporters. As the unchallenged voice of the landed interest, resistance to Liberal fiscal innovation focused particularly on land, which was treated as pivotal to the defence of all property rights. The 1909 Budget thus crystallised emerging divisions between the two parties and provoked an ill-considered Conservative revolt against what it perceived to be the 'quintessence of Socialism': a social revolution characterised by the combined threats from permanently rising taxation, income differentiation against one class of property, social reconstruction and the infringement of property rights.

Yet despite majority alarm and outrage at the social, economic and class implications of Liberal budgetary methods, after 1906 some Unionists were increasingly fearful of being left behind in the competition to exploit social reform to rally working class support. In this context, Conservative enthusiasm for tariff reform was a pragmatic response to a pressing doctrinal, policy and fiscal need. As Green argues, 'the reason the Conservative party embraced the politics of tariff reform in the early twentieth century is the one usually given by miscreant teenagers – it seemed like a good idea at the time.' To put it another way, tariff reform apparently offered a tantalising panacea for a range of fundamental problems besetting the party and the nation, rooted in fears about economic decline, military vulnerability, the imperial and social threat posed by welfare problems and the need for a robust foundation for Unionism when the Union was not under threat.[40] Just as the New Liberalism was an attempt to produce a uniquely Liberal answer to some of these questions, so tariff reform was an effort to provide a distinctively Unionist response. Moreover, when viewed from this perspective, the beauty of tariff reform was that it could accommodate so many different meanings, nuances and policy benefits under a single rhetorical umbrella. Unfortunately for the tariff reformers, not all Conservatives accepted either their diagnosis or their prescription. Nonetheless, like Emy's 'Social Radicals' in the Liberal ranks, Green's 'Radical Conservatives' often entertained bold thoughts about both social reform and the method of funding it, although in their case this was intended specifically as a riposte to the horrors of confiscatory direct taxation so menacingly embraced by New Liberalism.

5.5 Labour, the Progressive Alliance and the New Liberalism

The vigour of the New Liberalism created problems of an equally fundamental, if rather different, variety for Labour. In the Liberal landslide of 1906 the Labour party had won twenty-nine seats – most of them as a result of the secret Gladstone–MacDonald pact. Yet despite its promising start, the period between 1906 and 1914 was an extremely troubled one for what was still essentially a trade union 'pressure group under pressure'.[41] One obvious difficulty stemmed from the poor calibre and lack of experience of Labour MPs and only under MacDonald's chairmanship from 1911 did the PLP convey some sense of real direction and effectiveness. Another problem arose from the Osborne Judgment in 1909 which ruled that union subscriptions could not be used for political purposes; a major long-term constraint upon Labour growth given its dependence largely upon union funds.[42] A more frustrating dilemma concerned the high degree of doctrinal convergence which had existed between parliamentary Labour and Liberalism since 1900. Given the solidly Gladstonian heritage of most of the union-sponsored MPs, any Labour claim to doctrinal distinction was obscured by a more fundamental harmony about the traditional core of Liberal politics which still predominated in both parties. At the same time, the ethical and social foundations provided by Hobson and Hobhouse permitted a close identification between Social Radicals and moderate socialists like Ramsay MacDonald, through the *via media* of groups like the Rainbow Circle. On this basis, New Liberals and socialists often appeared indistinguishable in terms of their expectations and language. 'It is budgets, and not barricades which chiefly interest practical socialists', Keir Hardie declared in 1906: 'Taxation to extinction of unearned incomes' had taken the place of 'death to the capitalist classes'.[43]

Equally fundamental practical problems were engendered by the existence of an overwhelming Liberal majority in a highly adversarial two-party system. The effective choice confronting the PLP was thus between the unthinkable option of asserting its independence by voting with the Tory opposition and the almost equally demoralising prospect of slavishly supporting Liberal measures, thereby raising questions about their autonomy, role and effectiveness. In the short term, Labour effectively demonstrated its independence by campaigning on well-established trade union causes such as the reversal of the Taff Vale judgment and they achieved a notable early success with the Trades Dispute Act in 1906 when the government abandoned their own complicated Bill in favour of a Labour–TUC measure which went well beyond the *status quo ante* of 1875 on the right to strike and peaceful picketing. In the same year Labour's school meals measure was adopted by the government and it contributed to the improvement of a new Workmen's Compensation Act and the Medical Inspection Act. Although on occasions Labour rallied considerable support from backbench Social Radicals frustrated by the government's early lack of progress over social reform, at other times it sought to demonstrate its independence through sponsorship of the 'Right to

Work' Bill. Introduced for the first time in July 1907, at the heart of MacDonald's Private Member's Bill was the duty it imposed on local authorities to provide work or maintenance. Although initially prompted by frustration at government inertia and traditionalist reluctance to combat unemployment, the Bill provided Labour with a policy of direct appeal to organised labour which most Liberals were not prepared to countenance given its unbridled 'socialistic' ambitions.[44] Unfortunately, although Labour introduced the Bill annually until the outbreak of war (except in 1910), after 1908 the legislative momentum of New Liberalism reduced even this scope for Labour to assert its credentials as something more than a radical wing of a reforming Liberal party.

Ironically, the constitutional crisis and general elections of 1910 served to reinforce still further this sense of dependency. Deprived of its overall majority by two inconclusive elections, the Liberal government remained in office principally with Irish Nationalist support in return for another Home Rule Bill. In such circumstances, Labour held the balance of power only in the most theoretical sense given the absence of any realistic alternative. First, Labour's electoral success in 1910 depended entirely on their pact with the Liberals and where cooperation was not forthcoming it won no seats in January and only two seats in December. Second, they needed to preserve Asquith's government at all costs because two elections within a year had imposed such an intolerable burden on Labour finances that it had already been forced to reduce the number of candidates from 78 in January to only 56 in December. Finally, whatever the strategic desirability of appearing to be independent of the Liberals, in the short term Labour had far too much to lose from a change of ministry, given increasing Tory bellicosity towards the unions and its own desperate need to reverse the Osborne Judgment. Although payment for MPs was introduced in return for their support for National Insurance in 1911, it was not until 1913 that the Trade Union Act restored the financial links between the unions and Labour. In the interim, Labour MPs were forced to troop into the lobbies in support of Liberal measures reflecting Liberal priorities.

This apparent subservience to Liberalism inevitably created unrest among Labour's more militant socialist rank-and-file. In 1908, Ben Tillett's vitriolic pamphlet asked, *Is the Parliamentary Labour Party a Failure?* The answer was resoundingly in the affirmative as the docker's leader denounced the 'betrayal' perpetuated by a leadership more concerned with Liberal temperance and Welsh Disestablishment than putting capitalist exploiters on trial or dealing effectively with unemployment. Two years later, even the Parliamentary Committee of the TUC lamented the absence of any significant policy progress. The militant cause was given a substantial boost in July 1907 by socialist by-election victories for Pete Curran in Jarrow and Victor Grayson in Colne Valley. Grayson was ferocious in his condemnation of the PLP leadership as 'traitors to the working class'. Although defeated in 1910, Grayson and some fellow militants seceded from the ILP to join with the Social Democratic Party (the renamed SDF) and Clarion Fellowship to form the British Socialist Party. Yet although the BSP failed to make any more progress than the SDF and affiliated to Labour in 1916, the problem was not confined simply to parliamentary politics and tactics. Although principally economic in origin, the great 'labour unrest' of 1911–14 reflected growing support in some quarters for syndicalist ideas advocating 'Direct Action' through the general strike to overthrow capitalism and create a worker's state. Such challenges were a refutation of the PLP's strategic commitment to the constitutional road provoked by rank-and-file suspicion of the collaborationist tendencies of their own industrial and parliamentary leaders who appeared too closely incorporated into the prevailing system.[45] Undoubtedly, the rash of widespread and often violent strikes in these years made Labour a more militant force and the scale of such disputes was spectacular, reaching a peak of 40,890,000 working days lost in 1912.[46] Yet in reality, the 'labour unrest' was less an upsurge of revolutionary political consciousness than concerned with more mundane issues of trade union recognition, wages and conditions in circumstances in which full employment provided the industrial leverage to restore real wage levels eroded by recent inflation.[47]

Labour difficulties at Westminster should not obscure its very real achievements elsewhere. This is particularly so with regard to its developing extra-parliamentary organisation and support-base. Between 1906 and 1914, the number of trade unionists affiliated to the Labour party rose from 904,496 to 1,572,000, while socialist society membership increased from 17,000 to 33,000. In this context, the absence of a distinctive policy position or a 'socialist' programme was far from a handicap. What mattered was Labour's ability to present itself as the party of the organised working class able to draw freely upon the highly developed class-consciousness and intense class loyalties cultivated by the trade unions.[48] In this respect, a key event was the decision of the Miners' Federation of Great Britain (MFGB) to affiliate to Labour in May 1908, bringing with it almost 900,000 members and twelve additional MPs. Although the accession of these MPs exacerbated the problems of Labour identity through an often tenacious loyalty to Lib–Labism and many ordinary miners continued voting in the same way, in the country Labour could now at least claim to speak for 88 per cent of all trade union members. Moreover, although cooperation with Labour in the constituencies was patchy, particularly in the more prosperous Midland coalfields, the affiliation of the MFGB provided an embryonic organisational network spanning some of Britain's most cohesive working class communities which potentially controlled up to ninety seats.[49] Whatever Labour lacked in terms of a uniquely distinctive ideological programme, therefore, it arguably more than compensated through its emerging identity rooted in the authentic language of working class and trade union experience. Ultimately, it was on this basis of who Labour represented, rather than the principles and policies it articulated, that it acquired its momentum during a period in which government involvement in industrial disputes appeared increasingly to place the Liberals on the side of employers. As Pelling puts it, even among the majority of workers who were not socialists, 'a sort of undogmatic "Labourism" established itself, which consisted of little more than the opinion that the Labour Party, and not the Liberals, was the party for working men to belong to'.[50]

The capture of trade union support brought with it immediate benefits for Labour's organisational development. Among the most important were financial. Although the Trade Union Act (1913) required a secret ballot in each union before the establishment of a political fund to support Labour, all but three of sixty-three ballots voted to do so: events which 'ensured Labour's post-First World War electoral finances, and in themselves reflected an element of the explanation for the rise of the Labour party and the decline of the Liberal party in the early twentieth century'.[51] With more resources, the party organisation was strengthened – particularly as Grants-in-Aid to constituencies introduced in May 1912 increased central control. A larger staff emerged at head office, a National Agent was appointed with two full-time party agents touring the constituencies and twenty local agents were subsidised from the centre – a figure which had risen to eighty by 1918. Such developments encouraged the growth of a more extensive network of affiliated local bodies, trade councils and constituency parties, which increased from 76 in 1906 to 179 by 1914. In Scotland, the replacement of the separate Scottish Workers' Representation Committee with a more effective Scottish Council of the Labour party in 1906 and the imposition of control from London in 1909 improved organisational effectiveness, and there were corresponding enhancements in Wales.[52] Similarly, the formation of the London Labour Party in May 1914 represented a major breakthrough in a city previously bedevilled by SDF–BSP hostility to Labour.[53] At a broader level, in 1911 Lansbury founded the *Daily Herald* to support Labour's own *Daily Citizen* and the plethora of small local papers which gave activists a sense of identity and purpose.[54]

The implications of these developments have prompted a vigorous debate about the future of the Progressive Alliance at the general election planned for 1915. From one perspective, the alliance was already breaking down because the self-restraint upon which it depended was rapidly disappearing on both sides. Local Liberal mistrust of socialism meant the Progressive Alliance was not extended to municipal elections and after 1910 was breaking down at a parliamentary level given the depth of this hostility.[55] Similarly, between 1912 and 1914 Labour's destructive intervention in a series of three-corner by-elections, in seats it could not win but to the detriment of the Liberals, suggests that it would have been difficult to restrain local activists for much longer. According to Ross McKibbin, as Labour plans to field 120–150 candidates in 1915 would have brought it into direct conflict with far more Liberals, the escalation of party warfare would finally have destroyed any semblance of the alliance created in 1903.[56] While Labour may not have won many more seats, therefore, they could have prevented the Liberals from obtaining victory. Certainly, this was the lesson from Labour's intervention in the six by-elections lost to the Unionists between 1912 and 1914, and Asquith was well aware of the danger posed by a junior partner asserting its independence. On the other hand, Duncan Tanner plausibly argues that the

Progressive Alliance was far from dead and that Labour was in no position to make such a challenge given an insecure electoral base, limited resources and a still embryonic organisation. Besides its inability to win any genuine three-corner contest in either of the 1910 elections, the lesson of the fourteen three-corner by-elections after Hanley in 1912 was that without a pact Labour finished at the bottom of the poll while the Conservatives won six due to a Liberal–Labour clash. At a general election in 1915, therefore, the end of the 1903 agreement threatened to gratify a restive Labour rank-and-file only by obliterating the party as a parliamentary force and ushering in the horrors of a Tory government intent upon abolishing payment for MPs and revising the Trade Disputes Act. In this context, Tanner argues that most Labour interventions after 1910 were sanctioned by the leadership in the hope of forcing the Liberals into a more favourable allocation of seats within the Progressive Alliance rather than as a means of destroying it. Talk of running 150 candidates in 1915 was little more than part of the same calculated bluff to achieve this end as Labour would probably have fielded no more than 65 candidates in 1915, rather than the 150 proposed by McKibbin. The pact would thus probably have continued more or less in place into the general election of 1915, notwithstanding the grumbles and disappointment of eager local activists.[57]

Both interpretations contain some element of truth. In practice, the PLP (and even local party activists) had ambivalent attitudes towards tactics but consistently hoped to have the best of both worlds. This required some careful juggling as opportunity and need dictated. Tactically, MacDonald may have favoured a cautious extension of the pact in order to safeguard the seats won in 1910 and to secure further concessions. Yet he also understood the need to distance Labour from Liberalism in membership, loyalties and general aims, in circumstances in which the secret pact was becoming increasingly difficult to sustain. Such a balancing act could not be maintained indefinitely. Yet it says much about the ambiguous position of both partners in the alliance that in 1912 (and twice in 1914) Asquith offered, and MacDonald seriously considered, the prospect of senior Labour figures joining the Liberal ministry at a time when the party was supposedly contemplating independence.[58] Against this background, it may be reasonable to assert that for MacDonald, as for Bonar Law and Asquith, the Great War did not arrive a moment too soon as a release from seemingly intractable party problems of policy and strategy.

5.6 Rumours of a 'Strange Death', 1910–1914

Since the publication of George Dangerfield's impressionistic account of Edwardian politics, the events of the years immediately preceding the Great War have been immortalised as a period of acute political crisis. In particular, they have received closest attention for the clues they offer about the rapid decline of the Liberal party.[59] Confronted by a purportedly cumulative pattern of mounting political turmoil engendered by the constitutional crisis, escalating suffragette disorder, unprecedented syndicalist unrest and a violent recrudescence of the Irish problem, Dangerfield contended that Liberalism was devoid of answers to the challenges of a modern industrial society. In each instance, Dangerfield noted the willingness of Tory peers, militant suffragettes, striking miners and Ulster Protestants to abandon the established norms of liberal democracy to pursue their goals through more violent extra-parliamentary means, even to the extent that Tory leaders were prepared to subvert the constitution and condone civil war over Ulster. As a result, the values and assumptions which had crucially underpinned the flowering of Liberal England under Gladstone were rapidly and decisively eroded. At the same time, the emergence of Labour supposedly spelt the inevitable death of the Liberals, as Labour captured its 'natural' working class constituency leaving the Liberals without any obvious class base to represent. After 1910, therefore, Dangerfield already discerned the 'death knell of Liberalism' as the party began a process of decomposition which laid it to a strange but natural death by 1914.

Although influential in shaping the views of an entire generation of historians after its publication in 1935, today this crude 'sub-Marxian analysis' is easily dismissed as a 'literary confection' devoid of serious analysis.[60] While the pivotal importance of this period is still upheld by a wide range of historians, there is far less consensus about the political implications of these developments – or even about which party was actually most threatened by these events. One recent school of thought tends to depict these years more in terms of 'the Strange Death of Tory England' than as a harbinger of Liberal doom.[61] In the two elections of 1910, the Unionists had polled the largest share of the vote and the record of by-elections between 1910 and 1914 showed signs of distinct improvement. Yet such a performance at the polls was little consolation when the Progressive Alliance prevented them from making a parliamentary breakthrough to form a government. Moreover, Conservative gloom was intensified by continued onslaughts upon their most cherished institutions. The battle over the People's Budget ended with the emasculation of the Lords as an instrument of Conservative defence. Although they mobilised their delaying power against Home Rule and Welsh Disestablishment after 1912, both eventually became law in September 1914. At the same time, the reopening of the running sore over the position of 'food taxes' after the 1910 elections and the launch of the Land Campaign plunged the party still further into despair. In contrast with Dangerfield's picture of cumulative challenge to Liberalism, therefore, some historians present a more convincing vision of the Conservatives between 1910 and 1914 as a defeated, divided and demoralised party wallowing in a deepening 'crisis of Conservatism' because they had a 'problem but no solutions'.[62]

Efforts to find a solution often merely highlighted the scale of the problems. For those who believed the party would be more successful with a constructive programme of welfare reform, the unofficial Unionist Social Reform Committee was established in February 1911 to create a list of specific proposals. Over the next three years the USRC actively urged a range of reforms to the Poor Law, agriculture, education, housing, industrial unrest and health. Yet despite the USRC's efforts to provide 'a distinctive ideology of social reform – a synthesis of traditional Toryism, Fabian Socialism and contemporary ideas about rural regeneration', its brand of Conservative statism was never practical politics given the determined opposition of reactionary, business and propertied elements within the party committed to quietist passivity over social reform and bloody-minded resistance over everything else.[63] Nor were the Conservatives any more united or clear-sighted in addressing the specific problems identified by Dangerfield. Over labour unrest, Tory individualists saw the problem as one of industrial discipline in need of resolute resistance, while Radical Conservatives in the USRC looked to a more dirigiste approach involving a minimum wage, compulsory arbitration and an independent industrial court on the Australasian model. Conversely, over Ireland after 1911, Bonar Law successfully rallied the Unionists behind an uncompromising negativism which obscured and superseded other divisions while restoring leadership authority. At Blenheim Palace in July 1912 this strategy carried Law to the near-treasonable lengths of condoning (and even encouraging) armed resistance in Ulster: a stance which continued until the outbreak of the Great War. Yet even here, it has been suggested that Ireland raised as many difficulties for the Conservatives as for Liberals. In particular, Law's proposal for partition and the exclusion of Ulster from Home Rule opened divisions between Southern and Ulster Unionists, between advocates of partition (like Law and Carson) and those who sought constructive 'Home Rule All Round' (like Austen Chamberlain and Milner), and between those who believed the solution lay in a peaceful positive strategy of defence and those who preferred something more negative and violent. Far more alarming was the problem of where this strategy of fanatical resistance would leave the Unionists when the crisis finally broke. Bonar Law's stance may have contained a significant measure of 'bluff, bluster and brinkmanship' designed initially to unify his own party while extorting maximum concessions from the Liberal government, but as the nation lurched seemingly inexorably towards the prospect of civil war it was progressively less easy to control the forces that had been unleashed and encouraged. By July–August 1914, therefore, Law's high risk political strategy had left the Conservatives playing an extremely dangerous game, from which it was difficult to see a satisfactory outcome for the party, the constitution or the nation.[64]

This 'crisis of Conservatism' fuelled the so-called 'Revolt from the Right' as a loss of confidence in the eternal verities of their identity stimulated a deeper demagogic contempt for parliamentary institutions and party politics. Since the shocking revelations of manpower deficiencies in the Boer War, bodies like the National Service League, Navy League and Imperial Maritime League had flourished to correct these weaknesses. The confiscatory implications of the New Liberalism prompted the formation of the Anti-Socialist Union, Middle Class Defence League and the resurgence of the Liberty & Property Defence League. Collectively this miscellaneous assortment of the 'Radical Right' have been characterised as 'a collection of super-patriots unable for one reason or another to identify with their "natural" party' and alienated from all other existing political organisations. Yet although such discontents were a manifestation of a far wider crisis of European Conservatism between 1870 and 1914, perhaps the main difference in the British experience was the relative weakness and confusion of the extreme proto-fascist Radical Right which always left it confined to the margins of British politics.[65] Moreover, despite this 'legion of leagues', Frans Coetzee suggests that such bodies tended to complement rather than threaten official Conservatism, by mobilising sections of the middle class in support of their party. Ultimately, this may well have been a factor in the failure of British fascism between the wars, for while Continental fascism after 1918 was a continuation of an earlier trend rooted in the long-term failure of mainstream Conservatism, in Britain these populist, nationalist, anti-socialist Radical Right proto-fascist leagues did not gain any mass support.[66]

Although the idea of a 'Strange Death of Tory England' neatly inverts the Dangerfield thesis, a more direct challenge was posed by the emergence of a 'Liberal' Revisionist school which suggested that, far from being a doomed anachronism devoid of any natural class base, the New Liberalism provided a robust doctrinal and policy foundation which had enabled the party to adapt to class politics and capture the support of a responsive working class by 1914. As a result, this new 'social democratic' style of Liberal party had effectively secured its political future and contained the threat from Labour, which between 1910 and 1914 was suffering far more than the Liberals electorally and unable to break out of its position of subservient dependence within the Progressive Alliance.[67] For this 'Liberal' school, the years between 1910 and 1914 apparently provide ample evidence for the notion of 'Labour in decline'. At the two 1910 elections the Liberals had not extended the pact to other Labour candidates and the limitations of its electoral position were brought home by the fact that it came third in twenty-nine of its thirty-five three-cornered contests. Despite the increase in trade union affiliation, many members continued to regard the Liberals as the most effective alternative to Conservatism and the persistence of traditional confessional allegiances made it difficult to convince them that Labour was the answer to their felt needs.[68] Moreover, Labour's electoral situation deteriorated still further between 1910 and 1914 as it came bottom of the poll in fourteen by-elections, losing the four it was defending (two each to the other parties), and even performing poorly in industrial and mining areas. As Philip Snowden lamented in June 1913, the PLP existed 'mainly by the goodwill of the Liberals, and it will disappear when that goodwill is turned into active resentment'.[69]

In contrast, the rival 'Labour' school contends that Labour was already established on an inexorable upward path to replace the Liberals before 1914, through its identification as the authentic voice of organised labour at a time when class allegiances were becoming central to electoral choice.[70] Viewed from this perspective, Labour's disappointing electoral performances before 1914 are explained by reference to two factors. First, its ostensibly disastrous by-election reverses in seats like Hanley in 1912 and Chesterfield in August 1913 were a direct consequence of MacDonald's strategic desire to sever the connection with Lib–Labism, even if this required the short-term loss of a seat. Secondly, it is argued that parliamentary elections are not the best measure of prewar Labour progress, given a highly restrictive electoral system which excluded around half the working class and the still patchy organisational structure of a new party with few paid agents and handicapped by the Osborne Judgment. When the focus is shifted to municipal electoral performance, however, a far more promising picture emerges of significant incursions into Liberal support from 1909 and net gains every year until 1913.[71] Despite Tanner's view that Labour's municipal performance was still disappointing even in industrial areas, the fact remains that from an average of 87 municipal victories in England and Wales (outside London) between 1906 and 1910, Labour representation rose to 171 by 1913.[72] Among the reasons for this better municipal performance was Labour's ability to present a far more distinctive policy position when confronting what in many areas was the predominant Old Liberalism.[73] Thus, while too much should not be read into municipal results, these do not provide evidence of 'Labour in decline'. Indeed, although progress at local level was extremely patchy, in some areas (most notably Lancashire and Yorkshire) the base from which Labour would supersede the Liberals was arguably already present before 1914.

5.7 The electorate and the New Liberalism

Contemporary electoral attitudes towards reform provide a critical test of revisionist claims about the impact and viability of the New Liberalism. Given the political effort devoted to social reform in these years there is no doubt that significant bodies of opinion in all parties perceived the issue to be electorally popular. Yet the Liberals faced a particular dilemma. As Herbert Samuel once noted, it was 'the abiding problem of Liberal statesmanship to raise the enthusiasm of the working class without frightening the middle classes'.[74] The ability of New Liberals to achieve either of these goals in this period is vigorously debated among historians. Like its Edwardian champions, the revisionists tend to assume that the working class were naturally predisposed towards such reforms and that the New Liberalism provided 'a coherent social theory with direct relevance to political and social realities'.[75] The 'Labour' school, however, challenges both the assumption of instinctive support and the underlying belief that middle class perceptions of these 'realities' corresponded with those of the intended beneficiaries. As Pelling argued in his classic essay on the subject,

> the extension of the power of the state at the beginning of this century, which is generally regarded as having laid the foundations of the welfare state, was by no means welcomed by members of the working class, was indeed undertaken over the critical hostility of many of them, perhaps of most of them.[76]

According to Pelling, this hostility derived from working class mistrust of those existing institutions associated with national social policy. In the case of the Poor Law, with its hated workhouse and the stigma of outdoor relief, this was scarcely surprising. Yet there was equally vigorous opposition to compulsory vaccination, slum clearance and compulsory education which increased financial burdens by raising rents and removing child earnings. Working class hostility to the legal system as an instrument of class oppression was also subsequently extended to compulsory arbitration in trade disputes. Against this background, Pelling argued that while middle class Liberal reformers sponsored great measures of social reform in the interests of the working class, 'there is no evidence that social reform was in fact popular with the electorate as a whole until *after* it had been carried out'. Some go even further in arguing that even wartime collectivist developments did not necessarily make workers more receptive to the interventionist State.[77]

Conversely, Pat Thane has argued convincingly that both the working class and the trade unions adopted a far more pragmatic attitude towards specific reform measures on the basis of a personal cost–benefit analysis of their perceived impact. When measured in this manner, there is general agreement that non-contributory old age pensions were immensely popular and strong claims have been advanced for the popularity of the Land Campaign between 1912 and 1914. It is more difficult to assess response to National Insurance because these schemes were scarcely operational before 1914, but there was undoubtedly much initial resentment among workers compelled to contribute without the prospect of immediate benefit and this evidently cost by-election votes even in 1914. Trade unionists were also rightly suspicious of labour exchanges as a mechanism for the recruitment of strike-breakers. Beyond these material objections, however, there was a deeper working class resentment towards the elitist philosophy underpinning the New Liberalism. Social reform was thus something to be imposed from above in the best interests of the poor whether they wanted it or not and irrespective of whether it conformed with the norms of working class life. As a result, respectable working class opinion and organised labour tended to be hostile towards State interference where it undermined the traditional Liberal instincts of personal self-help and opened the way for middle class 'do-gooders' imposing their own standards upon communities they simply did not understand.[78] In this context, it is argued that New Liberals often failed to recognise that the working classes placed far greater emphasis upon 'independence' than 'charity', and so consequently favoured not social but economic reforms which empowered trade unions, increased real wages and enabled them to make their own choices. Similar problems confronted Liberal reformers in the industrial sphere.[79] Ultimately, then, it can be argued that the New Liberalism failed to capture and retain working class support because it emphasised what it did rather than what it was. Liberals pursued their integrative reformist strategy in the misguided hope that it would reduce the need for a distinct party of labour. They were wrong. Although at a general theoretical level revisionists may be correct in the view that 'there is no inconsistency between reformist politics and the development of a trade union consciousness among the working class',[80] the harsh reality was that Labour became the party of the working class rather than the Liberals because it was *of* the working class while Liberals were middle class reformers merely claiming to be *for* the working class as a disadvantaged section of a broader community.

The attitudes of the middle classes are equally contested. Roy Hay contends that business opinion partially accepted social reform as an instrument of 'social control' designed to improve the stability and efficiency of the capitalist system.[81] This was particularly so with regard to improved technical education, labour exchanges and where reforms like pensions and National Insurance enabled the transfer of some labour costs to the State. Yet they were far more hostile to the economic burdens which social reform imposed upon employers and these contributed sharply to the continued drift of middle class business support to the Conservatives during these years. Even before the full force of New Liberal legislation was felt, the proliferation of groups like the Middle Class Defence League, the Personal Rights Association, Income Tax Reduction Society and the Anti-Socialist Union all gave voice to 'the Bitter Cry of the Middle Classes' against the lavish use of ratepayers' money to 'keep thriftless people's children in ... luxury'.[82] This hostility was reflected in Tory municipal victories in November 1906 and the capture of the London County Council in March 1907 for the first time since its establishment in 1889. It was also apparent in the changing occupational profile of the parliamentary Liberal party, as the business contingent declined from some 43 per cent in 1892 to only 33 per cent by December 1910 while their places were taken increasingly by journalists, intellectuals and other men of social conscience. Thus, while businessmen like Alfred Pease, Richard Holt and D.A. Thomas remained on the Liberal benches, they were often enraged by concessions to 'socialism' at the expense of Liberal traditions and middle class taxpayers and such discontents may explain the abnormally high rate of retirements among Liberal MPs in 1910.[83] Yet even on this point historians differ about the impact of compositional changes. Although Clarke portrays this realignment as an essentially healthy development as the Liberals were transformed into a 'social democratic' party capable of addressing the needs of an industrial working class, Emy rightly points out that this was achieved at an extremely high cost in terms of traditional support and finance. In this context, the long-term drift of middle class support to Toryism which pre-dated Home Rule, but which perceptibly increased after 1886, accelerated still further after 1906. As one wealthy Liberal lamented in 1910, it was 'easier for a camel to pass through the eye of a needle than for a rich man to remain in the Liberal party'.[84]

In considering this debate it is important not to overstate the centrality of New Liberal ideas in winning and retaining electoral support in the country as a whole. Clarke's classic study of Lancashire concluded that the robust revival of New Liberalism in the county between 1906 and 1914 pointed to a more broadly applicable 'general theory which can subsume Lancashire as a special case'.[85] More recent local studies, however, cast considerable doubt upon this proposition. Kenneth Morgan suggests that in Wales an Old Liberalism firmly rooted in Nonconformity, Welsh nationalism and Gladstonian slogans survived in a healthy state while the 'New Liberalism barely existed'.[86] Similarly, in Scotland, the most remarkable feature of prewar politics was the

Liberal ability to retain its working class support on the basis of free trade, land reform and temperance and to mobilise it in 'a crusade against socialism'.[87] In other areas of the country, Nonconformity also played a far more important role in retaining both middle and working class support than New Liberalism.[88] Even by the two 1910 elections, there was some evidence that the Liberals were already less a party of either class than of the old Nonconformity of the Celtic fringe and industrial north. In West Yorkshire, Liberalism was controlled by an elite of Nonconformist woollen worsted manufacturing families unreceptive to New Liberal ideas and hostile to working class representation, the ILP and Labour, and a similar picture existed in the North East.[89] Conversely, in London, Edwardian Liberal recovery was due to a temporary combination of socialist hostility to the LRC, the pact with Labour and the resurrection of 'Old' Liberal issues like free trade, the Lords and land, but once the London Labour Party came into existence it made spectacular advances at Liberal expense because it offered better political prospects in an area of previously weak local allegiances on the left.[90]

Two central conclusions appear to emerge from this welter of conflicting evidence. First, the Liberals alienated a significant proportion of their middle class support with policies which also failed to arouse instinctive enthusiasm among the working class, for whom welfare reform was always subordinate to class and industrial interests. Second, where local Liberalism remained most resilient and robust it often did so on the basis of the tenacious hold of Old Liberal and Nonconformist allegiances: a cause for short-term consolation, perhaps, but a source of greater vulnerability in the longer term when confronting a more polarised class electorate. The critical nature of class as a key determinant of electoral behaviour should not be exaggerated. Labour's psephological advance was extremely patchy and the transition from political loyalties rooted in religion, locality and community to class voting was far from complete. Yet on the other hand, there is a tendency for the necessary qualifications and exceptions to obscure the fact that it was more class-based than some revisionists allow. Lancashire was a very different place from London where organised religion was weak and where voting was principally decided by class divisions after 1885.[91] Elsewhere the persistence of denominational loyalties conceals the fact that these were in themselves 'not so much an alternative to class loyalty as class in another guise'.[92] It is just possible that the trend towards voting for overtly class parties on the basis of intense class consciousness did not mean the doom of the Liberal party. Certainly, had it lost the planned peacetime election in 1915, it would not necessarily have been other than a recoverable electoral defeat. Yet these forces of class polarisation were advancing rapidly and the New Liberalism alienated middle class supporters without necessarily winning working class votes. The eventual doom of the Liberals stemmed largely from this problem. In the event, the war dramatically accelerated this process by destroying their ability to respond to the challenge at all.

5.8 Conclusion: the significance of the New Liberalism

Historians are generally agreed that it would be misleading to portray the New Liberalism as a revolutionary transformation in the nature of either Liberal theory or practice, from one immutable form of 'Old' Liberalism associated with Gladstonian individualism, to another antithetical form embodied by Lloyd George and wedded to the cause of direct taxation and uncompromising collectivism.[93] Yet while the philosophy of New Liberalism can be located within an evolving Liberal tradition, there are dangers in underestimating the radical nature of this reformulation for Liberal politics. Only by equating Liberalism loosely with individual liberty can the claim to continuity be sustained – and even then it begs fundamental questions as to the precise nature of that liberty and the constraints upon it. Similar concerns exist about the transformation of Liberal practice. The Victorian era undeniably witnessed significant departures from the minimal State towards State intervention, but blanket assertions of continuity conceal crucial elements of novelty. New Liberals saw the national State as the essential agent of reform within a collectivist framework quite different from the piecemeal exceptions to the prevailing individualist assumptions of the Victorian era. Powers were increasingly national and mandatory rather than permissive in form. The nature of State intervention also took new forms with regard to whom it protected and what it sought to do – particularly in areas previously considered the domain of personal responsibility and through the recognition of unemployment rather than just the unemployed. This implied the acceptance of a new responsibility on the national State rather than just the local taxpayer and such positions could be less easily sustained by traditional Liberal arguments than Victorian factory legislation.

If not exactly a revolution in the political tradition, such developments did at least constitute an unequivocal watershed between the nineteenth and twentieth centuries. Certainly contemporary observers were conscious that something important was happening and that things had changed in some fundamental way.[94] 'This is the last chance of English liberalism', Hobson warned in 1909.

> Unless it is prepared for the efforts, risks, and even sacrifices of expressing the older liberal principles in the new positive form of economic liberty and equality ... it is doomed to the same sort of impotence as has already befallen liberalism in most continental countries.

To reassure the more timid brethren, at times advocates of the New Liberalism presented it as a natural development of Cobdenite precepts. Having accepted the principle of factory legislation on moral and social grounds to protect children, the extension of interference to protect the unemployed was argued to involve a quantitative rather than qualitative change. Yet most of the time, men like Hobhouse, Hobson and Samuel contended that the classical doctrine had 'done its work' and now 'had the air of a creed that is becoming fossilised in an extinct form' (Hobhouse, *Liberalism* (1911), p. 110).[95]

It is difficult to prove the direct influence of a small group of committed New Liberals, supported at various times by a larger number of traditional Radicals and Labour. Yet by the end of 1909 the government had not only adopted most of the specific demands made in the previous four years, but had done so in language which suggested the direct influence of New Liberal philosophers; a remarkable degree of convergence between theory and practice most notable with regard to pensions, National Insurance and the fiscal policy of the 1909 and 1914 Budgets. By 1914 the interventionist collectivist State had arrived in a distinctly twentieth century form. Between 1888 and 1913 expenditure on 'social services' (excluding the Poor Law) rose disproportionately from £5,000,000 to £33,000,000 and appeared likely to continue its inexorable growth. In the same period, the proportion of revenue derived from direct taxation rose from 44 to 60 per cent.[96] The principles of ability to pay and social justice had superseded old notions of 'equality of sacrifice' and the primacy of indirect taxation. Such a transformation crystallised a new and fundamental cleavage between the parties which persisted, in one form or another, throughout the twentieth century. It also assisted the development of an appeal to class and economic self-interest as a central feature of the discourse between parties and voters to the extent that Gladstone would have felt deeply uncomfortable campaigning as a Liberal by 1910.

After the 1910 elections the unusual viciousness of party warfare was underpinned by the recognition that the victor would control social policy – with all this implied for taxation, land and the growth of State responsibility. The impact of New Liberalism thus extended well beyond the Liberal party. As a conscious response to the growing threat from Labour, the promotion of social harmony to head off class and sectional conflict was never going to be easy. Despite the massive impact of the war, however, the evidence appears to suggest that New Liberalism offered no more than a temporary respite to this electoral threat, even before 1914. Ultimately, this was not because of fundamental differences over policy, but rather because organised labour wanted a party of its own capable of mobilising working class aspirations and demands within the context of an authentic working class experience. Liberalism could change its ideological identity to deliver welfare legislation, but the Liberal party could not change its middle class character. Unionists were as divided as the Liberals with regard to the challenge of the New Liberalism. Moreover, this cleavage cannot be dismissed simply as a split between pro-reform Liberal Unionists and reactionary Tories. Nor was it a battle between traditional landed influence and the rising power of the 'Middle Class Monsters' as the Cecils described them. Rather it was a divide between a 'constructive' and 'quietist' approach to the challenge of a mass electorate and the advent of Labour. At one extreme, Radical Conservatives embraced bold schemes well beyond Joseph Chamberlain's own earlier enthusiasm for pensions and social reform. At the other end of the spectrum, the Liberty & Property Defence League denounced all State activity as undisguised 'socialism'.[97] Yet although the temporary ascendancy of the tariff reformers was nearly fatal to the party, as Martin Pugh notes, the tariff campaign itself was 'instrumental in drawing the Tory party towards the twentieth century notion of the State with its responsibility for managing the economy and maintaining the rising standards of the people'.[98] Moreover, although it lacked influence at the time, after 1911 the USRC equipped the Conservatives with a theory of the State with which it would subsequently seek to modernise British industrial life and refurbish its political appeal. This brand of Conservative statism came to fruition in the interwar years under disciples like Baldwin and Neville Chamberlain. Such divisions between, and within, the major parties defined the contours of twentieth century political competition and electoral allegiances.

Notes and references

The place of publication is London unless otherwise stated.

1 J.L. Garvin and J. Amery, *The Life of Joseph Chamberlain* 6 vols (1932–69), II, p. 407.

2 Lord George Hamilton, *Parliamentary Reminiscences and Reflections 1886–1906* (1922), p. 330. For the motives behind social reform see Bentley B. Gilbert, *The Evolution of National Insurance in Great Britain: The Origins of the Welfare State* (1966), pp. 59–80; José Harris, 'The transition to high politics in British social policy 1880–1914', in M. Bentley and J. Stevenson, eds, *High and Low Politics in Modern Britain: Ten Studies* (Oxford, 1983), pp. 58–79.

3 Michael Barker, *Gladstone and Radicalism: The Reconstruction of Liberal Policy in Britain, 1885–94* (Hassocks, 1975), p. 174. See also W.H. Greenleaf, *The British Political Tradition: Volume II, The Ideological Heritage* (1983), pp. 30–48.

4 Greenleaf, *The Ideological Heritage*, pp. 48–102.

5 Michael Freeden, *The New Liberalism: An Ideology of Social Reform* (Oxford, 1977); Peter Clarke, *Liberals and Social Democrats* (Cambridge, 1978).

6 Greenleaf, *The Ideological Heritage*, pp. 124–42. Also M. Richter, *The Politics of Conscience: T.H. Green and his Age* (1964).

7 L. T. Hobhouse, *Liberalism 1911*, p. 48, 81.

8 Greenleaf, *The Ideological Heritage*, p. 144. Emphasis is added.

9 Peter Clarke, 'Liberals and Social Democrats in historical perspective', in Vernon Bogdanor, ed., *Liberal Party Politics* (Oxford, 1983), pp. 27–34.

10 Barker, *Gladstone and Radicalism*, pp. 197–8, 254–6.

11 H.V. Emy, *Liberals, Radicals and Social Politics, 1892–1914* (Cambridge, 1973), pp. 48–9, 54–8, 62–3.

12 Ibid., pp. 94–5.

13 D.A. Hamer, *Liberal Politics in the Age of Gladstone and Rosebery: A Study in Leadership and Policy* (Oxford, 1972), pp. 321–3, 327.

14 George L. Bernstein, *Liberalism and Liberal Politics in Edwardian England* (1986), ch. 5.

15 José Harris and C. Hazelhurst, 'Campbell-Bannerman as Prime Minister', *History* 55 (1970), pp. 360–83.

16 Henry Pelling, *Popular Politics and Society in Late-Victorian Britain* (1968), p. 9.

17 Chris Cook, *A Short History of the Liberal Party 1900–1992* (1993), p. 39.

18 Michael Bentley, *The Climax of Liberal Politics: British Liberalism in Theory and Practice 1868–1918* (1987), pp. 144–5.

19 Emy, *Liberals, Radicals and Social Politics*, pp. 142–4, 185–7, 279, 284–9; Duncan Tanner, *Political Change and the Labour Party, 1900–18* (Cambridge, 1990), pp. 45, 344.

20 For this change in direction see José Harris, *Unemployment and Politics: A Study in English Social Policy 1886–1914* (Oxford, 1972), pp. 264–72.

21 For these reforms see Maurice Bruce, *The Coming of the Welfare State* 4th edn (1968), ch. 5.

22 Emy, *Liberals, Radicals and Social Politics*, pp. 192–3.

23 Ibid., pp. 106–13.

24 Harris, *Unemployment and Politics*, p. 265.

25 Bruce K. Murray, *The People's Budget 1909–10* (Oxford, 1980), p. 172.

26 Ibid., pp. 168–73.

27 For the constitutional crisis see R. Jenkins, *Mr Balfour's Poodle* (1954).

28 Roy Douglas, *Land, People and Politics: A History of the Land Question in the United Kingdom, 1878–1952* (1976), pp. 160–6; H.V. Emy, 'The Land Campaign: Lloyd George as social reformer, 1909–14', in A.J.P. Taylor, *Lloyd George: Twelve Essays* (1971), pp. 35–68; Ian Packer, 'Lloyd George and the Land Campaign 1912–14', in J. Loades, ed., *The Life and Times of David Lloyd George* (Bangor, 1991), pp. 143–52; Bentley B. Gilbert, 'David Lloyd George: the reform of British landholding and the budget of 1914', *Historical Journal* 21 (1978), pp. 117–41.

29 Emy, *Liberals, Radicals and Social Politics*, p. 219.

30 E.H.H. Green, *The Crisis of Conservatism: The Politics, Economics and Ideology of the British Conservative Party, 1880–1914* (1995), p. 1.

31 Harris and Hazelhurst, 'Campbell-Bannerman as Prime Minister', p. 375.

32 For a more optimistic view of electoral prospects see John Ramsden, *The Age of Balfour and Baldwin, 1902–1940* (1978), pp. 85–6.

33 Green, *Crisis of Conservatism*, p. 135.

34 David Dutton, 'The Unionist Party and social policy, 1906–1914', *Historical Journal* 24 (1981), p. 875.

35 Emy, *Liberals, Radicals and Social Politics*, p. 283.

36 Dutton, 'The Unionist Party and social policy', pp. 872–5.

37 Green, *Crisis of Conservatism*, chs 8–10.

38 Emy, *Liberals, Radicals and Social Politics*, p. 275.

39 Robert Taylor, *Lord Salisbury* (1975), p. 17.

40 Green, *Crisis of Conservatism*, p. 11.

41 Henry Pelling, *A Short History of the Labour Party* 8th edn (1985), p. 18.

42 Henry Pelling, 'The politics of the Osborne Judgement', *Historical Journal* 25 (1982), pp. 889–909.

43 Emy, *Liberals, Radicals and Social Politics*, pp. 135, 198; D. Martin, 'Ideology and composition', in K.D. Brown, ed., *The First Labour Party, 1906–1914* (1985), pp. 17–37.

44 K.D. Brown, 'The Labour Party and the unemployment question, 1906–1910', *Historical Journal* 14 (1971), pp. 599–616 and *Labour and Unemployment 1900–1914* (Newton Abbot, 1971).

45 Bob Holton, *British Syndicalism 1910–14* (1976).

46 Henry Pelling, *A History of British Trade Unionism* (1963), p. 293.

47 Henry Pelling, *Popular Politics and Society in Late-Victorian Britain* (1968), ch. 9.

48 Ross McKibbin, *The Evolution of the Labour Party 1910–1924* (Oxford, 1974), p. 243.

49 Ibid., ch. 2; R. Gregory, *The Miners and British Politics 1906–1914* (Oxford, 1968), pp. 11, 188–90.
50 Pelling, *Popular Politics*, p. 118.
51 Chris Wrigley, 'Labour and the trade unions', in Brown, ed., *The First Labour Party*, p. 151.
52 W. Hamish Fraser, 'The Labour Party in Scotland' and P. Stead, 'The Labour Party in Wales', in Brown, ed., *The First Labour Party*, pp. 38–88.
53 Paul Thompson, *Socialists, Liberals and Labour: The Struggle for London, 1885–1914* (1967), pp. 265–86.
54 Deian Hopkins, 'The Labour Party press', in Brown, ed., *The First Labour Party*, pp. 105–28.
55 Bernstein, *Liberalism and Liberal Politics*, pp. 4, 148–50.
56 McKibbin, *Evolution of the Labour Party*, chs 3–4.
57 Duncan Tanner, *Political Change and the Labour Party, 1900–1918* (Cambridge, 1990), pp. 317–37.
58 David Marquand, *Ramsay MacDonald* (1977), pp. 150–1, 159–62.
59 George Dangerfield, *The Strange Death of Liberal England* (1935). For a useful introduction to these events see David Powell, *The Edwardian Crisis: Britain, 1901–1914* (1996).
60 P.F. Clarke, *Lancashire and the New Liberalism* (Cambridge, 1971), p. 6; McKibbin, *Evolution of the Labour Party*, p. 236. Also Carolyn W. White, ' "The Strange Death of Liberal England" in its time', *Albion* 17 (1985), pp. 425–47.
61 E.H.H. Green, 'The Strange Death of Tory England', *Twentieth Century British History* 2 (1991), pp. 67–87; G.R. Searle, 'Critics of Edwardian society: the case of the radical right', in A. O'Day, ed., *The Edwardian Age 1900–14* (1979), p. 79; Dutton, 'The Unionist Party and social policy', p. 884.
62 Green, *Crisis of Conservatism*, p. 270; Ian Packer, 'The Conservatives and the ideology of landownership, 1910–1914', in Martin Francis and Ina Zweiniger-Bargielowska, eds, *The Conservatives and British Society, 1880–1990* (Cardiff, 1996), pp. 39–57.
63 Jane Ridley, 'The Unionist Social Reform Committee, 1911–14: wets before the deluge', *Historical Journal* 30 (1987), pp. 391–413, especially p. 394; Michael Fforde, *Conservatism and Collectivism, 1886–1914* (Edinburgh, 1990), pp. 96–102.
64 Jeremy Smith, 'Bluff, bluster and brinkmanship: Andrew Bonar Law and the third Home Rule Bill', *Historical Journal* 36 (1993), pp. 161–78 and 'Conservative ideology and representations of the Union with Ireland, 1885–1914', in Francis and Zweiniger-Bargielowska, eds, *The Conservatives and British Society*, pp. 34–5. See also Richard Murphy, 'Factions in the Conservative party and the Home Rule crisis, 1912–14', *History*, 1986.
65 Green, *Crisis of Conservatism*, pp. 319–33; Searle, 'Critics of Edwardian society', p. 85; Alan Sykes, 'The Radical Right and the crisis of Conservatism before the First World War', *Historical Journal* 26 (1983), pp. 661–76; Gregory D. Phillips, *The Diehards: Aristocratic Society and Politics in Edwardian England* (Cambridge, Massachusetts, 1979), chs 6–7.
66 Frans Coetzee, *For Party or Country: Nationalism and the Dilemmas of Popular Conservatism in Edwardian England* (New York, 1990), p. 164; Green, *Crisis of Conservatism*, p. 331.
67 Clarke, *Lancashire and the New Liberalism*, p. 6 and 'The electoral position of the Liberal and Labour Parties, 1910–1914', *English Historical Review* 90 (1975),

pp. 818–36; Roy Douglas, 'Labour in decline 1910–14', in K.D Brown, ed., *Essays in Anti-Labour History: Responses to the Rise of Labour* (1974), pp. 74–104.

68 Kenneth Wald, *Crosses on the Ballot: Patterns of British Voter Alignment since 1885* (Princeton, New Jersey, 1983), pp. 214–15, 251.

69 Brown, *The First Labour Party*, p. 1.

70 McKibbin, *Evolution of the Labour Party*; Keith Laybourn, 'The rise of Labour and the decline of Liberalism: the state of the debate', *History* 80 (1995), p. 207–26.

71 M.G. Shepperd and J.L. Halstead, 'Labour's municipal election performance in provincial England and Wales, 1901–13', *Bulletin of the Society for the Study of Labour History* 39 (1979), pp. 39–62.

72 Keith Laybourn, *The Rise of Labour, 1890–1970* (1988), p. 16.

73 M. Cahill, 'Labour in the municipalities', in Brown, ed., *The First Labour Party*, pp. 89–104. See also pp. 56–8.

74 Tanner, *Political Change and the Labour Party*, p. 60.

75 Freeden, *The New Liberalism*, p. 249.

76 Henry Pelling, 'The working class and the origins of the Welfare State', in *Popular Politics and Society in Late-Victorian Britain*, pp. 1–18.

77 T. Adams, 'Labour and the First World War: economy, politics and the erosion of local peculiarity?', *Journal of Regional and Local Studies* 10 (1990), pp. 29–30.

78 Pat Thane, 'The working class and State "Welfare" in Britain, 1880–1914', *Historical Journal* 27 (1984), pp. 885–6, 893–5.

79 David Powell, 'The New Liberalism and the rise of Labour, 1886–1906', *Historical Journal* 29 (1986), pp. 384–94.

80 Peter Clarke, 'Electoral sociology in modern Britain', *History* 57 (1972), p. 49.

81 J.R. Hay, 'Employers and social policy in Britain: the evolution of welfare legislation, 1905–14', *Social History* 4 (1977), pp. 435–55 and 'Employers' attitudes to social policy and the concept of social control, 1900–1920', in P. Thane, ed., *The Origins of British Social Policy* (1978).

82 Emy, *Liberals, Radicals and Social Politics*, pp. 171–3.

83 Ibid., pp. 94–103; Neal Blewett, *The Peers, the Parties and the People: The General Elections of 1910* (1972), pp. 211–15. Also G.R. Searle, 'The Edwardian Liberal Party and business', *English Historical Review* 98 (1993), pp. 28–60.

84 Ibid., p. 285; Clarke, *Lancashire and the New Liberalism*, p. 405.

85 Clarke, *Lancashire and the New Liberalism*, pp. 1–4, 397–8.

86 K.O. Morgan, 'The New Liberalism and the challenge of Labour: the Welsh experience, 1885–1929', in Brown, ed., *Essays in Anti-Labour History*, p. 164.

87 Fraser, 'The Labour Party in Scotland', in Brown, ed., *The First Labour Party*, pp. 49, 59–60; Hutchinson, *A Political History of Scotland 1832–1924: Parties, Elections and Issues* (Edinburgh, 1986), pp. 243–5.

88 Tanner, *Political Change and the Labour Party*, pp. 22, 317, 422.

89 Keith Laybourn and Jack Reynolds, *Liberalism and the Rise of Labour 1890–1918* (1984), pp. 129–30, 168–9; A.W. Purdue, 'The Liberal and Labour Parties in North-East politics, 1900–14: the struggle for supremacy', *International Review of Social History* 26 (1981), pp. 1–24.

90 Thompson, *Socialists, Liberals and Labour*, pp. 286–7. For an alternative view see Clarke, 'Electoral sociology', p. 50. G.L. Bernstein, 'Liberalism and the Progressive Alliance in the constituencies, 1900–14: three case studies', *Historical Journal* 26 (1983), pp. 617–40.

91 Thompson, *Socialists, Liberals and Labour*, pp. 86, 295; Henry Pelling, *Social Geography of British Elections, 1885–1910* (1967), p. 57.

92 José Harris, *Private Lives, Public Spirit: Britain 1870–1914* (Penguin edn, 1984), pp. 7–8; Pelling, *Social Geography*, pp. 418–28.
93 R. Pearson and G. Williams, *Political Thought and Public Policy in the Nineteenth Century: An Introduction* (1984), ch. 5.
94 Greenleaf, *The Ideological Heritage*, pp. 144–6, 161.
95 Edward David, 'The New Liberalism of C.F.G. Masterman, 1873–1927', in Brown, ed., *Essays in Anti-Labour History*, p. 24; Hobhouse, *Liberalism*, p. 110.
96 H.V. Emy, 'The impact of financial policy on English party politics before 1914', *English Historical Review* 15 (1972), p. 130.
97 Green, *Crisis of Conservatism*, p. 129.
98 Martin Pugh, 'Popular Conservatism in Britain: continuity and change, 1880–1987', *Journal of British Studies* 28 (1988), p. 63.

Chapter six

War and the party system

In contrast with the relatively limited and temporary nature of many of the domestic socio-economic changes prompted by the war, the impact on the British party system appears to have been far more dramatic in both scope and magnitude. As Martin Pugh suggests, 'the argument is not so much whether the war represented a major discontinuity, but whether it was *the* key discontinuity in modern British history'.[1] Yet underlying such a question lurk deeper controversies as to whether in party terms – as in socio-economic matters – the war represented a catalyst for total change or simply accelerated existing trends evident long before 1914. The most obvious point of contention concerns the argument that war fatally damaged the Liberal party, enabling Labour swiftly to supersede it as the alternative party of government. In 1914 the Liberals were still the dominant party and modestly confident of their prospects at the next general election. By January 1919 Labour occupied the opposition front bench and five years later it formed its first minority government while the Liberals looked on as impotent bystanders. The speed and drama of this transformation in Liberal fortunes inevitably focuses attention upon the impact of the war. Yet the war also transformed the fortunes of each of the other parties. For the Irish Nationalists, war robbed them of both purpose and appeal and prompted their eventual eclipse by the more radical demands of Sinn Fein. Labour was also divided by war, but it emerged from the experience a more confident and cohesive force. Similarly, the impact of war upon the Conservatives was far from negligible. Moreover, contrary to easy assumptions about the compatibility of war and Conservatism, its immediate effects were not altogether positive, although in the longer term it would become the principal beneficiary of several of these trends.

6.1 Liberalism divided

British entry to war in August 1914 was fraught with potential difficulties for the Cabinet and the Liberal party. Although Asquith initially rejoiced that European war had averted the imminent explosion of civil war in Ulster, the Irish problem could not be entirely ignored any more than the recent record of industrial militancy allowed the authorities to dismiss the threat of a general strike to prevent a capitalist war. In the event, however, these apprehensions proved groundless as patriotism and national unity prevailed. Asquith enjoyed an equally spectacular triumph in preserving the unity of the Cabinet, Liberal party and the Progressive Alliance. The Liberal party possessed a powerful Radical, Gladstonian wing with strong pacifist and 'pacificist' tendencies. On the eve of war, Asquith believed three-quarters of his backbenchers and 'a strong party' in Cabinet were 'against any kind of intervention in any event'.[2] Ultimately, however, German violation of 'poor little Belgium' resolved the Liberal dilemma. Grey's speech to the Commons on 3 August rallied a reluctant party behind a high-minded moral stand in defence of small nations and treaty obligations against the brutality of Prussian militarism. The only Cabinet resignations were those of John Burns and John Morley (with Charles Trevelyan from the junior ranks), but such losses were easily sustained, particularly as they made no effort to coordinate backbench dissent.

Asquith's handling of the other parties was equally adroit. Despite the deteriorating situation in Ireland in July 1914, Ulster Unionists and Irish Nationalists were soon harnessed to support the British war effort. The 'electoral truce' with the Conservatives and Labour on 28 August removed government anxiety at the divisive prospect of contested by-elections. Thereafter, the Conservatives adopted a stance of 'patriotic opposition' and began to wind down their party organisation. The appointment of a respected non-party soldier like Lord Kitchener to the War Office also represented a potentially promising tactic for deflecting future Conservative criticism from government conduct of the war. At the same time, Parliament effectively went into abeyance. Except for a brief session to deal with Irish Home Rule between 25 August and 15 September, it did not meet again until 11 November and its first division was delayed until July 1915. Against this background, there is some substance for the claim that Asquith had proved himself to be 'the essential Prime Minister' through his skill in leading Britain united into war.[3] Unfortunately for Asquith and the Liberal party, this reputation would not survive the challenges of a very different kind of war from that envisaged in August 1914. For all his early success, Asquith's political acumen could not resolve military problems. The war was not over by Christmas. Stalemate on the Western Front, spiralling casualty lists and the evident limitations of seapower on which military planners had placed their faith before 1914, all removed any prospect of an early victory. Outside Parliament, military disappointments fuelled a ferocious partisan attack upon the government from the right-wing press. In Parliament, they created the opportunity for bitter conflicts based on personal ambition and party rivalries. Military failure also provoked more fundamental, cross-party tensions between those who believed the war could still be won by 'traditional' means and those who came to recognise that only a wholesale reorganisation of State and economy would deliver victory.

The first major political crisis of the war erupted suddenly in May 1915 and ended with the collapse of the last Liberal government in British history.[4] The immediate causes of the crisis were twofold. First, the so-called 'shell scandal' exploded on 14 May. The public revelation of military allegations about a shortage of high explosive shells on the Western Front appalled public opinion and rendered the government extremely vulnerable. The second crisis broke on the following day, precipitated by the astonishing resignation of Admiral Lord Fisher as First Sea Lord in protest at Churchill's conduct of the Dardanelles campaign. Against this background, the backbench Unionist Business Committee threatened a debate on munitions in order to pressurise Bonar Law into demanding a more vigorous prosecution of the war. On 17 May Law consulted Lloyd George at the Treasury and both agreed that a coalition was necessary. Lloyd George then informed Asquith who also agreed. To everyone's surprise, the whole matter was allegedly settled within a quarter of an hour. The question ever since has been why these three key actors should all have agreed so readily to such a course.

In many ways Lloyd George's motives are least complex. He was known to be generally disenchanted with the conduct of the war – particularly Kitchener's incompetence at the War Office – and favoured coalition as a means of taking personal control of munitions production. In some accounts, Lloyd George's instinctive propensity for coalitionism also coalesced with an equally innate sense of personal ambition.[5] Yet Lloyd George's motives do not explain why Law and Asquith both acceded so swiftly to the idea. After all, Law did not share Lloyd George's coalitionist sympathies and had opposed the idea in August and December 1914 and again in March 1915. Similarly, Asquith had relatively little to fear from parliamentary defeat with so many Conservative MPs away at the front. In this context, the most plausible explanation for the actions of both Law and Asquith was that a coalition offered them the most convenient escape from their respective problems as party leaders. Certainly, the critical factor in changing Law's mind was the recognition that he could not confine Tory backbenchers to a restrained form of 'patriotic opposition'. The legacy of intense partisan passions since 1906 left an enduring bitterness which could not easily be assuaged by the acceptance of a limited electoral truce. The fragile nature of this party truce had been exposed by the passage of Home Rule and Welsh Disestablishment in a special session in September which many Conservatives regarded as a gross betrayal. By late January 1915 the difficulty of sustaining this posture of patriotic opposition was painfully exposed by an overt challenge to Law's strategy and authority as leader and the formation of a backbench Unionist Business Committee dedicated to the more effective conduct of the war. Although initially the UBC provided a valuable safety valve for pent-up backbench energy and frustrations, this positive role in reducing intra-party tensions came to an abrupt end on 29 March when Lloyd George's proposal for State purchase and control of the entire liquor trade inflamed Tory discontents. Although Law swiftly withdrew his initial support for the proposal when he recognised the strength of these feelings, his inept handling of the liquor question in April–May 1915 opened a gaping chasm between the leadership and its backbenchers. As such, John Stubbs argues that the liquor crisis was a third short-term explanation for the May 1915 coalition, alongside the shell scandal and Fisher's resignation.[6] In many respects, the UBC represented a greater threat to Law's leadership than to Asquith's government. By demanding a debate on the shell scandal it was effectively challenging Law's authority and the passive definition of 'patriotic opposition' to which he had committed them. In this context, coalition represented the lesser of two evils for Law by offering a convenient alternative to backbench revolt and a divisive wartime election.

Asquith's change of heart was the product of a similar calculation of pragmatic advantage. Despite the combined force of Law and Lloyd George, Asquith was in a far stronger position than is often recognised given his support in the Cabinet, parliamentary party and the country. With so many Conservative MPs absent on military duties he certainly did not expect the government to fall over either the shell scandal or Fisher.[7] Yet although he would have preferred to continue in office alone, he also recognised the dangers in such a course given no prospect of military success to insulate the government from right-wing criticism until Kitchener's New Army was ready for action in the summer of 1916. The need to renew the electoral truce on a monthly basis since March and the prospect of a general election by December 1915, thus conferred urgency on these calculations. In this context, Asquith's own explanation for his actions in May 1915 was that he was already convinced of the necessity for such an arrangement and merely needed a suitable pretext.[8] Law's intra-party difficulties and Fisher's resignation provided that opportunity. Thus, as Martin Pugh argues, the first wartime coalition was more a consequence of collusion than party conflict, as both leaders reluctantly imposed a convenient outcome upon their resentful supporters in order to resolve their own problems and avoid a damaging Khaki election.

Asquith made remarkably few concessions to his new allies when forming the coalition. Only eight Conservatives received Cabinet posts compared with twelve Liberals and one Labour; proportions reflected in the junior ministerial ranks.[9] While Balfour's appointment to the Admiralty effectively confirmed his existing membership of the War Council, both Asquith and Lloyd George were determined to exclude Law from anything more substantial than the Colonial Office. As a result, the new government 'was only halfway to coalition; ... a coalition of parties rather than a coalition of men, and it was run so as to maximise continuity'.[10] Yet in the longer term, this was its greatest source of vulnerability. Asquith hoped a coalition would compel his Conservative detractors to share the blame for the conduct of the war and in so doing restrain the right-wing press. Yet by limiting Conservative participation so effectively, the blame was not shared. On the contrary, the imbalance served only to increase Unionist resentment without creating any compensating sense of real loyalty or identification among mutually suspicious rivals. Moreover, by failing to consult his Liberal followers about coalition, Asquith also unsettled and alienated his own supporters – particularly as coalition required the sacrifice of Haldane to Tory prejudice.

The Asquith Coalition struggled on for nineteen agonising months. From the outset it was a story of chaos and mounting pessimism in the face of widespread military reverses on the Somme, the Dardanelles, Mesopotamia, Serbia, the Russian front and in the North Sea. Worse still, increasing pressure upon recruitment turned manpower into the most divisive issue confronting the government. Although by December 1914 some 1,186,000 men had enlisted in the first flush of patriotic zeal, voluntary recruitment was always problematical as a source of military manpower the longer hostilities continued. As casualty lists lengthened during 1915 the flow of men began to dwindle. In October 1915 Lord Derby, the Director of Recruiting, invited men to attest their willingness to serve if required and Asquith promised all single men would be taken before married men – a pledge which had the effect principally of stimulating a spate of marriages. Although the Derby Scheme was a 'shot-gun wedding between the fair maid of Liberal idealism and the ogre of Tory militarism', it failed to deliver the goods. In January 1916, the revelation that only 1,150,000 of the 2,179,231 single men on the National Register of manpower had attested, led immediately to the acceptance of compulsion for single men aged 18–41 years.[11] Three months later, full conscription for married men was adopted on similar terms. By 30 November 1916 it had been decided to extend conscription to all adults and all forms of employment.

Combined with military disappointment, this tortured progress towards conscription convinced many that the war could not be won under Asquith. Sympathetic historians argue that during the first eighteen months of the war Asquith's record was 'decidedly impressive', not least because 'among the potential leaders he was the one who, when he did not unite the country, divided it least'.[12] Yet from the spring of 1916 this ascendancy rapidly receded. His old shrewdness and intellectual dominance over his Cabinet were less evident. For many observers, his methods, leadership style and temperament had simply failed to adapt to the changing demands of war. Moreover, while his drinking gave new force to jibes about old 'Squiffy', his fondness for the company of young women and prewar relaxations smacked of dilettantism and made him an easy scapegoat for national misfortunes.[13] Thus, the more depressing the news from the front, the more insistent became the demands for a ruthless prosecution of the war by new men employing bold and novel methods. From the outset, Lloyd George's restless dynamism made him the embodiment of precisely this spirit. Although Conservatives retained their deep mistrust towards Lloyd George's politics, character and integrity, he was recognised as a symbol of the nation's will to victory. In late November the right-wing *Morning Post* called upon its readers to rally behind Lloyd George and subsequently attacked Law for his continued support for Asquith. A few days later, Unionist ministers resolved to put personal preferences aside and make Lloyd George Prime Minister to achieve the victory Asquith could not give them.

As in May 1915, the impetus came from the threat of Conservative backbenchers to repudiate Law's leadership. The formation of the Unionist War Committee with an active membership of around 150 provided backbench critics with considerable leverage – particularly as it coordinated action with the forty MPs in the like-minded Liberal War Committee (also established January 1916). Although the UWC enjoyed some initial success in coercing Law into more assertive demands for conscription, by the summer it was deeply discontented over Conservative ensnarement in the coalition under a leader apparently hypnotised by Asquith. Such tensions came to a climax on 8 November 1916 in the Nigeria debate. Although ostensibly about a relatively trivial question concerning the sale of enemy property in Nigeria, the underlying issue was a trial of strength between Law and his critics. In the event, although Law was supported by seventy-two Unionist MPs, to sixty-five against with thirty five abstaining, both the bitterness of the debate and the arithmetic convinced Law of the need to act decisively to realign himself with his own supporters. This meant a new government, possibly under Lloyd George. After considerable negotiation, manoeuvre, bluff and counter-bluff, during the first week in December the Lloyd Georgite strategy and Unionist need coincided. On 5 December 1916 Asquith resigned. When Asquith rejected Law's offer of a Cabinet place, the Unionist leader made way for Lloyd George to form a new coalition on 7 December 1916.[14]

The formation of the Lloyd George Coalition ushered in a new period in British party politics as well as a new style of war leadership. In the short term Lloyd George's accession to the premiership did not miraculously produce a reversal of military misfortunes or domestic problems. On the contrary, 1917 was a particularly gloomy period of the war. Yet the government enjoyed a far greater level of effectiveness than its predecessors – not least because it substituted Asquith's persistent partisanship with a new style of consensus and supra-party unity which Lloyd George cultivated well into the years of peace.[15] Although Lloyd George had a poor opinion of Law before the December crisis, they worked together astonishingly closely and a real bond of personal intimacy developed between them. As Leader of the Commons and deputy Prime Minister, Law provided loyal support and worked assiduously to avert threats to government unity – particularly during Lloyd George's battles with the generals which caused so much Tory consternation in 1917–18. Similarly, after initial mutterings of discontent, Labour was won over by promises of State enterprises, postwar reconstruction and places in the new ministry. By removing the partisan divisions and animosities so corrosive of the authority of Asquith's coalition from its inception, Lloyd George thus emerged as a truly national leader in a way in which Asquith never could.

While the Coalition remained united, Lloyd George had little to fear from Asquith or the Commons. Admittedly, Asquith faced an extremely delicate predicament, torn (like Law before him) between the imperative for 'patriotic opposition' and the appearance of passivity and political redundancy.[16] Equally evident was Asquith's profound disinclination to employ the sort of partisan tactics which had undermined his own position. Yet despite the constraints, during the last two years of the war Asquith showed himself at his worst as a leader. On one hand, his repeated refusal to serve under Lloyd George formalised the Liberal party split. On the other hand, his consistent failure to lead those Liberals who continued to support him condemned them all to a pathetic impotence on the margins of British politics from which they never re-emerged. While Asquithian backbenchers belaboured the Coalition over fundamental points of Liberal principle, their front bench either sat back as mute observers or absented themselves altogether. Only over control of military strategy did Asquith rouse himself from his political somnambulism to challenge Lloyd George. Yet when he made his stand during the Maurice debate in May 1918, over allegations that Lloyd George had lied to Parliament about starving Haig of troops on the Western Front, his inept speech let Lloyd George off the hook. The impact of this prolonged period of dismal non-leadership from the opposition front bench gravely impaired the credibility and confidence of the Asquithians in Parliament and the country.

In the longer term, the outcome of the December 1916 crisis was a devastating blow to the Liberal party. Arguably, it accelerated the process of Liberal demoralisation and decline from which it never recovered. To some degree these events substantiate the view of the 'contingency school' that Liberalism succumbed to its eventual fate through a variety of historical accidents, bad luck and poor judgement. In some respects, the Liberals were profoundly unfortunate simply in being in the wrong place at the wrong time in August 1914. Without the war, the Lloyd George–Asquith schism would probably never have occurred. Yet when it did, the bitter personal breach poisoned relations between the two mutually hostile groups throughout the interwar years. The perpetuation of this rift came to matter to many Asquithians more than even power itself. Everything was subordinated to the desire to exclude Lloyd George and prevent his rehabilitation to a Liberal state of grace. Yet the drama of the personal feud should not obscure the more fundamental ideological cleavage which lay at its root. It would be profoundly misleading to depict the crisis of December 1916 simply as a battle for personal ascendancy in which Lloyd George delivered a poisoned dagger to Asquith's noble back largely to satiate an unbridled lust for power. Ultimately, Lloyd George and Asquith parted company over different interpretations of Liberal principle, priorities and broader ideological agendas. Personal feud and ideological schizophrenia were not distinct, rival or exclusive explanations for Liberal decline during the war. Quite the reverse. In many crucial respects they represent mutually reinforcing cleavages which served fundamentally to undermine the viability of the British Liberal party, if not necessarily British Liberalism.

6.2 Liberal ideology and the strains of war

In October 1908 Churchill had declared prophetically that 'war is fatal to Liberalism'.[17] This theme has been widely echoed by historians. In its crudest form, this thesis suggests that the first two years of the war witnessed the 'last experiment in running a great war on the principles of *laissez faire*' before ending in collapse when it became clear that the real choices were between 'War Socialism or a negotiated peace'. December 1916 thus represented an ideological and policy watershed between nineteenth century *laissez-faire* and the collectivist interventionism of the twentieth century: rival positions in which Asquith's personification of the former was decisively defeated in 1916 by Lloyd George's determination to wage all-out war.[18] Yet to present December 1916 in this manner is scarcely convincing. First, the *laissez-faire* of the nineteenth century was never quite so austerely defined or so rigorously applied, and insofar as it ever was, New Liberal collectivism had already dealt it a mortal blow before 1914. Second, just as *laissez-faire* was less complete than suggested, so was wartime interventionism. Many of these measures were essentially pragmatic, short-term, piecemeal and cautious responses to the mounting crisis, with scarcely any roots in a new ideological approach to the State – hence the speed with which the State retreated again after the return of peace. Third, many key elements of this supposed collectivist transformation were introduced by Asquithians prior to 1916. Such men had no qualms about taking control of the railways, the sugar industry or maritime insurance to keep the merchant fleet at sea. Similarly, McKenna dramatically raised direct taxation, introduced Excess Profits Duty at 50 per cent and broke with free trade more than a year before the 1916 crisis without any ideological sympathy for Lloyd George's approach. Finally, in many respects, the transition from Asquith to Lloyd George was more a question of style than substance, and in some respects Lloyd George was significantly less bold than the Asquith Coalition – not least, in dealing with food rationing and the decision of November 1916 for full industrial and military conscription.[19]

A more sophisticated exposition of the 'contingency school' view that war played a crucial role in Liberal decline is presented by Trevor Wilson. In Wilson's memorable analogy, the Great War was the 'rampant omnibus' which mounted the pavement and ran down the ailing Liberal pedestrian before the severity of his symptoms of illness (Ireland, labour unrest and the suffragettes) could be diagnosed.

> After lingering painfully, he expired. A controversy has persisted ever since as to what killed him. One medical school argues that even without the bus he would soon have died ... Another school goes further, and says that the encounter with the bus would not have proved fatal had not the victim's health already been seriously impaired. Neither of these views is accepted here ... All that is known is that at one moment he was up and walking and at the next he was flat on his back, never to rise again; and in the interval he had been run over by a bus. If it is guess-work to say that the bus was mainly responsible for his demise, it is the most warrantable guess that can be made.[20]

Although according to Wilson the injury inflicted was partly attributable to the personal feud between Asquith and Lloyd George, at the core of his argument is the contention that the Great War exerted a far more corrosive influence upon Liberal doctrine with disastrous implications for the loyalties of those who subscribed to it. The successful conduct of the war required the abandonment or suspension of many defining Liberal principles. Those which were not compromised by war were often eclipsed and never to re-emerge – particularly the great Nonconformist issues of denominational education, temperance, Welsh Disestablishment and land reform which bound Dissenters to the party before 1914 but which rarely appeared on the political agenda after 1918.[21] There is much force in the view that 'the Liberal Party fell ... because of a revolution in ideas occurring in the minds of men'.[22] The McKenna duties introduced in September 1915 were a breach in the hallowed edifice of free trade which prompted thirty Liberal backbenchers to rebel. Runciman's acceptance of the protectionist Paris Resolutions in 1916 was a further nail in the coffin of Liberal free trade. The Treasury Agreement of March 1915 (and later the Munitions of War Act in 1916) rendered strikes illegal and disrupted the notion of freedom of contract. The Rent Restrictions Act of December 1915 enabled government to trample on the rights of private property in the interests of morale and war production, while the Defence of the Realm Act (DORA) conferred unprecedented powers over society, economy and individual. Press censorship, the internment of enemy aliens and the disenfranchisement of conscientious objectors, were all an affront to Liberal claims to be the party of individual conscience and liberty. Above all, there was the profoundly damaging slide into conscription. In January 1916, voluntarism and liberal values were defeated by a measure which many Liberals considered to be a triumph for the very Prussian authoritarianism against which the war was being fought. Moreover, in denouncing the Conscription Bill, the Liberal *Daily News* expressed the fears of many in opposing 'a principle which is alien to our spirit and which once introduced will remain a permanent menace to our conceptions of liberty'.[23]

It was possible to defend such measures by reference to the sheer scale of the conflagration. By 1915 it was simply unrealistic to talk of 'business as usual' when the war was costing more than £3 million per day to sustain two and a half million men in uniform; a figure which rose to almost four and a half million in 1917–18. Liberal pragmatists could also console themselves with the thought that the breach with past Liberal principle was neither so sharp nor so substantial as it appeared. After all, the peacetime Liberal government had introduced the Official Secrets Act in 1911 without too much anguish about the erosion of individual rights while DORA, the Aliens Registration Act, the National Register Act and strict censorship were also accepted by most as emergency wartime measures. For many Liberals, the absolute moral issue was thus compellingly transformed into a relative matter of accepting the lesser of two evils in order to ensure national survival and the restoration of all liberties after victory.[24] Furthermore, in acknowledging these adverse effects, it is important not to overstate the degree to which hallowed Liberal principles were sacrificed to the gods of war. Even the Asquith Cabinet could not be bullied into interning aliens with British naturalisation despite much xenophobic public pressure. Similarly, despite the demand for conscription, the government still granted exemptions to some 16,500 conscientious objectors. Although tribunals were often cursory, unsympathetic and harsh, the very fact that the concept was conceded at all in the midst of such a war represented a modest triumph for liberal values over blind patriotic compulsion.[25]

Yet among Liberal intellectuals such doctrinal compromises prompted gnawing doubts. Before 1914 New Liberalism had assumed that individual political and civil liberties were already secure and that the new challenge lay in the social and economic sphere where State compulsion was a condition of a larger freedom. Yet the impact of war compelled many New Liberals like Hobhouse and Hobson to rediscover liberty as the quintessential characteristic of Liberalism and to reconsider their optimistic faith in the State as a benevolent agent of social change for the common good. Ironically, they were moving in this direction at precisely the moment when many 'Old Liberals' came to accept restrictions on individual liberty and freedom of conscience for the common good, on the basis of a newly acquired patriotic, communal and quasi-organic view of society. There are a variety of explanations for this curious reorientation of Liberal thought during the war among the left-liberal intelligentsia. Some were out of sympathy with war aims and practice. Others drew a qualitative distinction between the limited ambitions of prewar New Liberalism directed at specific underprivileged groups and the universal application of wartime measures for the 'Prussianisation' of the State. Yet the outcome of such musings was two decades of Liberal ideological crisis during which 'hairline cracks widened into rifts that would not heal, and its edifice was revealed to contain ill-fitting sub-structures: "liberalisms" that could not be reduced to "liberalism".'[26] Such contradictions proved to be a substantial handicap for a party which had always celebrated the importance of ideas.

In many ways, Asquith's own predicament mirrored that confronting these sceptical Liberal intellectuals. Asquith attracted considerable criticism from both contemporaries and later historians for his handling of these doctrinal compromises, particularly over conscription. He is often portrayed as either temperamentally unsuited or intellectually too inflexible to adapt to the demands of war. Others go further in accusing him of moral cowardice in shirking measures he knew to be essential but whose partisan consequences he feared. Yet it could be argued equally plausibly, that Asquith rejected 'victory at all costs', not through some defect of character, excessive refinement or partisanship, but rather because war compelled him to adopt a strategy designed to achieve that which ultimately proved to be impossible. In this respect, John Bourne has compared Asquith's predicament with that confronting Lyndon Johnson over American involvement in Vietnam. Like LBJ, Asquith was forced into 'a policy of "enough, but not too much" ': enough to ensure military victory, but not so much as to compromise the survival of Liberal values for which Britain had gone to war and upon which all future social and political progress depended.[27] Although in retrospect it appears unlikely that this strategy could ever have been successful, this should not obscure the contemporary fact that as a Liberal, Asquith had no choice but to try, if 'Prussianism' was not to be defeated in the mud of Flanders only to prevail at home. Unfortunately for Asquith, the gamble was a costly one for his historical reputation. In seeking to achieve this balance, the concomitant appearance of drift and procrastination alienated Liberal pro-conscriptionists while his eventual failure equally appalled its opponents. Against this background, the wonder was not that Asquith ultimately failed in his quest, but that he was able to govern for so long when confronted by such immense contradictions in his position – particularly as his principal rival was constrained by no such sensibilities or doubts.

Ultimately, the devastating impact of war upon the Liberal creed can be judged by the bitterness of party divisions over how the war was to be won and the ideological price to be paid for that victory. Despite Taylor's much repeated claim that Liberal parliamentary schism was essentially decided by differences of temperament, social origin and education,[28] in reality it revolved around an ideological cleavage over how the war was to be fought: divisions which crystallised long-standing doctrinal differences over both domestic and foreign policy.[29] On the opposition benches after December 1916, Asquithian loyalists who had accepted the compromises of office joined an uncompromising group of Radical and 'pacificist' elements who had consistently defended Liberal principles from patriotic encroachment since August 1914. Although these two groups had occasionally voted together before 1916, after it they became the resolute defenders of 'true Liberalism' in the lobbies, despite Asquith's ineffectual leadership.[30] Conversely, the Coalition Liberals displayed a less consistent pattern of voting, depending on the degree to which Liberal principles conflicted with wartime demands. Given their 'patriotic' origins, it was not surprising that they loyally supported Lloyd George during the Maurice debate in May 1918 against a direct Asquithian challenge, but only nineteen of the seventy-two Coalition Liberals were prepared to support the disenfranchisement of conscientious objectors where vital war issues were not at stake.[31]

Despite the personal and doctrinal turmoil created by wartime experiences for national leaders, it should not be assumed that this torment was typical of the response of Liberal activists in the constituencies. It seems implausible that the periodic xenophobic attacks on those with German-sounding names were committed exclusively by Tory voters while Labour and Liberal supporters looked on aghast. Indeed, local studies suggest that as 'tension between policy and principle was a norm of Liberal politics', these activists accepted necessary doctrinal compromises and remained loyal to Asquith regardless.[32] Moreover, as most constituencies had never been converted to the New Liberalism in the first place, they felt little of the anguished disillusion of Hobhouse and Hobson when they continued to cling to their 'Old' Liberal commitments and mistrust of Lloyd George. Significantly, when the Manchester and Huddersfield local parties publicised their own programmes to rally wider support and pressurise Asquith into a more active lead, they did so largely on traditional Liberal foundations.[33]

6.3 Conservatism and the challenge of war

It is often suggested that the vigorous prosecution of war raised no fundamental problems for the Conservatives. In particular, Trevor Wilson makes much of the contrast in ideological tensions: 'If the war carried with it a certain menace for Liberals, Labour and Irish Nationalists, it was full of promise for the Conservatives.'[34] Unquestionably, as the party of chauvinism and Empire, war enabled them to speak the language of super-patriotism with a new fluency with which none of their rivals could plausibly compete. Once war was declared, Conservatives were equally confident in responding with an unswerving patriotic zeal unencumbered by political scruple, tradition or ideology. Official partisanship went into abeyance on 6 August and thereafter party officials and activists busied themselves with war work like the Parliamentary Recruiting Committee which ran the national campaign for the first eighteen months of the war through party rather than national channels.[35] In 1917, War Savings and the War Aims movement provided a new focus for Conservative patriotic endeavour. In this sense, therefore, war resolved many of the problems of Edwardian Conservatism by conferring a sense of overwhelming purpose. The negative spirit channelled into the battle for Ulster was turned more constructively and with greater confidence into the patriotic war.

War undoubtedly also brought the Conservatives some ideological benefits. For example, the McKenna duties breached the free trade edifice in a way that a decade of Chamberlainite campaigning had not. Yet in assessing the impact of war upon Conservative principles it is necessary to distinguish generally between legal–political issues and those in the socio-economic sphere. Certainly Conservatives experienced none of the difficulty of their Liberal adversaries in embracing the curtailment of individual liberty or conscription, but given all that had happened since 1906 it is more difficult to accept the argument that the Conservatives actually drew strength from the fact that it was 'sure about ends and pragmatic as to means', even where this involved the enlargement of the collectivist State.[36] Indeed, in the economic sphere, Conservatives were compelled to swallow some extremely unpalatable concessions over greater State interference with private property. The Rent Restrictions Act of 1915 showed how the government could be stampeded into curtailing the rights of property in favour of morale even where there was no proven profiteering. The State also took sweeping new powers of control over industry and agriculture which these disgruntled Conservatives rapidly dismantled after the Armistice. In the realm of taxation, war imposed a heavy burden on the party of property and the possessing classes. Income tax was raised from 9d (3p) to six shillings (30p) in the pound, while the tax threshold was reduced to only £120 p.a. Corresponding increases were introduced in super-tax and death duties, thereby accelerating the dramatic destruction of landed estates in the early postwar years.[37] Worse still, Conservatives were not only unable to resist such imposts when demanded as a patriotic duty, but they also recognised that once conceded the onus would be on property to justify their removal when peace returned. Hence their concern about postwar reconstruction, their fierce opposition to the alleged extravagance of Addison's social reform programme between 1919 and 1921 and Austen Chamberlain's determination at the Exchequer to restore prewar notions of Treasury control.

The Conservatives also paid the price of patriotism as the defender of the Irish Union and the Established Church. The passage of the Home Rule Bill in September 1914 deprived Unionism of one of the defining features of its political identity. As the right-wing *Morning Post* lamented in July 1916, 'The Unionist Party is, in fact, dead; the cause for which it existed has been surrendered.'[38] Similarly, although Tory High Churchmen were gravely concerned about the future of the Welsh Church in 1914, by 1920 Disestablishment aroused little controversy anywhere, even in Wales.[39] The issue of tithes and religious education suffered a correspondingly rapid demise. Periodically the Church re-emerged on the political agenda, as over the Prayer Book Measure in 1928 and arguments over tithes in the 1930s, but by then the Tories had lost some of their partisan intensity and entrenched certainties on these questions.

Arguments about Conservative benefits from the war also ignore the short-term alarm occasioned by concessions towards democracy. In reality, the Conservatives did well out of the private deal which widened the franchise in return for Liberal acceptance of the plural vote and an accompanying redistribution. Yet such gains could not entirely overcome nagging anxieties about the prospect of a mass democracy composed overwhelmingly of new voters expected to be as volatile as they were politically hostile. Although most Conservatives recognised that resistance to democracy was a lost cause before 1914, its onset still compelled them to consider more urgently the means to construct a broadly-based Conservatism capable of competing in difficult new conditions. Law had reassured a special party conference in November 1917 that they had nothing to fear and that their duty was now 'to make the best of the situation ... and to see that everything is done to make our Party what Disraeli called it and what, if it is to have any existence, it must be – a really national party'.[40] One response was to harness 'patriotic' working class support behind Milner's British Workers' League as an alternative to a trade union or 'socialist' focus for political loyalty.[41] Relabelled the National Democratic Labour party in 1918, it secured eleven MPs from its eighteen candidatures – all in Labour strongholds where neither Unionists nor Coalition Liberals stood a chance. Yet without roots, the movement had no long-term future.[42] Far more important, Tory anxieties about the future convinced their leaders that the perpetuation of the Coalition under Lloyd George represented the safest means of making the transition to peace in an unpredictable mass democracy. The intra-party tensions this decision engendered between 1919 and 1922 give particular force to Professor Ramsden's crucial distinction between the essentially long-term positive effects of the war for the Conservatives and the damaging short-term impact of Coalition – particularly after 1918. The beneficial effects of the former only really became evident after they deposed Lloyd George in October 1922. In contrast, the consequences of Coalition for the party were 'immediate and almost wholly negative'.[43]

Against this background, it is clear that the Liberals were not alone in suffering either ideological difficulties or leadership tensions as a direct result of wartime pressures. Yet for all that, it overstates the similarity of their predicament to suggest that 'it is not clear that the Liberals were uniquely or even especially undermined by the pressures of wartime politics'.[44] Both parties undoubtedly made painful compromises on cherished principles. Yet differences between the two parties in their ability to respond to these new challenges are far more important than any superficial similarity in the wartime origin of such problems. The Conservatives emerged from the war with their confidence and unity restored after the protracted nightmare of prewar futility. They believed national struggle had brought them closer to the electoral mood and had vindicated their credentials as the national patriotic party; a posture seemingly reaffirmed by the 1918 election. Thereafter, although compelled to adjust their programme and their doctrinal posture to adapt to a changed political environment, the experience of war conferred upon them the resilience and drive to meet this challenge. In stark contrast, the impact of war sapped Liberal confidence and gravely debilitated its capacity either to respond positively to these challenges or to redefine its faith in language relevant to a new mass electorate. Divided and demoralised by events since December 1916, the custodians of traditional Liberalism simply buried their heads in the sand. Unwilling and unable to contest the battle for hearts and minds once peace returned, Asquithian Liberals turned increasingly to a futile lament about lost political virtue, betrayal and honour and what constituted 'true' or 'false' Liberalism.[45] Consumed by their private agony, a divided and bewildered Liberal party found it particularly difficult to respond to the challenge from a newly reorganised, confident and more assertive Labour party seeking to supplant it as the principal party of anti-Conservative progressivism.

6.4 Collapse of the Progressive Alliance and Labour's bid for independence

If the war had adverse effects for Liberal ideology, its impact upon their electoral circumstances was equally damaging, particularly as it finally destroyed the Progressive Alliance. The war swiftly undermined the Irish dimension of the Progressive Alliance, along with the Irish Nationalist party. After 1912 Home Rule was increasingly interpreted as devolution rather than independence and Redmond's support for war in 1914 gave even this the tinge of British patriotism. Although Home Rule became law in September 1914, concessions over Ulster and the need to defer implementation until after the war prompted suspicions which further undermined the Nationalists and strengthened Sinn Fein's uncompromising republican belief that England's moment of crisis represented Ireland's opportunity. When Redmond was prevented by his party from joining the Asquith Coalition but Carson (the Ulster Unionist leader) became Attorney-General, both Home Rule and the Irish Nationalists appeared stranded. While Redmond's denunciation of the Dublin Rising in Easter 1916 made him appear an English stooge, the collapse of Asquith's efforts to use the crisis to grant some measure of Home Rule effectively destroyed the Nationalist party and deprived it of its doctrine and electoral confidence. It also transferred the loyal support and activism of many Irish voters in London, Liverpool and the Clyde over to Labour.[46]

In contrast, although Labour emerged strengthened from the war, this very vitality undermined the other pillar supporting the Progressive Alliance. In the short term, Labour was split by its support for intervention in 1914. Although it had prominently supported the position of the Second International since 1907, that an international general strike would be called to prevent a capitalist war, 'poor little Belgium' immediately transformed the situation. When an emotional meeting of the PLP resolved to support the war on 5 August, MacDonald resigned as Chairman. For Labour's war resisters, public and party responses to the outbreak of hostilities proved demoralising and disorientating. For Keir Hardie, it was a personal tragedy and he died a broken man in September 1915.[47] MacDonald was not a pacifist and resented the allegation that he was unpatriotic. Indeed, as he opposed the war because it was a blow to international socialism and the working class movement at home, he bitterly lamented the active support of his own party for intervention on the grounds that it risked becoming 'a mere echo of the old governing classes'.[48] Alongside MacDonald, the ILP and BSP both largely opposed war. In contrast, the bulk of the Labour movement responded with patriotic fervour to the national call to arms. As a result, the electoral truce was soon matched with an industrial truce which rapidly reduced the number of working days lost through strikes. As MacDonald's successor, Henderson swiftly came to recognise that once war had begun they had no choice but to support it. Yet although his membership of the Asquith Coalition and Lloyd George's five-man War Cabinet was a signal recognition of the importance of the trade unions to the war effort, Henderson remained pragmatic and opportunistic in his attitude and tactics throughout this experience. He joined the Asquith Coalition because the National Executive Committee and the trade unions believed this would best serve the interests of the working class; he joined Lloyd George after obtaining suitable pledges for precisely the same reason.

Participation in government was a mixed blessing. At a positive level, Labour undoubtedly acquired some enhanced status and prestige as a credible party of the State representing a crucial and 'patriotic' section of society. Yet there was a high cost to be paid for this recognition. Although Labour's influence over policy was often limited, its leaders were forced to accept responsibility for policies unpopular with their own supporters, especially over the dilution of labour and conscription. This produced tensions within the PLP after May 1915 when there were Labour MPs on both sides of the Commons and even greater ones with the rank-and-file who often saw few concessions for their cooperation. Such pressures increasingly manifested themselves in rising industrial unrest and the challenge from a militant shop stewards movement from the spring of 1917. Nevertheless, Henderson resisted calls for Labour's withdrawal from the government despite receiving a hostile reception from his own supporters – particularly over the deportation of trade unionists from the Clyde at the Labour party conference of 1917.[49]

Yet for all the tensions between both leadership and rank-and-file and between 'patriots' and war resisters, the Labour split was far less damaging than that in either the Liberal party at home or in socialist movements in France and Germany. Certainly Searle exaggerates in claiming that the degree of estrangement was so great that 'the very survival of a united Labour Party sometimes seemed to be in question'.[50] For a variety of reasons, Labour divisions were always sufficiently well contained that they were never allowed to develop into the irreconcilable breach it became in Liberal ranks. First, Henderson displayed a studied moderation in his treatment of Labour war resisters and refused to purge the party through expulsion, although he was less successful in restraining such efforts by 'patriotic' forces at the 1917 party conference.[51] Secondly, both sides conspicuously emphasised issues capable of generating consensus rather than division. In Parliament, opponents of the war abstained from waging a divisive campaign against its conduct by focusing on the role of international capitalism in causing the war and the need for democratic control of such forces through a new diplomacy. By channelling their activity through the Union of Democratic Control to achieve these goals, the possibility of direct conflict with the 'patriotic' wing of Labour was correspondingly reduced. Contrary to Pelling's assertion that the formation of the UDC in September 1914 meant 'new alignments ... cut across the ranks of the Labour Party, and threatened its continued existence as a political force', the reverse was true.[52] As MacDonald swiftly recognised that an alliance with anti-war Liberals did not represent a viable foundation for political realignment, the UDC provided the Labour movement with a vehicle for internal conflict-avoidance.

An even more important factor in containing internal conflict was the primacy of the campaign to defend class interests through alternative outlets within the broader movement. In part, this was achieved through trades councils where 'patriots' and 'pacifists' cooperated on a wide range of issues relevant to the working class. A more important focus for unity was provided by the War Emergency: Workers' National Committee, formed on the outbreak of war to defend working class living standards.[53] During the first part of the war the WNC adopted an essentially defensive strategy, coordinating campaigns on crucial day-to-day topics such as wartime unemployment, inflation, profiteering, food distribution, administration of relief, rent restrictions and the protection of employment conditions. After the introduction of conscription in 1916, however, it adopted a more aggressive posture – particularly with its 'Conscription of Wealth' campaign demanding the 'conscription of accumulated riches for the service of the nation' to match the conscription of working class men. The WNC thus called for higher rates of direct taxation, a capital levy, sequestration of all unearned incomes and the nationalisation of industries already under State control. Through its various campaigns, the WNC played a pivotal role in sustaining Labour's oppositional status as a party of dissent, while providing a unifying sense of common purpose among the heterogeneous members of an otherwise divided movement.

A critical watershed in Labour's wartime development arrived with Henderson's six-week visit to Russia in June–July 1917 and the so-called 'doormat incident' in August 1917. Having returned from Russia convinced that Kerensky needed decisive outside assistance to keep Russia in the war and to defeat the Bolsheviks pledged to an immediate separate peace, Henderson decided he must attend the Socialist Conference at Stockholm – despite the fact that German and Austrian delegates would also be present. After being left outside the Cabinet room while fellow ministers discussed this question, on 9 August Henderson resigned in protest. For the rest of the war, he devoted himself wholeheartedly to the doctrinal and structural reform of Labour in preparation for the forthcoming election. Cooperation between Henderson, MacDonald and Sidney Webb soon produced a Memorandum on War Aims in November 1917. In February 1918 the Henderson–Webb draft of the party's new constitution was adopted, which *inter alia* opened the way for individual membership, determined questions of NEC representation and articulated Labour's central aims – including the celebrated Clause IV Part 4 containing the commitment to common ownership of the means of production. In June, the party also adopted Webb's collectivist policy statement, *Labour and the New Social Order,* which enunciated four core principles: a national minimum wage, nationalisation of key industries, a 'Revolution in National Finance' including higher taxation and a capital levy and the use of 'the Surplus for the Common Good', in the form of expanded educational and cultural opportunities.[54] Above all, as Webb told the second party conference of 1918, the declaration was 'not an appeal to the converted but the basis of an appeal to the 20 million electors – 10 or 12 million of them being new electors'.[55]

At the same time, Henderson made considerable progress in rousing local party organisation from the torpor induced by the wartime electoral truce. Affiliated constituency bodies which had increased from 143 in 1913 to 199 in 1916, rose steeply to 389 by 1918; a crucial development as the redistribution of constituency boundaries in 1918 disrupted the established organisation of other parties at a time when Labour was embarking on major expansion in many areas for the first time. The number of full-time paid agents rose from seventeen in 1912 to eighty by 1918, while most of Labour's 388 candidates in 1918 were also placed during the last year of the war. Organisational expansion was paralleled and underpinned by a growth in resources, as levels of union affiliation to the Labour party increased from 2.6 million to 5.2 million – albeit that many remained erratic in their payments. Beyond all of this, after 1917 Labour inspired its followers through mass rallies which in many respects resembled the popular crusades to mobilise 'virtuous passion' so characteristic of Gladstone's brand of moral populism. As a result, despite the earlier divisions, Labour emerged from the war a far more cohesive and assertive force, with its extra-parliamentary organisation remodelled, its status enhanced and free from the constraints of the Progressive Alliance.

6.5 Labour, 'socialism' and the impact of war

One of the principal controversies about these events has focused on Labour's wartime adoption of its much-vaunted 'socialist commitment' in Clause IV of its new constitution. This clause contained the pledge:

> to secure for the workers by hand or by brain the full fruits of their industry and
> the most equitable distribution thereof that may be possible, upon the basis of the
> common ownership of the means of production and the best obtainable system of
> popular administration and control of each industry and service.

Interpretation of this commitment has been influenced principally by different
views of the nature of British socialism. Thus, historians on the left have
argued that Clause IV did not signal the adoption of socialism but rather 'that
Labour had finally done with its own version of Liberalism' and sought to
assert its innate 'Labourism'. As Miliband despairs, the new programme was
'much less the manifesto of a new social order ... than an explicit affirmation
by the Labour Party of its belief that piecemeal collectivism, within a
predominantly capitalist society, was the key to more welfare, higher efficiency,
and greater social justice'.[56] Conversely, many others have accepted uncritically
the view that this was the fundamental turning point at which Labour was
transformed from a social reformist to a truly socialist party.[57]

Perhaps the most far-reaching exposition of this latter argument has been
advanced by Jay Winter.[58] According to Winter, Labour's adoption of Clause
IV stemmed directly from the seismic impact of war upon both the political
attitudes and the very nature of the British working class – a process which
radically transformed Labour's prospects, ideology and policy. Central to this
argument is the claim that war turned the working class into a more
homogeneous force through an erosion of wage and status differentials to the
benefit of semi-skilled and unskilled workers. Through better living standards,
war also improved working class health and life expectancy – particularly for
the poorest sections of the labouring population.[59] Although in the short term
the impact of such changes was complex and often divisive, the outcome was
allegedly to create a far greater sense of working class consciousness and unity.
In its turn, this trend had a profoundly radicalising effect upon the British
working class, to which Labour leaders were compelled to respond by
promulgating a coherent and comprehensive socialist programme, including
the explicitly 'socialist aim' embodied in Clause IV, in order to fill the
ideological vacuum which had left Labour a directionless force before 1914.[60]

Winter's thesis has aroused considerable controversy with regard to its
arguments about both socio-economic causes and political outcomes. At one
level, a variety of reservations and caveats have been advanced about the claim
to greater class homogeneity. Arguments about rising living standards run
counter to much research on the negative effects of war on health, nutrition
and life expectancy. Others emphasise the critical distinction between wage
rates and actual take-home earnings to conclude that in general 'there was no
major narrowing of the gap between skilled and unskilled workers in Britain
during World War I'.[61] Nor did the occupational and status cleavages which
stratified the working class before 1914 easily succumb to the impact of war,
and where they did come under pressure, the effect was often to intensify
working class divisions as skilled men became resentful of the unskilled.[62] In

this respect, Winter is also accused of confusing growing 'class awareness' towards 'the rich' during the war with a unifying 'class-consciousness'. Thus, while resentment at inequalities in food distribution and profiteering did sharpen hostility towards the possessing classes during the war, the reality was that class distinctions *within* the working class remained acute and bitterly contested throughout.[63] Finally, others suggest that generalisations about any uniform working class experience conceal a wide range of regional and sectoral variations – even among those most directly involved in war work.[64]

A second challenge to the Winter thesis relates to the supposed impact of war on Labour's fortunes and the significance of Clause IV. For Ross McKibbin and the 'Labour' school, far from being a directionless force before 1914, Labour was already making substantial headway on the basis of a developing class politics and its evolving familial relationship with the unions (see section 5.5 above). The war thus represented a continuation of a well-established upward trend rather than a catalyst for change. Moreover, although there were a variety of compelling reasons for the adoption of a new party constitution in 1918, McKibbin contends that none of them had much to do with the acceptance of socialism by either the working class or its leaders. Indeed, the central fact about the 1918 constitution was that it 'embodied not an ideology but a system by which power in the Labour Party was distributed: an arrangement which was unequivocally favourable to the trade unions'. Against this background, the key issue throughout the debates about the new constitution was not the socialist commitment but 'who elected whom to the national executive'. On all of these essentials, the unions had their way, enshrining the position of the block vote and their in-built predominance in what they considered to be their own party. In contrast, decisions about ideology were of relatively little consequence although the unions accepted the so-called 'socialist' objective 'partly because they had always been collectivist, ... partly to indulge the Fabians, and partly because they did not think it mattered very much'.[65] As such, Clause IV was largely an irrelevance and an 'uncharacteristic adornment' to the constitution rather than a symbol of profound ideological transformation.

Against this background, McKibbin accepts that Clause IV was significant – but not because of its 'socialism'. First, by indicating a distinctive programme and direction, it sharpened the divide from the Liberals in such a way as to resolve Labour's prewar problem of an undifferentiated identity on the left of the Progressive Alliance. Yet as Rodney Barker perceptively emphasised

> there was a sense ... in which the Labour Party did not strike out for electoral and parliamentary independence from the Liberals solely because it was socialist, but in which the reverse was true: the identification of the party as socialist was a means of sustaining and publicising its independence.[66]

Second, Clause IV was believed by the Webbs, Cole and others to be electorally popular – but not because the working class had become socialist, but because a section of the middle class had.[67] Thus while 'a sop to the professional bourgeoisie', there is considerable evidence to suggest that even among trade unions in more statist occupational groups like mining and the railways, 'support for "socialist" state control was the preserve of the few'.[68] A final factor in the appeal of Clause IV was that it was not the precision of its commitment, but rather its vagueness and lack of rigour which permitted it to fulfil an 'umbrella function' capable of uniting a party where there was otherwise little doctrinal agreement. As Royden Harrison argues, Clause IV provided

> a rallying point around which the adherents of different ideologies and representatives of different interests assembled ... The adoption of Clause IV did not imply the whole membership came to have a common objective, but rather that an objective had been proclaimed which both accommodated and concealed a large diversity of particular concerns.[69]

Or as Rodney Barker puts it, Clause IV was part of a broader unifying 'political myth' necessary for a new party slowly gaining a sense of identity in a body which was far from united.[70]

While the period after the 'doormat incident' was a turning point of sorts for Labour, there must thus be considerable doubt as to how far it actually transformed Labour ideology. Arguably, the events of 1914–18 were a natural continuation and acceleration of two crucial prewar trends. First, for many disillusioned Liberals, wartime cooperation in the UDC and the No Conscription Fellowship suggested that Labour was a more reliable guarantor of shared values and ideals than the Liberal party. As a result, the war represented a major step towards Labour's victory in the battle for the moral and intellectual leadership of progressivism.[71] Secondly, always less a socialist party than a party which contained socialists, Labour seized the opportunity created by wartime collectivism to consolidate its position with statist trade unions. War did not fundamentally transform and radicalise either working class consciousness or Labour ideology, but it did create the conditions for Labour to benefit from the misfortunes of its principal rival. Furthermore, the Representation of the People Act in 1918 created a new political environment in which these changes would prove decisive. Yet at the end of the war the battle was still far from completely won. Many trade unionists were apathetic about electoral politics, the party organisation was often weak and sketchy and doctrinal tensions remained to be resolved. Moreover, where Liberalism had strong roots, the wartime party split and coupon election could not altogether destroy its popular appeal. Nevertheless, on these established foundations, the balance of probability increasingly appeared to suggest that Labour would prevail.

6.6 The 'coupon' election of December 1918

In the expectation that a general election could not be long delayed, the Coalition partners agreed on the allocation of seats in mid-July 1918. In the event, the so-called 'coupons' – the letters signed by the two party leaders endorsing the recipient – were distributed to 362 Unionists and 159 Coalition Liberals: a disparity reflective less of Tory dominance than the quantity of available Coalition Liberal candidates and finance. These negotiations had taken place on the assumption of a wartime election, as most expected fighting to continue well into 1919. Yet in the event, the end came with an astonishing suddenness. On 8 August the British counter-offensive started a hundred-day rolling advance which ended with the Armistice on 11 November. Lloyd George immediately obtained a dissolution and an election was scheduled for 14 December. The outcome was never in doubt. The Coalition won a total of 473 of the 707 seats – and with various other supporters it had a maximum possible total of 554. Of these, the Unionists obtained 382 MPs, some three-quarters of the government side of the Commons. In contrast, although the Coalition Liberals obtained 127 seats, many were in industrial working class areas extremely vulnerable to Labour advance should Conservative support be withdrawn. This factor, combined with the limitation to 159 coupons, proved particularly damaging for any prospect of Liberal recovery after the fall of the Coalition, simply because Liberals of both varieties found it far more difficult to recapture lost territory than Conservatives.[72]

Besides the sheer size of the Coalition majority, the other notable feature of the election result was the complete collapse of the old Progressive Alliance. In Ireland, the Nationalists were reduced from eighty-four MPs in December 1910 to a meagre seven, while Sinn Fein took seventy-three seats on a platform of outright separation. Similarly, the Asquithians were utterly annihilated, winning only thirty-six seats – of whom nine immediately accepted the Coalition whip. Among the fallen were Asquith and virtually the entire prewar leadership. Besides their humiliating numerical weakness, these results reflected signs of long-term vulnerability. First, while Coalition Liberal representation corresponded with areas of Liberal strength since 1885, the Asquithians were 'a collection of fragments' devoid of any uniform socio-regional base.[73] Second, the existence of only 276 candidates meant that in many areas the absence of an Asquithian forced progressive Liberals to choose between abstention or voting Labour – an enforced discontinuity in voting allegiance which became a recurrent problem throughout the decade. Third, the results suggested little scope for future optimism, particularly as in their 144 three-corner contests the Asquithians came third in no fewer than 92.

For Labour the electoral signs were more mixed. On a negative level, there was undoubtedly disappointment at obtaining only fifty-seven MPs (although a further four independent MPs joined Labour immediately). Second, the profile of the PLP gave little reason for optimism given the predominance of stolid trade union MPs and the defeat of many promising anti-war socialist leaders like MacDonald and Snowden; a factor which played a significant role in weakening the PLP's effectiveness throughout the 1918–22 Parliament. Third, in electoral terms, the increase in Labour's poll from only 6.4 per cent in December 1910 to 22.6 per cent in 1918 came almost entirely from extra candidates. Moreover, its regional distribution was still heavily concentrated in northern England (especially Lancashire) and Scotland, while it made only partial inroads into mining seats in South Wales, West Lancashire and West Yorkshire. In urban areas, Labour also performed disappointingly, obtaining only eight of the eighty-seven seats in the twelve largest provincial towns. Yet at a more positive level, Labour's 388 candidates reflected a qualitatively stronger position than its prewar maximum of 78 in January 1910. Moreover, for the first time, Labour could claim theoretically to be bidding for power. Some consolation could also be derived from the existence of specific disadvantages in 1918. A low poll of only 57.2 per cent probably disproportionately reduced Labour's share of the vote – particularly as only 900,000 of the 3.9 million servicemen actually voted.[74] Anti-patriotic smears were also inevitably harmful during a 'Khaki' election, as was the impact of the coupon which meant that for each contested seat Labour won, it polled an average of 48,821 votes, compared with 12,474 votes for each Coalition supporter. Without the coupon, Labour had every expectation of obtaining far more seats for the same level of support. While not a quantum leap in Labour's forward march, then, the war did at least bring with it some advantages which assisted the steady continuation of positive prewar trends.

Notes and references

The place of publication is London unless otherwise stated.

1 Martin Pugh, 'Domestic politics', in Stephen Constantine, Maurice K. Kirby and Mary B. Rose, eds, *The First World War in British History* (1995), p. 10.

2 Michael and Eleanor Brock, eds, *H.H. Asquith: Letters to Venetia Stanley* (Oxford, 1982), p. 146.

3 Trevor Wilson, *The Myriad Faces of War: Britain and the Great War, 1914–1918* (Oxford, 1982), p. 408.

4 Ibid., ch. 18; Cameron Hazelhurst, *Politicians at War, July 1914 to May 1915: A Prologue to the Triumph of Lloyd George* (1971), pp. 235–60.

5 Trevor Wilson, *The Downfall of the Liberal Party, 1914–1935* (Fontana edn, 1968), pp. 54–6.

6 John Stubbs, 'The impact of the Great War on the Conservative Party', in Gillian Peele and Chris Cook, eds, *The Politics of Reappraisal, 1918–1939* (1975), pp. 23–6.

7 Martin Pugh, 'Asquith, Bonar Law and the first Coalition', *Historical Journal* 17 (1974), p. 818.

8 Hazelhurst, *Politicians at War*, pp. 114–15, 261; Wilson, *Downfall of the Liberal Party*, pp. 65–6; Pugh, 'Asquith, Bonar Law and the first Coalition', pp. 813, 835–6.

9 G.R. Searle, *Country Before Party: Coalition and the Idea of 'National Government' in Modern Britain, 1885–1987* (1995), p. 91.

10 John Ramsden, *The Age of Balfour and Baldwin, 1902–1940* (1978), p. 131.

11 Arthur Marwick, *The Deluge: British Society and the First World War* (1965), pp. 80, 82.

12 Wilson, *Myriad Faces of War*, pp. 408–10.

13 Brock and Brock, *H.H. Asquith*, pp. 117–18.

14 John Turner, *British Politics and the Great War: Coalition and Conflict 1915–18* (New Haven, 1992), pp. 112–51.

15 Kenneth O. Morgan, *Consensus and Disunity: The Lloyd George Coalition Government, 1918–1922* (Oxford, 1979), pp. 13–14.

16 B. McGill, 'Asquith's predicament, 1914–1918', *Journal of Modern History* 39 (1967), p. 297.

17 P.F. Clarke, *Lancashire and the New Liberalism* (Cambridge, 1971), p. 394.

18 A.J.P. Taylor, 'Politics in the First World War', in *Essays in English History* (Penguin edn, 1975), p. 76. Also *English History 1914–1945* (Pelican edn, 1975), pp. 64–5, 98–101, 113.

19 Keith Grieves, *The Politics of Manpower, 1914–1918* (Manchester, 1988), pp. 4–5, 114.

20 Wilson, *Downfall of the Liberal Party*, p. 20.

21 Ibid., pp. 23–4. Also Michael Bentley, *The Climax of Liberal Politics: British Liberalism in Theory and Practice, 1868–1918* (1987), pp. 121–2; Stephen Koss, *Nonconformity in Modern British Politics* (1975), pp. 135–8. William L. Miller, *Electoral Dynamics in Britain Since 1918* (1977), pp. 3–8, 20, 24.

22 Ibid., p. 390.

23 Michael Freeden, *Liberalism Divided: A Study in British Political Thought, 1914–1939* (Oxford, 1986), p. 21.

24 Ibid., p. 20.

25 John Rae, *Conscience and Politics: The British Government and the Conscientious Objector to Military Service, 1916–1919* (Oxford, 1970).

26 Freeden, *Liberalism Divided*, pp. 1, 41.

27 J.M. Bourne, *Britain and the Great War, 1914–1918* (1989), p. 116. The phrase is from George C. Herring, *America's Longest War: The United States and Vietnam, 1950–1975* (1979).

28 Taylor, *English History 1914–1945*, p. 67. See also Morgan, *Consensus and Disunity*, p. 14; Chris Cook, *A Short History of the Liberal Party, 1900–1992* (1993), p. 72.

29 Edward S. David, 'The Liberal Party divided, 1916–1918', *Historical Journal* 13 (1970), pp. 527–31. Also Peter Clarke, *Liberals and Social Democrats* (Cambridge, 1978), ch. 3.

30 Ibid., pp. 514–18.

31 Ibid., pp. 522–5.

32 G.L. Bernstein, 'Yorkshire Liberalism during the First World War', *Historical Journal* 32 (1989), p. 126.

33 Duncan Tanner, *Political Change and the Labour Party, 1900–1918* (Cambridge, 1990), pp. 379–81, 404–8, 430.

34 Wilson, *Myriad Faces of War*, pp. 198, 412 and *Downfall of the Liberal Party*, p. 28. Also Robert Blake, *The Conservative Party from Peel to Thatcher* (Fontana edn, 1985), pp. 195–6; Martin Pugh, *The Making of Modern British Politics, 1867–1939* 2nd edn (Oxford, 1993), p. 165; Stuart Ball, *The Conservative Party and British Politics, 1902–1951* (1995), p. 56.

35 Ramsden, *The Age of Balfour and Baldwin*, pp. 112, 123–5.

36 Ibid., p. 115. Also Ball, *The Conservative Party and British Politics*, p. 59.

37 F.M.L. Thompson, *English Landed Society in the Nineteenth Century* (1963), ch.12.

38 Stubbs, 'The impact of the Great War on the Conservative Party', pp. 31–2. Also J. Stubbs, 'The Unionists and Ireland, 1914–1918', *Historical Journal* 33 (1990).

39 Morgan, *Consensus and Disunity*, pp. 34, 160; Michael Kinnear, *The Fall of Lloyd George: The Political Crisis of 1922* (1973), p. 139.

40 Ramsden, *The Age of Balfour and Baldwin*, p. 119.

41 J.O. Stubbs, 'Lord Milner and Patriotic Labour, 1914–1918', *English Historical Review* 87 (1972), pp. 717–54.
42 Roy Douglas, 'The National Democratic Labour Party and the British Workers' League', *Historical Journal* 15 (1972), pp. 533–52.
43 Ramsden, *The Age of Balfour and Baldwin*, p. 110.
44 Pugh, 'Domestic politics', p. 16.
45 Michael Bentley, *The Liberal Mind 1914–1929* (Cambridge, 1977), pp. 1–3.
46 D. George Boyce, *Nationalism in Ireland* (1982), pp. 283–90; Turner, *British Politics and the Great War*, pp. 397–8.
47 Kenneth O. Morgan, *Keir Hardie* (1974), pp. 265–7.
48 J.M. Winter, *Socialism and the Challenge of War: Ideas and Politics in Britain, 1912–1918* (1974), pp. 234–40.
49 Ibid., pp. 241–2.
50 G.R. Searle, *The Liberal Party: Triumph and Disintegration, 1886–1929* (1992), pp. 135–6.
51 Henry Pelling, *A Short History of the Labour Party* 8th edn (1985), pp. 39–40.
52 Ibid., p. 37.
53 Royden Harrison, 'The War Emergency Workers' National Committee, 1914–1920', in A. Briggs and J. Saville, eds, *Essays in Labour History, 1886–1923* (1971), pp. 211–59; Winter, *Socialism and the Challenge of War*, ch. 2.
54 Pelling, *Short History*, pp. 44–5.
55 Rodney Barker, 'Political myth: Ramsay MacDonald and the Labour Party', *History* 61 (1976), p. 54.
56 Ralph Miliband, *Parliamentary Socialism: A Study in the Politics of Labour* (1961), p. 62.
57 Pelling, *Short History*, pp. 43–4.
58 Winter, *Socialism and the Challenge of War*, chs 8–9 and 'Labour politics in the Great War,' *Bulletin of the Society for the Study of Labour History* 34 (1977).
59 J.M. Winter, *The Great War and the British People* (1985), pp. 153, 244–5.
60 For echoes of this interpretation see James Hinton, *Labour and Socialism: A History of the British Labour Movement 1867–1974* (Brighton, 1983), pp. 96–7; Searle, *The Liberal Party*, p. 138; Wilson, *Myriad Faces of War*, ch. 68.
61 Alastair Reid, 'World War I and the working class in Britain', in A. Marwick, ed., *Total War and Social Change* (1988), pp. 20–1.
62 Wilson, *Myriad Faces of War*, pp. 526–7; Tanner, *Political Change and the Labour Party*, pp. 363–4.
63 Bernard Waites, *A Class Society at War: England 1914–1918* (Leamington Spa, 1987), p. 22 and 'The government of the Home Front and the "moral economy" of the working class', in P.H. Liddle, ed., *Home Fires and Foreign Fields* (1985), pp. 175–94.
64 Tanner, *Political Change and the Labour Party*, pp. 351–61.
65 Ross McKibbin, *The Evolution of the Labour Party 1910–1924* (Oxford, 1974), pp. 91, 102.
66 Barker, 'Political myth', p. 48.
67 McKibbin, *Evolution of the Labour Party*, p. 97.
68 Tanner, *Political Change and the Labour Party*, p. 372; T. Adams, 'Labour and the First World War: economy, politics and the erosion of local peculiarity?', *Journal of Regional and Local Studies* 10 (1990), pp. 29–30.
69 Harrison, 'The War Emergency Workers' National Committee', p. 259.
70 Barker, 'Political myth', pp. 48–9.

71 Tanner, *Political Change and the Labour Party*, p. 382; Catherine Anne Cline, *Recruits to Labour: The British Labour Party 1914–1931* (Syracuse, 1963), pp. 8–23.

72 Turner, *British Politics and the Great War*, pp. 333–4. See also Roy Douglas, 'The background to the "Coupon" election arrangements', *English Historical Review* 86 (1971), pp. 318–36.

73 Michael Kinnear, *The British Voter: An Atlas and Survey since 1885* 2nd edn (1981), pp. 39, 83; Wilson, *Downfall of the Liberal Party*, ch. 8.

74 Pugh, *The Making of Modern British Politics*, p. 196.

Chapter seven

The Lloyd George Coalition, 1918–1922

7.1 The impact of Labour

In retrospect, it is tempting to regard the postwar Coalition as an anachronistic vestige left over from the war, before the resumption of a 'normal' pattern of party conflict in 1922. Yet in reality, the Coalition represented a premeditated effort permanently to reconstruct anti-socialist party politics to address the twin challenges of Labour and mass democracy. The boldness of this ambition and the urgency with which it was pursued are explicable only in terms of the political disorientation left by a war which had swept away most of the great party controversies that had imparted meaning to Edwardian electoral allegiance. In this strange new political world, Liberal and Conservative leaders echoed Lord Hugh Cecil's lament that 'our old landmarks are submerged and it is not easy to find a resting place for the soles of one's feet'. The challenge confronting politicians after the war was the need to erect fresh landmarks to guide a new mass electorate they feared less because it was unpredictable than because it was potentially more capricious, ignorant and gullible to irresponsible Labour promises. 'What shall we inscribe on our standard?' Austen Chamberlain asked his half-brother in 1917. 'How and for what seek to rally Unionist and conservative ... forces after the war for the problems which then confront us?' In particular, his mind settled on a future 'full of difficulty and dangers, strikes, discontents and much revolutionary feeling'. Above all, there was the need to combat 'what its exponents called a "class consciousness", but what [he] should call a class prejudice, which is something new in our political life'.[1] More recent historians have labelled this challenge 'the impact of Labour'.[2]

Immediately after the war, it was the industrial threat from the Labour movement which most preoccupied its opponents. In the wake of the February 1917 revolution in Russia, an upsurge of rank-and-file militancy saw the number of days lost in disputes rise sharply from 2,450,000 in 1916 to 5,650,000 in 1917. In June, at the Leeds Convention organised by the anti-war ILP and BSP, some 1,150 delegates had even briefly conjured up the spectre of Workers' and Soldiers' Councils on Russian lines. Although even the most radical trade union leaders had urged patriotic restraint in face of Ludendorff's offensive in the spring of 1918, after it collapsed in late July it was clear that industrial militancy could not be held in check for long and with the return to peace the nation witnessed a massive upsurge of actual and threatened industrial action to maintain the gains of the war years and restore prewar union prerogatives. During 1919 there was strife in mining, engineering, shipbuilding, the railways, London Underground and even a police strike in London and Liverpool. In total, 1,352 stoppages cost 34,970,000 working days in 1919. During the first half of 1920, economic boom, inflationary pay rises and more skilful ministerial leadership substantially improved the state of labour relations. As the economy collapsed into an intense slump during 1921, however, the latitude for concession and manoeuvre on all sides was removed. The outcome was an unprecedented total of 85,870,000 days lost to strikes in 1921 – a figure more than double its prewar peak in 1912.[3]

Underlying Cabinet concern at the scale of industrial disruption was the omnipresent spectre of revolutionary working class unrest and Bolshevism. Fears that disillusioned ex-servicemen without jobs may become a resentful threat to political stability had encouraged prudent concessions on unemployment insurance and disabled service pensions in 1919. Elsewhere, however, the government was prepared to adopt a tough line to defeat assertive trade unionism and revolutionary discontents. As early as the spring of 1919, Lloyd George responded to a threatened coal strike with talk of starving mining communities into submission because they had 'challenged society to a duel'. 'Once the strike begins it is imperative that the state should win', he warned in March. 'Failure to do so would inevitably lead to a Soviet Republic.'[4] In these circumstances, there was little reluctance about the use of military force. In January 1919, a Glasgow engineering strike ended with cavalry and armoured cars patrolling the streets.[5] In readiness for the clash with the MFGB in April 1921, the government had the equivalent of fifty-six infantry battalions and six cavalry regiments assembled for action. In addition, various schemes were considered for the use of a local militia composed of battalions of university dons, clerks, stockbrokers and other patriots mobilised in defence of constitutional government.[6]

With the threat of a general strike looming ever larger, the political temperature on both sides inevitably increased. The transition to peace and the postwar boom coincided with an attempt to revive the Edwardian syndicalist dream of achieving working class political objectives through direct industrial action. Such a vision held considerable sway in the minds of union leaders like Smillie, Hodges and Robert Williams. Such men cared little for the aspirations of parliamentary leaders seeking to project Labour as something more than a class movement rooted in trade unionism. Yet, by definition, 'Direct Action' was a reactive force. At various times it was discussed as a means to force Lloyd George to follow President Wilson's line at the Paris Peace Conference (January 1919), to nationalise the mines (September 1919) or withdraw troops from Ireland and Russia (July 1920). Undoubtedly the most legendary challenge from the forces of Direct Action came in August 1920, when Councils of Action were established after London dockers refused to load the *Jolly George* with arms for anti-Bolshevik forces in Poland.

Although the incident has entered socialist folklore as a victory which prevented further British intervention, the reality was that Direct Action was 'pushing on a door that was already open', given Lloyd George's reluctance to confront the unions at home or embark on reckless adventures abroad.[7] The illusion of victory, however, led the advocates of Direct Action to overstep themselves in the following year in the depths of severe economic slump as they sought to resist unemployment and wage cuts. This came to a catastrophic climax when the recently revived Triple Alliance of mining and transport unions collapsed in the face of a coal owner's lockout on 'Black Friday' on 15 April 1921 (see section 7.3 below). The outcome of this long-awaited confrontation brought defeat for the MFGB, humiliation for the Triple Alliance and a bitter disillusionment for those who placed their faith in Direct Action. After 'Black Friday' the syndicalist threat receded in conditions profoundly unfavourable to industrial militancy.

As Direct Action represented a challenge to the democratic road to socialism, 'Black Friday' also strengthened the hand of PLP leaders who emphasised the need to transform the system from within, rather than through industrial confrontation from without. Despite their disappointing performance at the 1918 general election, the electoral tide soon confirmed the wisdom of the official party strategy. In the municipal elections in November 1919 Labour made sweeping gains – particularly in the London boroughs where its representation rose from 48 to 573 seats, giving it control of twelve of twenty-eight metropolitan boroughs. Although during 1920 Labour experienced a check to both its by-election and municipal progress, with the sudden onset of the slump, the electoral threat returned with a vengeance at a time when Direct Action went into an equally dramatic decline. During March 1921 Labour made three by-election gains in as many days. Two more followed later that year, with four in the first half of 1922, culminating in the defeat of a junior minister at Pontypridd in July. The precise significance of this electoral progress is open to debate. Despite its fourteen victories between 1918 and 1922, it is easy to exaggerate the extent of Labour advance, as all but two were in classical working class seats and these exceptions were won on protest votes or a split in the anti-socialist front.[8] Yet on the other hand, Labour could derive some satisfaction from the fact that in only two by-elections during this period did its share of the vote actually go down, while its improved performance in a diverse range of seats from northern and industrial Widnes to southern and suburban St Albans, Bromley and Woodbridge was evidence of an unmistakable 'psephological earthquake'.[9]

To comprehend the full extent of anti-socialist alarm at this advance, it is important to understand that opponents saw it as far more than simply a bid for majority control of the House of Commons. Labour was also perceived to be a formidable menace to property and the stability of the entire economic, social and political order. As such, it had to be stopped at all costs. How this was to be achieved became the dominant preoccupation of anti-socialist politicians until the question finally resolved itself with the outcome of the 1924 general election. As Maurice Cowling puts it, the debate which went on in the Conservative party and elsewhere was 'a struggle about method rather than about policy. It was a struggle to decide what to say, and what tone to say it in, in attempting to construct a broad-based body of resistance to "socialism".'[10] Between 1918 and 1924 this dilemma resolved itself essentially into a choice between two broad strategies. The option which ultimately triumphed under Law and Baldwin after 1922 was for an independent Conservative party informally to absorb most of the disparate elements of anti-socialism within its broad church. In the immediate aftermath of the war, however, the dominant mode of resistance to socialism was embodied by Lloyd George's attempt to transform the wartime Coalition into a permanent method of government based on a more formal realignment of the centre-right and 'sane' Labour in opposition to socialist extremism.

7.2 Coalition, reconstruction and resistance to socialism

How seriously Lloyd George took his own rhetoric about Labour and the Bolshevik menace is open to debate.[11] Yet whether real or manufactured, the emergence of a credible Labour threat made 'resistance to socialism' a viable political platform for the first time. Lloyd George's long-standing passion for coalition is legendary. At the height of the constitutional crisis in 1910 he boldly proposed a Liberal–Conservative coalition to divert national energies towards the supreme priorities of social reform and military preparedness, while putting aside the old controversies about the Lords, the Welsh Church, Ireland and even free trade. After December 1916 he got his chance. As he told the Reconstruction Committee in March 1917, 'The nation was in a molten condition, it was malleable now, and would continue to be so for a short while after the war, but not for long.'[12] In such circumstances, Lloyd George resolved to perpetuate wartime consensus as the basis for a permanent realignment of British party connection on the rhetorical and policy bedrock of 'Reconstruction'. Under the leadership of Christopher Addison, Lloyd George's closest Liberal confidant, the Ministry of Reconstruction (established July 1917) rapidly developed into 'a species of Government-supported ideas factory for a postwar party that would evolve under the leadership of Lloyd George'.[13] War had created the demand for such a programme by drawing attention to manifest social need (as in housing and education), and by engendering a collective conviction that, as all sections of society had contributed to victory, they were equally entitled to share in Lloyd George's vision of 'a fit land for heroes to live in'. Moreover, by helping to transform attitudes towards State intervention and collectivism, war had also legitimised the means to achieve those ends.

Historical assessments of the Ministry of Reconstruction have differed widely. In his valuable detailed history of reconstruction planning, Paul Barton Johnson has been dismissive of a confused institution, handicapped by an overly ambitious remit and inadequate resources, powers and ministerial leadership.[14] Conversely, Kenneth Morgan contends that the Ministry was taken seriously as a new departure in social policy and that under Addison 'reconstruction' became a practical theme capable of achieving Lloyd George's supra-party aspirations. Certainly, during the later stages of the war, Addison prepared a new social agenda including ambitious programmes for housing, slum clearance, demobilisation linked to land settlement, a new Ministry of Health, technical and secondary education, substitution of the Poor Law with new public assistance committees, comprehensive unemployment insurance and 'Whitleyism' through Joint Industrial Councils.[15] If anti-socialism was the negative purpose of coalitionism, therefore, 'reconstruction' represented a positive face which conformed well with Lloyd George's leadership of the New Liberalism before the war. It was also a missionary theme which belies two frequently repeated misapprehensions about the Coalition: that Lloyd George was the prisoner of the Tories from the outset, and that the postwar Coalition was devoid of a coherent philosophy to sustain either its sense of purpose or the loyalty of its supporters beyond the pursuit of power. Alongside its commitment to industrial cooperation at home and a correspondingly conciliatory stance abroad, social reform was one of the three crucial pillars upon which Lloyd George hoped to construct this new consensus.

Social reform undoubtedly dominated the Cabinet's early labours and during 1919–20 a flood of suitable legislation emerged from the Home Affairs Committee. The Unemployment Insurance Act of 1920 extended coverage to some 12,000,000 workers in all trades covered by health insurance, except farm labourers and domestic servants. Old age pensions rose by 80 per cent. Fisher's Education Act in 1918 created greater access to secondary schools and a Ministry of Health was created in June 1919 with the intention of centralising control over medical and hospital provision. Above all, there was Addison's ambitious and expensive housing scheme which became his obsession and the acid test of the Coalition's sincerity. Militant working class unrest during and immediately after the war had raised awareness of the housing problem and kept it near the top of the political agenda. Indeed, Swenarton goes so far as to argue that Addison's housing programme (and the high design specification it embodied) was consciously advanced as an 'insurance against revolution', by buying off the more affluent and organised working class who would be the most likely source of trouble and the only ones capable of affording the rents for such dwellings.[16] Addison's Housing and Town Planning Act of 1919 imposed obligations on local authorities to meet working class housing needs and laid a corresponding duty on central government to finance such schemes. In retrospect, these social reforming dreams were soon dashed. Within two years the housing scheme was dead and its principal architect sacrificed to those unwilling to pay the price for this supposed bulwark against Bolshevism. Nevertheless, until the intervention of the slump, the government's initial enthusiasm, energy and sincere commitment cannot be denied.

Rather less optimism attended the Coalition's early efforts at national unity and reconstruction in the industrial sphere. The trade unions had emerged from the war with an enhanced status and a new consciousness of their power, particularly as membership had undergone a heady expansion, rising from

4,145,000 in 1914 to a peak of 8,348,000 in 1920 at the height of the postwar boom. Despite a massive rash of postwar strikes, Lloyd George initially remained hopeful of carrying wartime cooperation and proto-corporatist structures into peacetime. This was to be achieved through a combination of Prime Ministerial intervention and structural efforts to divert capital and labour into more constructive avenues conducive to cooperation, such as an extension of trade boards and minimum wage schemes and through bodies like Whitley Councils and a National Industrial Council. In the event, such methods did little to improve the climate of labour relations, made no impact upon government policy and encountered widespread resistance from both employers and unions.[17] Nevertheless, until the end of 1920, the Coalition could still claim that its strategy of preserving industrial harmony on a progressive basis remained viable, even if the omens in mining were scarcely promising.

The importance of social reform and industrial conciliation to a government seeking to turn 'national unity' into a durable platform for political realignment is self-evident. For those who view Lloyd George's project in social imperialist terms, as an effort to drive a wedge between 'sane' labour and revolutionary working class militancy, their centrality is equally apparent. Although the role of overseas policy is less immediately obvious, according to Kenneth Morgan, 'as Lloyd George's interpretation of the wartime consensus essentially linked conciliation and non-intervention abroad as the corollary of industrial peace and social reconstruction at home, his government took its tone from the direction of foreign affairs.'[18] Although perhaps a rather sweeping claim, there can be little doubt that his studied moderation towards Germany did reflect the intimacy of the perceived connection between the revival of domestic trade, the reduction of unemployment and the settlement of reparations and war debts. After mid-1920, the assumption that domestic slump and unemployment were a direct consequence of the political and economic chaos prevailing throughout Europe drove Lloyd George on in his struggle for Anglo-French diplomatic cooperation. He did so in the belief that a solution to the problem of reparations would settle Europe, restore dislocated trade channels, increase British exports, eradicate domestic unemployment and guarantee social stability. After a long series of international conferences, this bold quest to settle Europe culminated at Genoa in April–May 1922 in the collapse of Lloyd George's diplomacy and a severe blow to his credibility.

7.3 Slump and the destruction of 'national unity'

Despite some setbacks with social reform and industrial reconciliation, until the end of 1920 Lloyd George's project to perpetuate the Coalition on a more permanent basis did not appear to be impossible. Certainly the political drive and economic stability necessary to achieve these domestic objectives were both present in abundance during the first eighteen months of the Coalition. Yet after mid-1920, it became painfully evident that the economic boom had broken, as unemployment rose rapidly from 287,000 (1 per cent) in June 1920 to a registered peak of 2,178,000 in June 1921 (23 per cent of the insured workforce) – with another 832,000 on short-time.[19] Thereafter, some time during 1922, the slump 'did not so much end as peter out', as the economy became becalmed for the remainder of the decade in what Pigou described as the 'doldrums'; a period of economic stagnation and unhealthy quasi-equilibrium characterised by the existence of the 'intractable million', that 10 per cent of the insured workforce who appeared to be permanently surplus to employment requirements.[20] Ultimately, mass unemployment and slump spelt disaster for Lloyd George's hopes of 'reconstruction' and the consensus necessary to realign anti-socialism. During the winter of 1920–1 the social reform programme perceptibly slowed, before going into sharp reverse in face of mounting economic crisis and the political pressure exerted by Addison's critics.

Although Unionist leaders had initially accepted the logic of social reform, they rapidly became alarmed by the cost of fulfilling grandiose pledges about 'a fit land for heroes to live in'. Even before the slump they thoroughly mistrusted Addison's radicalism and were sensitive to middle class anger at the persistence of income tax at six shillings (30p) in the pound. Yet the launch of the Anti-Waste League in January 1921, in protest at continued high taxation and government 'extravagance', transformed the nature of the challenge to the Coalition – particularly given the support of the Rothermere press. From the outset the AWL became a focus for disaffected middle class Tory voters in London and the Home Counties, whose material comfort had been eroded by the war and its subsequent inflationary boom, and who felt squeezed between proletariat and profiteers.[21] In January 1921, the AWL won an astonishing victory in Dover over the official Unionist candidate. In June there were two further victories over Unionists in St George's (Westminster) and Hertford and it was a measure of its underlying electoral appeal that at the Abbey (Westminster) by-election in August all three candidates stood on an anti-waste platform consciously distancing themselves from the Coalition. Although the official Unionist won the by-election, he did so under the 'Constitutional and Independent Conservative Anti-Waste' label; an embarrassment for Coalition Unionism repeated at West Lewisham in the following month. Although the AWL's electoral threat receded after Lewisham, by then the movement had enjoyed considerable success when combined with growing Cabinet opposition to Addison's extravagance. Soon after the AWL's first by-election victory, drastic new curbs were placed upon the cost and the projected scale of the housing programme. In March 1921 Addison's demotion to Minister without Portfolio represented a signal defeat for the social reform project, and on 13 July 1921 he resigned, an unwilling sacrifice to Lloyd George's desire to placate his Tory allies. The establishment of the Geddes Committee two weeks later, with its infamous 'Geddes Axe', merely completed the process by laying waste all earlier dreams of national consensus built on social reform.

Slump dealt a comparable blow to the corporatist impulses fostered during the war. Mining was among the principal victims of trade depression as coal exports collapsed and prices halved. With losses of £5,000,000 per month in the first quarter of 1921, the government announced that State control would come to an end on 31 March. In response, the coal owners announced a return to district agreements, which meant wage cuts of up to 50 per cent in some areas. As the MFGB was determined to resist, a lockout commenced on 1 April. In the event, leaders of the Triple Alliance lost patience with the miners' leadership and called off the threatened collective action on 15 April 1921. 'Black Friday' dealt a devastating blow to almost all concerned. The Triple Alliance collapsed and would never be reconstructed. Defeat for the 'Cripple Alliance', as it became known, removed the threat of a general strike and decisively undermined the illusion that Direct Action represented a viable alternative to the parliamentary road. For the trade unions, membership fell by more than a third from its peak of 8,300,000 in 1920 to 5,400,000 by 1923. The miners were eventually starved back to work in June to accept appalling conditions, worse than those offered before the lockout, by some of the most notoriously callous employers in British industry. Wages in mining fell to 47 per cent of their prewar level and victimisation was rife. Moreover, for workers generally, the defeat of the miners was the prelude to a widespread employer offensive with devastating consequences. By the end of 1921, the *Economist* calculated that workers as a whole had lost three-quarters of their wartime wage increases and the gap between skilled and unskilled rates was narrowed, never to be restored.[22] For the remainder of the Coalition the number of stoppages declined but a menacing state of sullen industrial truce prevailed. Similarly, for Lloyd Georgian hopes of a permanent coalition based on national unity, 'Black Friday' was an even greater defeat. After losing ground electorally in 1920, 'Black Friday' and the slump enabled Labour to make a spectacular revival in municipal and parliamentary by-elections. The bitterness engendered by such a reverse gravely damaged Lloyd George's reputation as a friend of organised labour and destroyed any hope of continued industrial partnership on wartime lines. Contrary to his repeated claims that he wished to maintain a proper balance between classes, after 'Black Friday' the Coalition appeared irrevocably committed to the cause of capital, property and big business at the direct expense of organised labour and the working class. Thereafter, despite a series of panic-inspired half-measures designed to ameliorate unemployment, an increasingly beleaguered government settled down simply to await either the natural recovery of the economy or a diplomatic miracle capable of resolving the European economic dislocation which lay at the heart of British industrial distress.

In industrial relations as with social reform, Kenneth Morgan persuasively argues for more balance in considering the initial priorities, aspirations and optimism of 1919–20, alongside the often dismal policy outcome in 1921–22.[23] Given high levels of class consciousness, it is debatable how far Lloyd George's hopes of national unity transcending class cleavages were ever realisable. Yet the slump revealed the extent of the divergence between the two Coalition partners in their perceptions of the purpose of this arrangement. For

Lloyd George and Addison, coalition was a means to carry national politics on to a more elevated plane on the basis of a positive policy of reconstruction and reform for all. In contrast, most Conservatives had a far more limited and essentially negative vision of coalition as a means to restrain socialism at a time of acute political uncertainty. While the former implied a permanent new state of anti-socialist synthesis, the latter suggested a strictly temporary marriage of convenience. In this context, the real significance of the slump was that it dealt a devastating body-blow to any hopes of building a new political order on the foundations of wartime cooperation. Without either a positive agenda or the latitude to create one, the Coalition drifted to the right as its unifying *raison d'être* came to depend upon little more than a negative defence of the constitution from the threat of 'Bolshevism' – a fear which itself began to recede to more manageable proportions after mid-1921.

7.4 Anti-socialist 'fusion' and the realignment of the centre-right

After Lloyd George's return from the Paris Peace Conference in July 1919, plans for permanent anti-socialist realignment took the form of a movement towards 'fusion' in a new Centre party. The logic of 'fusion' was not confined simply to Lloyd George. The formation of the New Members' Coalition Group by Walter Elliot and Oswald Mosley in April 1919 reflected a high-minded cross-party determination to ensure that the appalling sacrifices of the war should not be in vain. Often fresh from the trenches, the strong social conscience of this group of around a hundred Conservative and Coalition Liberal MPs initially provided a solid bedrock for Coalition and fusion.[24] By the spring of 1920 many within the Conservative leadership had also come to accept that 'fusion' (in one way or another) was inevitable in order to contain socialism, although in Bonar Law's case this meant on the 1886 model in which the two allies retained separate organisations and gradually grew together, rather than Lloyd George's idea of immediate formal amalgamation. Within the National Union and the constituencies, however, there was little enthusiasm for such a step even at this juncture – as the demands for independence at the annual party conference at Birmingham in June 1920 demonstrated.[25]

In the event, Bonar Law was saved from an uncomfortable and divisive dilemma by the partisan attachments of Lloyd George's followers. Always assuming that the Tories represented the principal obstacle to his plans, Lloyd George took the acquiescence of his own supporters for granted. His meeting with Liberal ministers on 16 March disabused him of this illusion. Only Addison and Churchill were enthusiastic about fusion – the former as a positive means of promoting reconstruction, the latter as a negative bastion to defend the social order from the 'foul baboonery of Bolshevism'. The reluctance of the others to discard their Liberal traditions, however, compelled a surprised Prime Minister to shift his ground from 'fusion' to the less ominous prospect of closer cooperation. Yet when addressing Coalition Liberal MPs two days later he enjoyed equally little success even on these lines.

Although 'fusion' would have provided the organisational foundation they desperately needed to assure their future against Asquithian and Labour encroachment, these events clearly demonstrated the potency and resilience of party labels and traditions, even when assailed by so persuasive a figure as the Welsh Wizard. The Asquithians had equally few doubts about their hostility to any form of cooperation with Lloyd George. In the absence of political effectiveness, independence represented a symbol of their adherence to the true faith. During the spring of 1919 their creation of a separate parliamentary organisation with its own whips formally institutionalised the party split. At the NLF conference at Leamington on 7 May 1920 the breach was completed when concerted Asquithian heckling forced a walkout of those Coalition Liberal ministers and MPs who dared to show their faces. Unable to consummate either fusion with the Tories or Liberal reunion, the Coalition Liberals established their own political organisation. With lavish financial assistance from the notorious Lloyd George fund, a party magazine was launched in October 1920 and 224 nominal constituency associations were established in 1921 to create the semblance of a party organisation, albeit one without real grassroots support even in Scotland and Wales.[26] Of the twenty-five by-election seats defended between 1919 and 1922, the Coalition Liberals lost nine (eight to Labour) and retained the others only with Conservative support.

In retrospect, historians agree that the failure of 'fusion' marked a significant watershed in the decline of the postwar Coalition.[27] Yet such a view is far more compelling with hindsight than it was even to the majority of alienated Conservative MPs who went to the Carlton Club meeting on 19 October 1922 determined to oppose the continuation of the Coalition but convinced they would not destroy it. For the enthusiasts of fusion, failure to achieve their objective by direct advance in 1920 merely suggested the need for a less forthright means to achieve their goal by stealth. By December 1921 the revival of government fortunes with the Irish Treaty had imbued them with a mood of heady optimism in which the possibility of an immediate election to achieve fusion by the back door was discussed for the first time. If formal agreement to fuse into a Centre party could not be obtained by direct agreement, Coalition leaders of both parties assumed that another five years of cooperation in office would bring about merger indirectly by habit and routine after more than a decade in alliance together. In the event, this plotting came to grief on the rock of Tory partisanship mobilised by the Conservative Chairman and fellow party managers in support of Austen Chamberlain's leadership and his more cautious strategy of gradual organic convergence.[28] The abandonment of these election plans in mid-February 1922 was a far more severe blow to the credibility of the Coalition and its joint leadership than the failure of 'fusion' in 1920.

7.5 The fall of the Coalition

The Carlton Club revolt on 19 October 1922 was one of the most decisive single turning points in the development of the modern party system. In the aftermath of the 1918 election, Bonar Law believed that 'Lloyd George can be Prime Minister for life if he wants'.[29] Four turbulent years later, the Coalition was destroyed by Conservative MPs anxiously defending their party's distinctive identity and independence from just such a possibility. No single factor or explanation adequately explains the fall of the Coalition. In the event, it was not defeated by external threats whether from Labour, disaffected Tory Diehards or Lord Robert Cecil's patrician conspiracy to thrust Lord Grey forward as the champion of a more principled brand of anti-socialism. Contrary to Bonar Law's subsequent claim, nor did the Coalition fall because of a 'deeply rooted' feeling in the constituencies which impelled Conservative MPs to depose the Prime Minister and their own leaders in favour of independence.[30] Instead, the Coalition was destroyed from within, by serious policy failure and even worse leadership. After four extremely difficult years in office, disillusionment over policy was inevitable. Equally inevitably, blame would focus upon a Prime Minister whose highly personalised style of leadership and apparent rootless opportunism made him an obvious target for attack.

'Black Friday' and the betrayal of the bold rhetoric of 'a fit land for heroes to live in', provoked working class bitterness and the despair of reformers of all political hues. Although Conservatives rejoiced rather than lamented at Black Friday and the nemesis of Addison, they nursed their own deep grievances over other policy betrayals. Although the 1920 Agriculture Act which fixed farm prices and wages was declared to be the 'permanent policy of the government', within six months tumbling cereal prices and a government liability of £40,000,000 prompted the repeal of the price guarantees in Part I of the Act while cynically leaving the trivial clauses in Parts II and III on the Statute Book to comply with the pledge not to repeal the measure for four years. The 'Great Betrayal' of agriculture in 1921 infuriated and alienated the 150 or so Conservative MPs representing rural constituencies whose electoral significance and effective parliamentary organisation ensured their opinions mattered at the Carlton Club meeting. Similarly, the limits of coalition as a means of transcending old party divisions were exposed by the running sore over fiscal policy as the need to accommodate the free trade sensibilities of the Coalition Liberals increasingly infuriated the now solidly protectionist Tory backbenches. The settlement of the Irish Treaty in December 1921 revived old hostilities and exacerbated new tensions within both the Coalition and the Conservative party by providing the Diehards with a new oppositional coherence, and rousing Bonar Law from his detached retirement on one of only two issues about which he really cared deeply. The failure to honour the joint manifesto pledges of 1918 about House of Lords reform was another area for tension which the National Union executive denounced in May 1921 as 'a breach of the understanding upon which the allegiance of the Unionist Party to its leaders depends'. The 'honours scandal', following the publication of the notorious Birthday Honours list in June 1922, was a major embarrassment for the government. Although the practice of selling honours disgusted some high-minded moderate Tories, what outraged many others in the summer of

1922 was less the practice than the fact that a Liberal Prime Minister had turned it into a business on purely commercial lines and was 'nobbling our men' by selling honours to those who would otherwise provide funds for their own party coffers.[31] Beneath the hypocrisy and cant, such activities appeared to many to epitomise everything that was wrong with the Coalition's method of doing things. Finally, Lloyd George's Palmerstonian sense of destiny in foreign affairs played an equally major role in discrediting the Coalition and increasing internal tensions during its final six months. Although the failure of the Genoa Conference over German reparations was a major blow, when Lloyd George's pro-Greek stand against Turkey in Asia Minor brought Britain isolated to the brink of war at Chanak in late September, the crisis provided a unifying focus for an unprecedented revolt within the traditionally pro-Turk Conservative party.

Although some historians emphasise the importance of these acute divisions over policy, it is important not to exaggerate their significance in determining the outcome of events. First, despite many setbacks in 1921–2, Lloyd George and his pro-coalition Conservative counterparts were still relatively firmly in the saddle until September 1922. Second, despite rumblings of discontent, the absence of any credible alternative leader tended to reinforce the argument that coalition offered the only real alternative to Labour. Third, tensions over policy should not obscure the fact that the government remained remarkably united in its quest for a new anti-socialist consensus. Morgan even goes so far as to suggest that the Cabinet's 'inner coherence compares favourably with that of most British governments during the course of the present century'.[32] Ultimately, it was a measure of this consensus that most of the key policy directions pursued by the Coalition were continued without apparent protest or difficulty by a purely Conservative government after 1922. Finally, Michael Kinnear's detailed analysis of the Carlton Club rebels suggests that ultimately most voted to reject the Coalition through the intransigence of Austen Chamberlain and Lloyd George rather than through policy failure and that Conservative MPs 'were unwilling to smash the keystone of postwar political alignments because of disagreements over one or two policies'.[33] Rather, the Coalition was destroyed by the revival of Conservative partisanship, compounded by some of the worst and most misguided party leadership of the twentieth century.

Participation in the peacetime Coalition engendered a variety of tensions within the Conservative party which would have tested even the most skilled leadership. Given the need to accommodate Lloyd George's Liberals, Coalition implied a greater than usual sense of frustrated ambition because of the corresponding reduction in the career opportunities open to aspiring Conservative MPs. After 1918 the Conservatives had three times as many MPs as their Coalition allies, but they occupied only ten of twenty-one Cabinet seats and less than half the total number of government posts. This meant that about a dozen Tories were not ministers and about thirty others did not hold junior office as a direct consequence of Coalition.[34] As the web of patronage ensnares those who aspire to office as well as those who actually obtain it, the impact of such frustration encompassed a significant section of the parliamentary party. A more important tension, attributable directly to the Coalition, concerns the fundamental gulf it opened between the collective leadership of both parties and their followers in Parliament and the constituencies. The cohesion and unity of the Lloyd George Cabinet was no illusion. Even an 'old-fashioned Tory' like Griffith-Boscawen, who had no love for Lloyd George's methods and emerged as the first Cabinet rebel in early October 1922, conceded that almost to the end the Cabinet was 'a really happy family'.[35] Undoubtedly this harmony owed much to Lloyd George's almost hypnotic charm over those who worked closely with him. The closeness of the relationship with Bonar Law gave substance to the jibe that the Coalition represented a deal between a flock of sheep led by crook and a flock of crooks led by a sheep.[36] Despite his earlier intense antipathy, Austen Chamberlain fell even more dramatically under the spell of the Welsh Wizard after succeeding Law as Conservative leader in March 1921.[37] Such reactions fully substantiate Professor Ramsden's view that coalition was 'not ... only a political creed, but also a web of friendships and habits that underpinned political cooperation'.[38] Yet the problem was that the experience of coalition differed dramatically depending on where one stood. The camaraderie felt within the tight confines of Cabinet was not matched by instinctive sympathy or enthusiasm further down the party structures. For Tories in the Commons lobbies, the National Union and the constituencies, who were beyond the mesmeric personal charms of the Welsh Wizard, old political prejudices, personal animosities and partisan instincts were never extinguished. Ultimately this divergence of sentiment and experience lay at the core of the Coalition's disintegration.

The barrenness of Austen Chamberlain's inheritance as leader became evident soon after his succession in March 1921. With the economy in the depths of slump, over the next weeks the entire basis of Lloyd George's programme collapsed, as 'Black Friday' in mid-April was followed by Addison's removal from the Ministry of Health in June. From the right, the government also found itself under attack from the Anti-Waste League, while the Diehards took on a new lease of life with the commencement of the Irish negotiations in July 1921. None of these problems need have proved fatal had Austen Chamberlain been a more tactful, sensitive and flexible leader. Unfortunately, he was peculiarly devoid of all of the necessary talents demanded by the particular circumstances. As a result, perhaps more than any other single actor in the crisis, his personality and leadership style were directly responsible for the nemesis which overwhelmed the Coalition. Chamberlain's conviction about the imperative need to maintain coalition and move towards gradual fusion was not in itself the problem. It is easy to exaggerate the degree to which there was opposition to coalition *per se*, as opposed to a Lloyd George-led combination of the sort prevailing in 1922. Far from rejecting coalition, even after the Carlton Club revolt the Conservative rebels were prepared to be pragmatic if circumstances demanded a new arrangement.[39] Ultimately, what they wanted was not a total renunciation of anti-socialist coalition so much as a change of leadership to displace Lloyd George, curb the influence of his Cabinet followers and to reflect Conservative dominance.

In this context, Chamberlain and the Coalition fell because he made two fatal errors in managing the growing partisanship within his own party; mistakes which placed him on an almost inexorable collision course with those who would have followed him given more communication and coaxing. First, Chamberlain's honourable but wholly misguided loyalty to Lloyd George meant that he never gave his supporters the reassurance they wanted, to the effect that he shared their views about the future leadership and organisation of the Coalition. This failure bred the damaging impression that he was so mesmerised by the Welsh Wizard that he was either unwilling or unable to defend party interests at a time when these demanded a proper share of power. Second, during the critical final months, Chamberlain's autocratic leadership style and arrogantly aloof personality became a fatal handicap.[40] During his extended political apprenticeship he had developed a highly tuned sense of loyalty to the Conservative party and its leaders and he felt justified in making the same demands of unquestioning obedience from his own followers. While Bonar Law used his personal capital to balance factions to keep the government on an even keel, for Chamberlain leadership consisted of exercising authority and giving orders rather than synthesising opinion and explaining actions. Throughout, he dismissed critics with the assertion that the Conservative leaders were united and it was the duty of others to follow without equivocation. Worse still, this 'superiority complex' was based on a misplaced belief in his own indispensability. As early as March 1922 he had made it clear that if the party would not follow him, it should look elsewhere for leadership. As the crisis developed during the autumn his mood became increasingly autocratic, domineering and brutally intolerant of all those who opposed another Coalition election in November 1922.

During the final days of the Coalition, Chamberlain and his fellow leaders unerringly mishandled almost every aspect of a delicate personal and political situation. By the eve of the revolt, at least six different groups, comprising rebellious ministers, under-secretaries, backbenchers and party managers, were all united in opposition to the Coalition by the determination of their leaders to force them into a corner into which they would not be driven.[41] Similarly, at the Carlton Club meeting on 19 October, Chamberlain's 'uncompromising and somewhat aggressive attitude' surprised many MPs present and turned the meeting into a vote of confidence in his leadership.[42] With more sensitivity, defeat was probably avoidable even at this stage had he revealed his private belief that the perpetuation of the Coalition did not necessarily mean under Lloyd George, but instead Chamberlain compelled those present to choose blindly between loyalty to the Coalition under its existing leadership (without any indication of future change), or loyalty to their party without its current leaders. Conservative MPs chose by the substantial margin of 187 votes to 87 to fight the election 'as an independent party with its own leader and its own programme'. Although much mythology subsequently developed about the impact of a variety of last minute factors in determining the outcome, in the absence of leadership compromise, the Coalition's fate had already been sealed by the time Conservative MPs gathered at the Carlton Club, although very few realised it at the time. Of the 107 MPs whose views can be determined, the overwhelming majority had made up their minds before the meeting and only eight probably decided at the Carlton Club itself. As such, for all the dramatic spectacle and surprise, the outcome was merely a collective affirmation of a widespread prior discontent.[43] The foundation for this collective resistance was the desire to defend their own distinctive Tory traditions and party label against a leadership apparently intent upon submerging that independent identity in a new anti-socialist amalgam. In March 1920 the Coalition Liberals had demonstrated the critical importance attached to party labels by vetoing 'fusion' although it offered them electoral salvation. In October 1922 the Conservatives overthrew the Coalition for precisely the same reason, in circumstances in which the political and electoral logic for its perpetuation appeared much less compelling. Conservatives were not turning their backs upon the possibility of any future anti-socialist combination, but the Carlton Club revolt was an unequivocal rejection of Lloyd George's dream of making his particular brand of coalitionism the dominant mode of resistance to socialism.

Notes and references

The place of publication is London unless otherwise stated.

1 Robert Self, ed., *The Austen Chamberlain Diary Letters, 1916–1937* (Cambridge, 1995), pp. 31–2.

2 Maurice Cowling, *The Impact of Labour, 1920–1924: The Beginning of Modern British Politics* (Cambridge, 1971), p. 1.

3 Henry Pelling, *A History of British Trade Unionism* (1963), p. 294.

4 Kenneth O. Morgan, *Consensus and Disunity: The Lloyd George Coalition Government 1918–1922* (Oxford, 1979), p. 49.

5 Chris Wrigley, *David Lloyd George and the Challenge of Labour: The Post-War Coalition, 1918–1922* (Hemel Hempstead, 1990), pp. 105–12.

6 R. Geary, *Policing Industrial Disputes, 1893 to 1985* (Cambridge, 1985), pp. 53–6.

7 Morgan, *Consensus and Disunity*, pp. 68, 221.

8 Chris Cook, *The Age of Alignment: Electoral Politics in Britain 1922–1929* (1975), pp. 11–12.

9 Cowling, *The Impact of Labour*, pp. 25–6.

10 Ibid., pp. 2–3.

11 See Michael Bentley, *The Liberal Mind, 1914–1929* (Cambridge, 1977), pp. 134–5; Wrigley, *Lloyd George and the Challenge of Labour*, pp. 14, 17.

12 R.J. Scally, *The Origins of the Lloyd George Coalition: The Politics of Social Imperialism, 1900–1918* (Princeton, 1975), p. 354.

13 Bentley B. Gilbert, *British Social Policy 1914–1939* (1970), p. 9. Kenneth and Jane Morgan, *Portrait of a Progressive: The Political Career of Christopher, Viscount Addison* (Oxford, 1980), pp. 71–3, 80–2.

14 Paul B. Johnson, *Land Fit for Heroes: The Planning of British Reconstruction, 1916–1919* (Chicago, 1968).

15 Morgan, *Consensus and Disunity*, pp. 23–5.

16 M. Swenarton, 'An insurance against revolution: ideological objectives of the provision and design of public housing in Britain after the First World War', *Bulletin of the Institute of Historical Research* 51 (1981) and *Homes Fit for Heroes* (1981).

17 Rodney Lowe, 'The erosion of state intervention in Britain, 1917–24', *Economic History Review* 31 (1978), pp. 270–86.

18 Morgan, *Consensus and Disunity*, p. 116.

19 Henry Clay, *The Post-War Unemployment Problem* (1929), p. 34.

20 A.C. Pigou, *Aspects of British Economic Policy, 1918–1925* (1947), pp. 7, 42–3.

21 See Cowling, *The Impact of Labour*, pp. 56–9.

22 Patrick Renshaw, 'The Depression years', in Ben Pimlott and Chris Cook, eds, *Trade Unions in British Politics* (1982), pp. 102–4.

23 Morgan, *Consensus and Disunity*, p. 106.

24 G.R. Searle, *Country before Party: Coalition and the Idea of 'National Government' in Modern Britain, 1885–1987* (1995), pp. 119–20.

25 John Ramsden, *The Age of Balfour and Baldwin, 1902–1940* (1978), pp. 143–4.

26 Michael Kinnear, *The British Voter: An Atlas and Survey since 1885* 2nd edn (1981), pp. 88–93.

27 Morgan, *Consensus and Disunity*, p. 187; Ramsden, *Age of Balfour and Baldwin*, p. 144.

28 Self, *Austen Chamberlain Diary Letters*, pp. 173–7.

29 Martin Pugh, *Lloyd George* (1988), p. 128.

30 Michael Kinnear, *The Fall of Lloyd George: The Political Crisis of 1922* (1973), ch. 3.

31 J.A. Ramsden, 'The organisation of the Conservative and Unionist Party in Britain, 1910–1930'. Unpublished D.Phil, Oxford, 1974, pp. 342–4.

32 Morgan, *Consensus and Disunity*, p. 177.

33 Kinnear, *Fall of Lloyd George*, pp. 87–8.

34 Ramsden, *Age of Balfour and Baldwin*, pp. 134–5.

35 Sir Arthur Griffith-Boscawen, *Memories* (1925), pp. 214–15, 232, 260–2.

36 Kinnear, *Fall of Lloyd George*, p. 4.

37 Self, *Austen Chamberlain Diary Letters*, pp. 147–8.

38 Ramsden, *Age of Balfour and Baldwin*, p. 133.

39 Kinnear, *Fall of Lloyd George*, pp. 106–7.

40 Self, *Austen Chamberlain Diary Letters*, pp. 14–15, 197–200.

41 Cowling, *The Impact of Labour*, pp. 194–212.

42 Lord Hemingford, *Backbencher and Chairman: Some Parliamentary Reminiscences* (1946), p. 42.

43 Kinnear, *Fall of Lloyd George*, pp. 131–3.

Chapter eight

Three-party confusion in the 1920s

8.1 Explanations for party realignment

The period between the fall of the Coalition and the 1929 general election established the pattern of British party politics for the remainder of the interwar period and determined its broad contours for the rest of the century. Two-party politics were eventually restored after a period of three-party instability although the earlier Liberal–Conservative cleavage had now given way to a Conservative–Labour contest for power. During the 1920s the two successful parties came to terms with the doctrinal and organisational implications of mass democracy in a less deferential, more secular and more class-conscious society. In contrast, the Liberals failed to respond until it was too late, although whether this was a cause or consequence of more profound decline, and whether this demise owed more to accidental factors or a 'natural' process of socio-economic change remains the subject of often heated debate.[1]

Despite the intense confusion of the 1922 campaign and the astonishing closeness of the vote, for each of the parties the election produced a result of long-term significance. Although only 3,738 Conservatives voting for the second party in thirty constituencies would have denied them effective parliamentary control,[2] the overall Conservative majority of seventy-seven removed the need for another coalition. Thereafter, they remained in office for all but three years of the interwar period and obtained most votes in all five subsequent elections. At the same time Labour emerged from the 1922 election as the principal party of opposition with 29.7 per cent of the vote and 142 MPs. Although not yet the party of the entire working class so much as a section of it, within a year Labour formed its first government with only 200,000 more votes and forty-nine more MPs. Thereafter, Labour's share of the vote showed a slow but steady increase to 37.1 per cent in 1929 when it formed a second minority government. In 1922 the Liberals collectively obtained 28.8 per cent of the vote and 115 MPs – scarcely fewer than Labour. Yet the election was significant for the Liberals for two reasons. First, they fought not as a single party but rather as a bitterly divided force unable to decide who were the real enemy. As they never fully overcame either of these difficulties, consideration of collective performance is virtually meaningless except in assessing the full tragedy of Liberal self-immolation in these years. Secondly, after 1922, both major parties became markedly more aggressive in their determination to destroy Liberalism completely. After a brief tantalising 'recovery' in 1923, the Liberals swiftly collapsed into a state of abject decline on the margins of power, although they proved too stubborn simply to lie down and die. From 159 MPs in 1923, Liberal parliamentary representation plummeted to 40 in 1924, mostly at the sufferance of the Tories and without any solid socio-regional base. The party which had 399 MPs in 1906 was reduced to a pathetic vestige of just 21 MPs and 6.4 per cent of the vote by 1935.

Unfortunately, although the facts are clear, the problem for the historian of party is that the debate about the causes of these trends is long on controversy and very short on undisputed truths. One school of thought contends that whatever the balance of probabilities, there was nothing inevitable about any of these party trends, even after 1918. All three parties had the opportunity to win the support of new voters before they committed themselves. After the war the Conservatives could have fumbled their opportunity as they did before 1914, and in 1922–3 many believed this was a real possibility. Similarly, although Labour went from strength to strength, it should not be forgotten that in 1918 the Liberals collectively obtained 350,000 more votes than Labour and even at the 1923 election, which brought the first Labour government to power, Labour only polled 138,299 votes more than the Liberals. Against this background, the 'contingency' school tends to emphasise the pivotal significance of accidental factors in explaining the Liberal inability to prevent Labour slipping past them within a plurality electoral system which systematically discriminated against national third parties. Errors of judgement, poor leadership, bad luck, hostility from their opponents and more than a touch of suicidal mania all played their part in the process by denying the Liberals any credibility as a serious challenger for power while retarding their ability to formulate a rhetoric relevant to the new electorate. From such a perspective, advocates of the 'contingency' thesis point to the obvious dangers in 'simply *assuming* the Liberals were losers, as a consequence of which all successes have to be dismissed as "aberrations".'[3]

On the other hand, for many historians there is something profoundly unsatisfactory about explaining these dramatic shifts in party dominance simply as a version of the 'one damned thing after another' school of history. If nothing else, emphasis upon the sorts of accidents usually discussed often begs more fundamental questions. From this perspective, the intrinsically linked processes of Liberal decline and Labour rise are presented as the product of long-term structural changes in British society, as regional, religious and traditional electoral alignments gave way to highly developed class loyalties. For historians like Pelling and McKibbin, this trend was already evident in the Progressive Alliance before 1914 and at most, 'the war did not act so much as a generator as an accelerator' of change.[4] For this 'class school' generally, the Liberal party was fatally handicapped by its inability to make a claim upon the loyalties of any particular class and the extension of the electorate in 1918 sealed its fate. The New Liberalism had been the last bold attempt to transcend class as populist reformers capable of winning votes from the 'community' as a whole. Although all claimed to be 'a party of the nation' rather than a section or a class, Liberals alone depended upon making such an aspiration come true. In the view of the 'class school', the quest would always prove fruitless for cultural as well as political reasons.

8.2 The 'franchise factor' and the Fourth Reform Act of 1918

A much discussed structural explanation for the rapid replacement of the Liberals by Labour relates to the 'franchise factor'. Even with the significant exception of women, the Edwardian electoral system was a long way from a mature participatory democracy given a systematic class bias which not only excluded 40–45 per cent of the male population (predominantly the industrial working class), but through plural voting also doubled the electoral significance of middle class voters who accounted for perhaps 40 per cent of the electorate but little more than 20 per cent of the population (see section 2.3 above). The Representation of the People Act in 1918 fundamentally transformed this situation. Henceforth, the voting qualification was based on age and citizenship rather than the complexities of property tenure, while the previously crucial function of electoral registration now became the responsibility of neutral officials. These changes drastically extended the size of the electorate from just 7,709,981 in 1910 to 21,392,322 in 1918, by enfranchising all men over the age of 21 and women over 30 if they were either local government electors in their own right or the wives of those who were. Soldiers on active service over the age of 19 were also given the vote in recognition of their war service, the plural vote was reduced to only two constituencies whether by virtue of a business or university qualification and conscientious objectors were disenfranchised for five years. These reforms were accompanied by a wholesale revision of constituency boundaries which disrupted much established organisation.

Although hotly contested on many fronts, exponents of the 'franchise factor' argue that these reforms radically transformed the very structure of British politics in two key respects. First, this massive 277 per cent increase in the size of the electorate inevitably changed its class profile by enfranchising a very substantial proportion of working class men and women previously excluded from the vote but who were largely predisposed towards Labour. Second, the combination of a mass electorate and new constituency boundaries imposed unprecedented demands upon the electoral organisation of the parties to which they responded with very different levels of commitment and success. According to Matthew, McKibbin and Kay, together these two effects had a decisive impact upon Labour's rise and Liberal decline after 1918 and were certainly 'at least as significant as chronological developments' such as the war. Moreover, it is argued that Labour also benefited from the defection of Liberal voters who either did not have a Liberal candidate to support or who switched allegiances. Although a solid core of 25–30 per cent of Liberal loyalists remained unwilling to vote for any other party throughout the 1920s, the remainder split almost evenly between Labour and Conservatives with a marginal advantage to the latter.[5]

Despite its seductive charm, the 'franchise factor' has been questioned on two main grounds. A first line of criticism concerns the apparent absence of any immediate impact of this structural change. Labour did advance from 42 MPs in December 1910 to 57 in 1918 and 142 by 1922. Its share of the vote rose in the same period from 7.2 per cent to 22.7 per cent in 1918 and then 29.7 per cent in 1922. Yet sceptics argue this was scarcely an explosive advance, particularly given the far more dramatic increase in its number of candidates from 56 in 1910 to 361 in 1918 and 414 in 1922. Nor is this progress considered to be impressive given the fact that Labour continued to be concentrated in areas of traditional prewar strength – most notably in the coalfields which provided nearly two-thirds of its MPs in 1918.[6] Overall, then, sceptics argue that in 1918, far from experiencing a dramatic 'big bang' in its electoral fortunes as a direct result of franchise reform, at best the party was the beneficiary of steady advance.[7] A second and rather different reservation focuses upon doubts about the actual size of the franchise increase and its supposed class bias. First, according to Duncan Tanner, many historians underestimate the size of the prewar working class electorate and thus exaggerate the impact of the Fourth Reform Act in 1918. As Duncan Tanner calculates that the actual increase in working class voters in 1918 was from 67 to 78 per cent of the total electorate, it follows that Labour's interwar rise cannot be attributed solely to new voters and the 'franchise factor'. Secondly, although the electoral system discriminated against young unmarried men living at home and those in high mobility occupations, Tanner argues that these circumstances were by no means confined to Labour's natural supporters among the working class.[8] Engineers, commercial travellers, Wesleyan ministers, teachers and government employees were among many professions afflicted with high residential mobility. Similarly, given the obstacles to registration under the lodger franchise, in 1915 250–350,000 single, middle class men were voteless out of around three million single men in the population as a whole. At the same time, changes in the law and procedure of registration and rating increasingly enabled working class tenants to obtain access to the vote.[9] As a result, it is concluded that while the very poorest were 'slightly under-represented, ... Labour's inability to win elections [before 1914] was not caused by a structural bias in a system which systematically discriminated against working class men'.[10] Rather, the discrimination within the system was not a class bias, but one in favour of householders of all classes against lodgers.

Although much recent work has endorsed these reservations about the effect of the 'franchise factor', the counter-case should not be carried too far. First, it seems reasonable to assume that prewar working class Labour supporters were less likely than Liberal or Conservative supporters to uphold their claim to the vote at a registration court, given the fact that (outside Scotland) registration conditions ensured that it was almost impossible to obtain the lodger franchise without the aid of an agent. As Labour had only seventeen full-time agents in 1912 compared with around 300 for the Liberals this must have been a substantial handicap. Second, it does not necessarily follow that the middle classes would be more likely to surrender their vote to resist intrusion into their private circumstances at a registration court, when a labourer lost a day's pay to uphold his claim. Third, even if Tanner's upper estimate of 350,000 single voteless middle class men is accepted, it still represents a small proportion of the almost five million unenfranchised men before 1914. Moreover, given the rising commitment to the trade union movement and its increasing alignment with Labour, there must be some grounds for assuming that a fair proportion of these men would have been Labour voters. Finally, as the lowest prewar enfranchisement levels were largely in London, northern towns and industrial areas with a high proportion of poorer and Catholic inhabitants, the transition to adult male enfranchisement after 1918 did represent a significant structural change because within such constituencies many households had no established patterns of voting allegiance to pass on from a pre-Labour generation.

In this context, analysis of the generational profile of the electorate in the period of Labour's emergence tends to confirm the general importance of a franchise factor, even if not in its classic form.[11] Contrary to the assertion of Tanner and others, that the new voters after 1918 would be expected to reflect the political opinions of their parents, Michael Childs concludes that among the younger generation entering the electorate between 1910 and 1929, a significant realignment of party allegiances was taking place. This highly unusual discontinuity between generations may have been the consequence of an increasing class-consciousness within the political culture in which socialisation took place after 1900, at a time when denominational socialisation influences were in steep decline.[12] Alternatively, it may be due to the unifying homogeneity of working class experience in education, work and leisure as it came down to youth in the decade before the First World War.[13] Either way, when seen from this perspective, Labour's real problem in expanding before 1914 was perhaps less that a large section of the working class were denied the vote, than that Labour confronted a working class whose political loyalties had been formed in a very different era, in which community and confessional affiliations rather than class identity had been crucial determinants of the socialisation process. In the longer term, however, new political socialisation influences produced a slow but steady haemorrhaging of support away from the Liberals. Thus, although among the generational cohort born before 1875 the Liberal share was 38 per cent, this figure fell steadily from 25 per cent among those born between 1875 and 1897 to only 13 per cent among those born between 1901 and 1914. As a result, evidence of generational replacement suggests that the established parties were not so much abandoned by their older working class supporters, but rather they were progressively less successful in appealing to each new cohort of working class electors entering the electorate after 1918. There was thus no 'big bang' because Labour did not come into its class inheritance overnight. Nevertheless, the reality was that the working class Liberal vote socialised in a pre-Labour era was an ageing and wasting asset, while Labour's support was being increased and replenished with each generational cohort entering the electorate after 1918.

Despite the importance of the enfranchisement provisions of the 1918 Act, its impact was not confined exclusively to the number of voters or the conditions of eligibility. The Act also reduced the plural vote to only one at a time when the advent of the motor car made multiple qualifications a practical reality. Henceforth elections would also take place on a single day, thereby substantially enhancing the importance of the national campaign and party image over local influences. Arguably, both of these factors offered some assistance to Labour, either directly by creating a more level playing field or by increasing the problems for its opponents. Above all else, the 1918 Act was accompanied by a wholesale revision of constituency boundaries. This had a variety of important implications for party competition. First, redistribution disrupted the structures of the older parties far more than it did Labour whose often embryonic organisation in many areas only emerged in 1917–18 specifically in response to the stimulus of the Act. Second, redistribution delivered a severe blow to the Liberals by reducing their over-represented bedrock of once safe seats in the rural Celtic fringe, while assisting Labour to consolidate its own electoral base through the creation of more socially homogeneous industrial seats and by increasing the number of mining constituencies from forty to sixty-six.[14] After 1918 perhaps a third of all British seats were dominated by working class or mining groups compared with a quarter before 1914. The importance of such a structural change in British politics during this formative period cannot be overestimated given the close competition between Labour and Liberals in the early 1920s. Finally, these structural challenges came at a moment when the Liberals were in maximum disarray and thus least able to respond effectively – if only because they could not field a full slate of candidates or maintain a consistent local challenge.

Although a host of other factors may have influenced the effectiveness of the parties in meeting these new challenges, it would appear perverse to deny the significant, if complex, impact of the 1918 Act in disrupting established parties and intensifying the sense of fluidity which existed in the aftermath of the Great War. In this context, one of the greatest accidents or errors often overlooked by the 'contingency school' was Lloyd George's failure to implement the unanimous recommendation of the Speaker's Conference on Electoral Reform in favour of the Single Transferable Vote for borough elections returning three or more MPs and the majority proposal for the Alternative Vote in other constituencies.[15] Had the AV system been introduced in 1918, it has been calculated that the Liberals would have held the balance of power not only in 1923 and 1929, but also in 1922 and 1924.[16] On this basis, some historians believe that the Liberals could have created a more enduring role for themselves either as a true centre party[17] or as a party of rural radicalism within an electoral system capable of sustaining genuine three-party politics.[18] Yet in the event, the Liberals either ignored the possibility or proved remarkably resistant to this new role until it was far too late.

8.3 The organisational factor in Labour rise and Liberal decline

Controversies about the impact of the 'franchise factor' are partly mirrored in debates about the different attitudes of the parties towards the role of electoral mobilisation within a mass democracy. From the outset, apprehensions about the ignorance and volatility of these new electors prompted the belief that robust organisation would be an essential prerequisite for those parties who wished to succeed in new conditions. One of the central motives behind Henderson's party reorganisation in 1917–18 was the recognition that the existing party structure simply could not cope with the demands of the mass democracy. The reorganisation of NEC activity and the appointment of Egerton Wake as National Agent provided the impetus to carry Labour's crusade to the regions through the creation of constituency Labour parties (CLPs) rather than the trade councils which had predominated before the war. As a result, the number of CLPs increased from 239 in 1916 to 397 by 1918. Stimulated by three elections in less than two years, by 1924 only nineteen constituencies were not covered by some sort of local organisation – however rudimentary and makeshift that may have been.[19] The number of full-time agents increased correspondingly from 17 in 1912 to 80 by 1918 and then reached a plateau of around 112 in 1920–4 before rising steadily to 169 in 1929. Candidates increased with the growth of local organisation (and often preceded it), to reach an interwar peak of 569 in 1929, only 21 fewer than the Tories. As a direct consequence of this increase in the number of candidates, Labour's vote rose steadily from 4,237,349 (29.7 per cent) in 1922 to 8,370,417 (37.1 per cent) in 1929. Underlying such advances was the continued financial and organisational commitment of the unions to what most now regarded as their party.

Inevitably there were defects and weaknesses in such an organisation given the speed of its development. Many CLPs were scarcely more than nominal, ramshackle improvisations. Despite the introduction of individual membership in 1918, the total had risen to only 227,897 by 1929 and only forty-seven CLPs in England and Wales claimed more than 1,000 individual members by 1930. Similarly, the creation of separate Women's Sections with their own NEC representatives and regional organisers attracted only 120,000 members by 1923. Finance was also an obvious constraint upon organisational growth given the speed with which it had taken place. The need for 'contracting-in' to the political levy, introduced in the 1927 Trade Disputes Act, was also a severe blow to Labour finances – although less devastating than expected. Yet trade union control over the party's purse strings was a longer-term problem given their extremely defensive and parochial attitude towards the use of their cash. This explains why full-time agents were concentrated in union-controlled safe seats where they were least needed, while the unions resisted Henderson's plans to redirect resources to assist the development of organisation in more marginal constituencies.[20]

Yet despite the improvised nature of Labour's organisation, the structures it created were remarkably resilient. Trade union branches and trades councils played a key role as a nucleus to sustain continuity of local organisation and finance, as well as mobilising support in the seats they controlled. Equally important, deficiencies in formal structure were often compensated for by a passionate sense of class loyalty and the sheer vitality of grassroots activists.[21] When systematically channelled into mass doorstep canvassing, as in London during the early 1920s, such enthusiasm yielded some remarkable by-election successes which startled opponents sought to emulate. Against this background, it is important to retain a proper sense of perspective in assessing claims about the supposed 'illusion' of Labour's organisational strength.[22] For all its deficiencies, Labour's rivals were aware of their own corresponding weaknesses, while 'outside the rural, semi-rural, and overwhelmingly bourgeois constituencies, the enemy was taken aback by the intensity and vigour of Labour's attack'.[23] Even in a city like Birmingham, with its strong Chamberlainite Unionist tradition and recently reorganised and strengthened party machine, the Labour onslaught provoked grave alarm. As a special meeting of the Birmingham Conservative Association heard in December 1922:

> We must not forget that conditions were now very different to what they had been in the days of [Joseph Chamberlain], when his personal influence had been so overwhelming that there was really no need for organisation. It was no longer a fight between Unionists and Liberals, but between Unionists and Socialists, who exploited the sufferings of the poor, setting class against class, and particularly appealed to the out-of-works who were in such a hopeless state that they were only too ready to believe that their sufferings were due to political causes. This propaganda was going on day in and day out; not alone at public meetings, but from house to house and at street corners.

The degree of emphasis which Conservatives placed upon organisational development and propaganda during the 1920s and the proliferation of anti-socialist alliances at local and national elections were indicative of the seriousness with which interwar opponents regarded Labour's local organisational strength.[24]

Certainly Labour's vigour appeared astonishing when compared with the parlous state of Liberal organisation. Although there were signs of decay in areas as diverse as Wales, Lancashire and London before 1914, after the war this disintegration became substantially more severe. Nor was this entirely a problem of structure, finance and mechanics. According to Matthew, McKibbin and Kay, a crucial element of the 'franchise factor' was the reluctance of the Liberal party either to take electoral organisation seriously or to make the necessary demagogic appeals to the mass electorate; an error based on an excessive commitment to the norms of a pre-democratic era of limited franchises and their failure to recognise that 1918 had fundamentally transformed the character of the electorate. Centralised control, formal party membership and crude demagoguery were never wholly comfortable notions for a party which prided itself on its faith in active appeals to citizenship and democratic rationalism. The decentralised, ramshackle and undoubtedly decaying organisation before 1914 was thus supposedly incapable of coping with the demands of a mass electorate and (unlike both their opponents) the Liberals allegedly did little to address the problem because of these anachronistic attitudes towards the political community and the nature of electoral politics itself.[25] Although it is undoubtedly true that the Liberal party did fail to adapt from its nineteenth century roots as a cadre party dependent on a few large subscribers, such an argument is only partly convincing. Between the wars Lloyd George lost none of his earlier capacity for demagoguery and 'Limehousing', as he demonstrated in defence of free trade in 1923 and in his campaigns on land and unemployment in 1925–9. More important, perhaps the real problem confronting the Liberals in this respect was less one of attitudes than of resources.

The 1918 general election and its outcome dealt a devastating blow to the Liberal organisation from which it never recovered. By April 1923 party managers conceded that 'Liberalism as an active missionary force is almost dead in numbers of constituencies and needs strengthening in almost all'.[26] In practice, organisational paralysis, financial crisis and electoral failure usually went hand-in-hand to form a vicious spiral of decline. Derelict and impoverished local associations were both a cause and a consequence of a more dramatic decline in local activism, which often left constituency associations totally dependent on a single wealthy candidate or central subsidy and once either was withdrawn the whole organisation tended to collapse. These problems were most damagingly reflected in the inability to contest elections. In 1918 the Asquithians had fielded only 276 candidates. Although this rose to 333 in 1922, it was still little more than half the total number of constituencies and 81 fewer than Labour. Such failures were profoundly damaging because they disrupted the very habit of Liberal voting by compelling potential supporters to consider their second preference, while enabling Labour to stake an uncontested claim to be the principal representative of progressive opinion. Among the new voters entering the electorate after 1918 the effect must have been particularly damaging.[27] This is not to suggest that the Liberals could not win seats. Their problem was the inability to contest and retain them with any degree of continuity. In the five elections between 1918 and 1929, the Liberals won 281 seats at least once – only slightly fewer than Labour's 304 seats. Yet the Liberals won only 22 of these 281 seats on all five occasions and only 75 seats on three or more occasions, compared with 160 of 304 for Labour and 335 of 445 for the Conservatives.[28] Beyond a few isolated strongholds on the Celtic fringe, therefore, the declining number of Liberal victories appeared less a pattern of regional strength than a random hotchpotch of freak wins devoid of obvious socio-regional coherence and gained only as a second-rate substitute for Conservatism.[29] Without a solid bedrock of support, like Labour's mining districts or the Conservatives' suburbs and agricultural seats, the Liberals confronted a major handicap in a class-based competition conducted under the rules of an unforgiving winner-take-all electoral system. Whatever the cause, the fact remained that only political marginalisation beckoned for a party incapable of consistently fielding sufficient candidates either to sustain electoral loyalty or to claim credibility to be a genuine party of government.

Atrophy within local organisation undoubtedly reflected the demoralising state of party division at national level. Aged 70 in 1922, Asquith's inertia since 1916 had robbed the party of all vestiges of leadership and direction and he was equally determined to prevent Lloyd George from filling this void. Thus, while the fall of the Coalition in October 1922 opened the way for possible reunion, as a crucial prerequisite for the restoration of the party's organisation, finances and morale, Asquithians were prepared to destroy the party rather than permit it. Ironically, Lloyd George's forcible rehabilitation within the party was brought about by his principal enemy when Baldwin resurrected tariff reform in October 1923. Although in the short term the fight against protectionism stimulated a renewal of constituency activity and the appearance of 457 candidates, beneath the surface reunion came too late for the Liberals to become an effective electoral machine. Moreover, although constituency opinion generally supported the decision to put Labour into office in January 1924, the divisions and humiliations of the parliamentary party during the first Labour government were a disaster for activist morale. In consequence, during 1924 their brief revival was not consolidated through any concerted effort to restore grassroots local organisation.

Finance was in many respects a key obstacle to organisational recovery and party reunion. Access to the 'Lloyd George millions', raised by the sale of honours during the Coalition, was not a substitute for high morale or local activism, but it was a partial precondition for it because while Lloyd George had all the money and no national organisation, the Asquithians controlled the party machine but were virtually bankrupt. Unfortunately for the party they led, reciprocity of need could not overcome accumulated hatreds. Given their personal vendetta, this meant that Asquithians wanted the fund but not its possessor, while Lloyd George would not spend any money without obtaining control over the entire party. The outcome was a protracted and debilitating feud over money after 1923. Lack of preparedness due to these financial wranglings was by no means the principal cause of the Liberal massacre in 1924, but it certainly did not help when agents were unpaid and the party headquarters considered closing down altogether. Thus, by the time Lloyd George became leader in 1926, the party was probably beyond anything but divine intervention. Despite Lloyd George's dynamic efforts to refurbish Liberal ideology and Sir Herbert Samuel's party reorganisation, the 1929 election came as a crushing blow to a party hopelessly squeezed between the hostile forces of left and right and imprisoned within a particularly unforgiving form of electoral system.

8.4 Labour, Liberals and the battle of ideas

Although organisational and electoral forces are important, other factors are necessary to explain the behaviour of voters once coaxed or cajoled to the polling station by party activists whose fervour and awareness they (almost by definition) did not share. Yet the impact of ideas and ideology upon the electoral fortunes of the three parties during the 1920s represents a complex conundrum. For example, ideological failure would appear to be at least plausible as a factor in explaining some of the problems confronting the Liberals at municipal level. The wartime decline of most of the essentially denominational issues which had brought many into local politics before 1914, removed much of the incentive to participate in this arena after 1918, except where Nonconformity remained powerful or in those few areas of Yorkshire, the East Midlands and London where local Liberals fought on a refurbished radical programme.[30] Elsewhere, however, municipal Liberalism suffered because it failed to excite activists or even to distinguish itself from Conservatism. Yet on the other hand, at a national level, the relationship between the health of Liberal doctrine and the Liberal party is far more ambiguous. If nothing else, some extraordinarily bold claims have been advanced for the Liberal Summer School (LSS) movement as

> the linchpin of liberal and progressive thought during the 1920s. It witnessed the only serious attempt to revive Liberalism as an intellectual force; it supplied the Liberal party with a radical ideology that gradually assumed salience and centrality in its programmes; and it served as a source of inspiration, often discreet, sometimes acknowledged, for a wider spectrum of political activists outside the Liberal party.[31]

The LSS had been inspired by E.D. Simon, a wealthy Manchester industrialist and Liberal MP. Frustrated by the intellectual malaise of the leadership, Simon sought to replace vague outmoded generalities with definite policy. An initial meeting of radical Liberals in the summer of 1920 produced Ramsay Muir's bold statement, *Liberalism and Industry*, committed to rail and coal nationalisation, major public investment in housing, health and education and the minimum wage. On the fiscal side, it embraced a comprehensive shift to higher direct taxation, an emergency capital levy, taxation of land values and profit limitation for the public good. From these roots, the LSS rapidly developed into an institutionalised forum for theorising about liberal ideology, free from the constraints inseparable from a direct party political purpose. After its first meeting at Grasmere in September 1921, the annual week-long meetings held alternatively at Oxford and Cambridge brought together the greatest minds of liberal economics and political science including Keynes, Walter Layton, Gilbert Murray, Graham Wallas, Hobhouse and Tawney. Attracted by such a glittering array of talent, attendance soon rose to 1,000 during its heyday in the mid-1920s, while LSS ideas were disseminated to a broader audience through the *Nation*. As Keynes told the 1925 meeting, the objective was 'to invent a new wisdom for a new age'. Given this unofficial intellectual vigour, Liberal decline is thus rightly described as 'no simple tale of ideological regression'.[32] Through Lloyd George's campaigns of 1926–29 and 1935, the Liberal intelligentsia infused political discourse with refurbished notions of State planning, deficit finance, welfare and internationalism which arguably came to fruition in the supposed political consensus of the 1950s.[33]

Unfortunately, this triumph of Liberal ideas and values would only occur after all these party leaders were long dead. During the early 1920s, when the party most needed intellectual creativity to maintain its challenge, its leadership proved astonishingly incompetent at propagating any ideas. In full-scale retreat from the harsh realities of a new political world, they were even uncertain as to where they stood on the political spectrum. At times they masqueraded as a progressive force, either proclaiming a radical policy of their own as in 1926–9, or by supporting a Labour government as in January 1924 and after June 1930. At other times they associated themselves with the Conservative party, as in 1918–22 and in October 1924 when they were instrumental in the destruction of a Labour government. On many occasions they presented themselves in both guises depending on local circumstances, to the extent that the elections of the 1920s witnessed overt or tacit local pacts with both Conservatives and Labour – even in 1923, when the defence of free trade was often subordinated to the perpetuation of anti-socialist pacts in parts of Scotland, industrial Lancashire and the mining areas of South Wales and the North East.[34] Neither wholeheartedly a radical party nor an alternative anti-socialist force, under Asquith's indolent mockery of 'leadership' the Liberals increasingly occupied a centre ground wholly devoid of any positive *raison d'être*. As one disillusioned Liberal noted in 1927: 'The Liberal Party has no creed, no cause ... It is ... a kind of shelter for timid passengers in the middle of a busy street. It rouses no enthusiasm. It enlists no zeal.'[35]

Insofar as it stood for anything at all after 1918, this intellectual malaise encouraged Asquithian leaders to fall back on the enunciation of ancient platitudes and irrelevant articles of faith. This often meant a rehash of the Gladstonian formula of 'peace, retrenchment and reform' in an era in which such shibboleths cut little ice.[36] Against this background, it is not surprising that the only bright spot of Liberal revival in the early 1920s should have been stimulated by Baldwin's declaration in favour of tariff reform in October 1923, although even here the recital of familiar Edwardian slogans was accompanied by conspicuously little that was constructive or even specific, beyond a neo-Gladstonian commitment to the League of Nations. It is tempting to lay much of the blame for this demoralising failure at the feet of Asquith. Hopes that his return to the Commons in February 1920 would stimulate more energetic leadership were rapidly dispelled by the cumulative effects of his age, temperamental indolence, a surfeit of alcohol and the bitterness which had frozen his soul. Unfortunately, Asquith's obstinate inertia was symptomatic of the mentality pervading the 'Holy Family' surrounding him during the 1920s. Every new disappointment and rebuff further sapped their political will and increased their propensity to find solace in nostalgic introspection. From such a perspective, it is not too fanciful to compare the Asquithian party in these years to a primitive millenarian cult impotently lamenting the problems of the present, looking back wistfully to an idealised Golden Age lost through the actions of man (specifically one man, Lloyd George) and impatiently awaiting a new Liberal heaven on earth in which they would be restored to their proper position as true believers. In the absence of anything but the incantation of a fossilised creed, the Asquithian guide to the future was reduced to nothing more than keeping faith with the past.

Lloyd George adopted a characteristically more dynamic approach towards interwar Liberal doctrine. Convinced that Liberal failure was due to the absence of a positive fighting policy, after 1924 he employed the Liberal Summer School as a think-tank to prepare policy statements for a new managed capitalism. The first fruit of this collaboration was *Coal and Power*, published in July 1924. *Land and the Nation*, the so-called 'Green Book' from the colour of its cover, followed in October 1925 and a few weeks later its sequel, *Towns and the Land*, appeared with its emphasis on site value rating. Far more significant was *Britain's Industrial Future*, published in February 1928. The 'Yellow Book' offered 'a vigorous policy of national reconstruction and development' designed to get 'the best of both worlds, harmonising individual liberty with the general good, and personal initiative with a common plan'.[37] To capitalise on the electoral potential of these 500 dense pages, *We Can Conquer Unemployment* was produced in March 1929 as a pamphlet, spelling out a concrete and costed loan-financed programme of infrastructural development capable of putting 600,000 men back to work for two years at a cost of £250,000,000. While proclaiming a more cautious approach to collectivism and the State than the prewar New Liberalism, *Britain's Industrial Future* was perhaps a decisive stage in the incorporation of State intervention into Liberal ideology. In the short term, although Liberal leaders were predictably divided, Lloyd George's dynamism and multi-coloured array of schemes rekindled a revivalist spirit within the rank-and-file. Despite the lavish praise of historians for *Britain's Industrial Future* and its sequels, however, they failed to excite electoral enthusiasm or to overcome the now customary perception of politics as a battle between Labour and Conservatism. By 1929 the problem was less that Liberals were incapable of refurbishing their policy and doctrine, than that they did so too late and under the wrong leader to restore their credibility as a real contender for office.

In contrast to this picture of Liberal intellectual vigour and electoral decline, in the 1920s Labour apparently succeeded despite rather than because of the quality and novelty of its policy ideas. In February 1920 Churchill told his Dundee constituents that 'Labour was unfit to govern' because it was a divisive party led by leaders fighting for class interests without a constructive programme for the great national questions of the hour. Intemperate attacks of this sort became the staple diet served up by the bellicose anti-socialist class warriors of the interwar years. Yet it is an indictment echoed by many historians. In such versions, Labour in the early 1920s is characterised more as a protest movement than a party of government, 'pitchforked into office in 1924 before it was either intellectually or psychologically ready to govern in a socialist sense'. Just as Edwardian Labour ideology is easily dismissed as a simplistic defensive 'Labourist' creed, its post-1918 ideas are often condemned as vague, unimaginatively orthodox and woefully derivative.[38] Although on foreign affairs and imperialism its Gladstonian and UDC internationalist heritage provided Labour with moral fervour, on social reform there was remarkably little detail and policy adhered closely to the New Liberal conception of protecting vulnerable groups rather than adopting a more comprehensive approach to State responsibilities. Over economic policy, Labour's essential continuity with the prewar progressive tradition was even more evident. As Labour's Chancellor, Philip Snowden was the living embodiment of the party's adherence to the Gladstonian orthodoxy of balanced budgets and free trade and under his withering influence Labour had nothing new or even coherent to say about the revitalisation of British industry, planning and economic management.

Besides public ownership, the one apparent exception to this rule concerned Labour's advocacy of a graduated capital levy. On the face of it, this had considerable propaganda value as a radical socialist proposal which combined notions of 'fair play' and moral outrage at wartime 'profiteering' with necessary fiscal reform. Yet in reality, the claim to 'socialism' was always illusory as the primary objective was to soak up inflation and pay off the war debt rather than to provide social services or achieve radical economic redistribution.[39] Moreover, as inflation gave way to deflation in 1920–1, the need and the opportunity for even this receded and in office during 1924 Labour leaders simply ignored it. In the absence of any distinctive policy solutions, they thus declared that their objective was to prepare for a new 'socialist' society rather than repair the existing one. In this context, Labour did have something novel to say, insofar as 'socialism' was often synonymous with public ownership. Yet nationalisation was compelled to carry an enormous burden as a panacea for all manner of ills, and even here Labour scarcely moved beyond vague generalities with regard to the detailed organisational and philosophical blueprint.

In interpreting this evidence, historians often appear particularly obsessed with the notion that Labour was handicapped by the fact that it did not have a distinctive economic policy of its own. Cowling is correct in asserting that 'the Labour movement in the early 1920s was a rag-bag of attitudes, purposes, programmes and intentions which were held together by a common language, a small number of common objectives and the Trade Union movement'.[40] Yet it does not follow, as Tanner and Morgan suggest, 'that Labour was ill-prepared if not unfit to govern, in that they had no new analysis of the economic troubles of the nation'.[41] Emphasis upon such a test would appear to be misguided for three reasons. First, the absence of a 'new analysis' had never stopped a government taking office before or since. Second, for Labour's immediate purposes the intellectual poverty of its policy prescriptions simply did not matter given the massive impact of class in determining electoral preferences and the low salience of detailed manifesto positions. Finally, and most important, such concerns ignore the cardinal general rule that in the twentieth century, British governments lost elections rather than oppositions winning them. It was not the belief that Labour could solve national problems that alarmed its opponents, but rather the well-justified fear that if Labour said it often enough, the electorate would come to believe that they could. As the *Daily Herald* proclaimed in November 1917, 'Liberal, Coalition and Lloyd George Governments have failed – *then let Labour try its hand.*'[42] After 1921 the persistent failure of anti-socialist governments to ameliorate the unemployment problem massively increased the potency of the Labour challenge without obliging them to offer any constructive proposals of their own. Thus, while Morgan is correct in saying that Labour would not have done any better, that was not the point. From 1921 onwards, Labour claimed they could do better because they uniquely understood this working class problem and they had the inestimable advantage of not having to put their claims to the test. In that sense, anti-socialists feared the presumed gullibility of the new mass electorate almost as much as Labour itself.

Such evidence would appear to refute any simple relationship between doctrinal vigour and the relative electoral fortunes of the Labour and Liberal parties. Indeed, if programmatic coherence and novelty are employed as benchmarks for evaluation, it appears that Labour rose and Liberals declined in the 1920s, despite rather than because of the quality of their policy and thought. Yet in reality, Labour's overwhelming debt to prewar Liberal progressivism was less of a weakness than a significant source of strength. Given the violation of Liberal principles during the war, Labour's appeal to disillusioned progressives depended on its ability to present itself as a more effective vehicle for the propagation of established values than a demoralised and compromised Liberal party. In this context, untainted continuity with a common progressive–internationalist heritage was a positive advantage.[43] Moreover, these continuities extended beyond a broad policy agenda to encompass a shared sense of idealism and a common Gladstonian heritage of moral outrage towards inequality and injustice. Baldwin was keenly aware of this emotional dimension in Labour success. As he told his party in February 1924, the experience of war had left people 'peculiarly open to the presentation of ideals; and it is perfectly useless ... to think you can secure the support of a majority of the nation as it exists today ... unless your appeal is not only to their head but to their heart.'[44] Thus, just as Conservative resistance to socialism after 1922 involved their absorption of like-minded Liberal elements into a *de facto* anti-socialist coalition, so Labour effectively recreated the old Progressive Alliance under its party banner to win the support of radical Liberals without either a formal alliance or the need to accommodate discordant elements of the 'Old Liberal' right. By October 1924 Labour had been fully accepted as the true inheritor of this progressive mantle.

As the party's principal propagandist, evangelist and myth-maker it is difficult to overstate the role played by Ramsay MacDonald in this process. His election as leader in 1922, at the head of a conspicuously more middle class PLP, brought a new polish, charisma and effectiveness to the front bench so painfully absent under Adamson and Clynes. His grand style of platform oratory attracted vast audiences and inspired a truly Gladstonian sense of 'virtuous passion' across a broad spectrum of supporters. As a prolific writer, his great gift (or sin, depending on perspective) was to propagate a vision which could at different times meet the varying needs of middle class radicals, sectionalist trade unionists or ILP socialists. At the heart of his message was a compelling moral vision of socialism as the hereditary heir of Liberalism, to be achieved not by class war but rather by steady evolutionary progress towards a better, more harmonious and fairer society; an aspiration conveyed with an almost Biblical certainty of absolute victory.[45] Although historians are often contemptuous of the vacuous simplicity of MacDonald's writings on socialist 'theory' and economics, such criticisms often fail to recognise that his primary purpose was more the practical task of propagating a vision and a political myth than the creation of an intellectually coherent ideology. In the context of the 1920s, vagueness and obfuscation were not defects, but rather a crucial strength in appealing to the broader progressive audience with a flexible rhetoric which served as a substitute for coherent ideology and detailed programmes.[46] This was essential for a party which was attempting to appeal to progressive opinion while basing itself primarily upon a developing working class consciousness and the intense class loyalties this engendered. Arguments about the primacy of class loyalties in Labour's rise conform well with the dominant 'Party Identification' or 'Expressive' model of British electoral behaviour which emerged in these years and which prevailed until the electoral watershed of 1974.[47] Through its trade union links and by articulating the authentic language of working class experience, Labour increasingly appropriated its natural class constituency with each new cohort of voters entering the electorate after 1918. Although emphasis and tone varied with occasion, these sectionalist appeals were rendered less crude and more uplifting when shrouded in the heady ethical language of equality, brotherhood, the dignity of labour and the need for a fairer society based on cooperation and redistribution. This did not amount to 'socialism', but many Labour leaders intended it to be so, and it was easily mistaken for such by those who wanted to believe it was, within a movement where allegiance to a class mattered more than commitment to any specific ideological principles.

In recent years, a vigorous revisionist assault had been launched upon many of the certainties of the so-called 'class explains all' school of thought.[48] This critique tends to assert variously the importance of ideas, the role of State influence, the restructuring of economic and social relations and the impact of female enfranchisement in promoting a new style of politics based around the expansion of public services and emphasising consumer rather than producer needs. Yet, although based on a variety of case studies from Preston to boom towns like Slough, much regional evidence from Labour's heartland still exists to substantiate the claims of the 'class' school about the predominance of working class norms and the ethos of organised labour over ideology. In practice, the trade union mentality represented something of a long-term constraint within the somewhat inchoate coalition of sections Labour represented at this juncture. Tensions between trade union barons and ILP socialists were often severe and the essentially sectionalist nature of Labour's appeal tended to discourage some potential middle class defectors from Liberalism. This may have inhibited Labour's electoral growth from its traditional heavy industry strongholds into socially more diverse areas such as those of new industries and the major cities, just as its male-dominated producer-focused ethos may have deterred women.[49] Yet in the 1920s, Labour's pursuit of its 'natural' class base still offered vast scope for advance and this prospect held real terrors for its opponents. Moreover, its credibility as the only real hope for the progressive cause, as well as that of the working class, would be dramatically reinforced by the first Labour government in 1924.

8.5 The impact of the first Labour government

The Labour government installed in office in January 1924 lasted only nine months but it marked a decisive turning point in determining (or at least, confirming) the pattern of interwar party development. The existence of a secure Conservative majority in 1922 had encouraged Labour to settle down for a long haul, until Baldwin's unexpected tariff election a year later deprived the government of its legitimacy along with its overall majority. During the next ten months the three-party uncertainty of the past five years was finally resolved by three key developments. First, the disgruntled Conservative Coalitionists under Austen Chamberlain and Birkenhead made a last unsuccessful attempt to impose their preferred strategy on the party by displacing Baldwin and creating an anti-socialist coalition to exclude Labour from office. When this failed in December–January 1924 they were compelled to accept their uneasy subordination to Baldwin and the mode of resistance to socialism that he had come to epitomise. Second, during its short period in office, Labour finally dispelled the myth that it was either too dangerous or too incompetent to be trusted with power and it emerged from the experience as a credible alternative party of government. Finally, in the language of the era, during this period the Liberals were finally crushed between the 'upper and nether millstones' of their two rivals. Between December 1923 and October 1924 Britain arguably witnessed 'A Stranger Death of Liberal England' than anything envisaged by Dangerfield.[50] The novelty of Chris Cook's influential reassessment of this neglected period lies in the suggestion that it marked the critical moment at which serious, but still reversible, Liberal decline turned into an inevitable downfall. Ironically, this downfall stemmed from Liberal success in defending free trade during the tariff election. Although the best Liberal performance since 1910, the harsh reality was that the Liberals narrowly failed to win sufficient seats to emerge as the principal party of opposition. Had they done so, they would have formed a minority administration and possibly restored their confidence, while dispelling the damaging impression of political redundancy. Instead, as the third party, the Liberals were condemned to hold the balance of power rather than exercise it themselves. The experience finally destroyed them.

The fateful decision to install a minority Labour government has engendered much mythology about the so-called 'Liberal miscalculation'. By putting Labour into office without playing for a minority Liberal government or, at the very least, imposing definite terms in return for their support (particularly a commitment to electoral reform), Asquith has been accused of committing 'the most disastrous single action ever performed by a Liberal towards his party'.[51] Unfortunately, such criticisms are founded upon the wholly erroneous assumption that the Liberals were masters of the situation. Yet in reality, Baldwin and MacDonald were the pivotal actors in this drama, not Asquith or Lloyd George, and they were far more clear-sighted in their determination to exploit Liberal discomfiture to destroy their weaker rival. By refusing all anti-socialist overtures for an arrangement, Baldwin forced the Liberals to accept the blame for installing Labour when Parliament reassembled. Similarly, MacDonald's determination that the government should do little beyond conclusively demonstrating its moderation, respectability and fitness to govern disastrously torpedoed fond Liberal illusions of establishing a positive role as a brake upon Labour's revolutionary ambitions or legislative incompetence. 'They are all engaged in looking as respectable as lather and blather will make them', a frustrated Lloyd George wrote to his daughter on 4 February. 'They are out to soothe ruffled nerves ... Ramsay is just a fussy Baldwin – and no more.'[52] In the event, the 1924 government became a Liberal nightmare, as the first flush of optimism rapidly withered under the weight of Labour contempt. Ignored and deliberately humiliated by a minority government dependent on their parliamentary support, these disappointments devastated an already fragile Liberal unity at Westminster. Tensions between Lloyd George and Asquith over strategy soon boiled to the surface. At the same time, Churchill made his transition back to the Conservatives during 1924, while a self-styled group of up to thirty-five anti-socialist 'Liberal Imperialists' under Grigg, Hilton Young and Guest prepared tentatively to do the same. To the delight of their opponents, ideological fragmentation produced chaotic indiscipline in the division lobbies, with Liberals regularly voting for each side while a third group (including the leadership) were either absent or abstained.[53]

In contrast, Labour became a double beneficiary of its short period in office, for not only did they fatally damage their Liberal opponents, but they also established their own credibility as a respectable party of government. This was a vital prerequisite for the party's further development. Since the Russian revolutions in 1917, Labour leaders had vigorously differentiated their outlook from that of Bolshevism and had overwhelmingly defeated three efforts by the Communist party (established 1919) to affiliate to the party. Yet despite these efforts, on the eve of the 1923 election anti-socialists still denounced them as 'slaves of the Third Internationale' determined to 'effect a social revolution like the Reformation' through a minority government intent on the abolition of private property.[54] A few short months in office did much to expose the hysterical idiocy of such smears. Having recognised from the outset that a minority government could usefully achieve little by domestic legislation, MacDonald decided upon a strategy of 'steady effort which even if not quite successful will gain respect and confidence in the country'. Or as Buxton put it, 'MacDonald's idea is to show how respectable they are.'[55]

This priority upon an image of respectability and competence became obvious from the outset. The Cabinet included ex-Liberals like Haldane, Trevelyan, Buxton and Wedgwood along with former Conservatives like Lords Parmoor and Chelmsford, but the Labour left was confined to Wheatley and Jowett. In the Commons, MacDonald's authority and command were valuable tools which impressed even the most critical opponents. Nor were these successes confined solely to matters of presentation. As his own Foreign Secretary, MacDonald scored a notable success as the mediator of Europe, while Snowden's Budget was sound and successful. Beyond this, Wheatley's Housing Act and Trevelyan's reversal of the worst of the unpopular Geddes cuts were the government's only positive legislative triumphs. Equally significant, the capital levy was shelved and the nationalisation of coal (and everything else) was the subject of studied silence from the front bench. Moreover, despite the presence of seven trade unionists in office, the government also soon asserted its distance from its trade union paymasters by invoking the Emergency Powers Act (1920) to defeat a dock strike in February and a London tramway dispute in March. When assessed against MacDonald's primary goal of demonstrating Labour's respectability and fitness to govern, therefore, the first Labour government was a remarkable success. By October, MacDonald could seriously reassure the Palace that 'the genuine Labour movement may be regarded as the stoutest buffer between the Constitution and Communism'.[56]

As the Conservatives also desired Liberal destruction in order to return to a more advantageous two-party competition, their tacit indulgence enabled Labour to remain in office long enough to achieve their common objective. In the event, the fall of the government on 8 October led to the third general election in as many years. Although immortalised by the *Daily Mail's* publication of a letter fraudulently purporting to be from the President of the Third International inciting class war in Britain, in many ways the Zinoviev Letter was merely the culmination of a long-term propaganda campaign seeking to equate British Labour and Soviet Bolshevism.[57] Fighting on such advantageous ground, a rejuvenated Tory party emerged from its landslide victory with 7,854,523 votes (46.8 per cent) and 412 MPs. Despite the largest parliamentary majority since 1832, however, the Conservatives were almost completely unable to penetrate mining areas, rural Wales, East London, Glasgow and most of the Black Country.[58] Labour had also entered the campaign in relatively confident mood after a series of encouraging by-elections. Fighting on the broadest front in its history, Labour fielded a total of 514 candidates – 50 in seats never previously contested. Only in Preston was a formal pact with the Liberals preserved, while the existence of anti-socialist pacts denied it as many as twenty-seven seats. Although Labour's parliamentary representation fell by 40 to 151, its 5,489,087 votes (33.3 per cent) constituted an increase of over a million on an increased turnout of 2,100,000 electors. Particularly significant was its consolidation of the bedrock of safe seats in working class industrial areas.[59]

Total and unmitigated disaster is almost too modest a description for the Liberal plight in October 1924. The vulnerability of the Liberal gains of 1923, and the growing ambivalence of Liberal opinion towards support for Labour, were both apparent in the nine contested by-elections of 1924. Labouring pathetically under every conceivable handicap of finance and organisation, the Liberals eventually fielded 399 candidates but this was still too little and too late to claim credibly to be a real contender for power at a time when the need for a period of stable government was a key election issue. The fundamental bankruptcy of policy was also painfully exposed during an abysmal campaign in which Liberals offered little more than a 'bastard Nonconformist Toryism' at a time when the Conservatives were at their apogee and could provide the real thing.[60] Worse still, having polled towards the peak of their strength on a uniquely favourable issue in the previous year, in 1924 the Liberals found themselves squeezed between the frustrated expectations of both wings of the party. For its more conservative supporters, the decision to put Labour into office in January often stretched their loyalty to breaking point. Conversely, working class and more radical supporters were alienated by Liberal cooperation with the Conservative enemy to destroy Labour in October. For both wings of the Liberal party, the logic of all that had happened during 1924 was that the real choice now lay between Labour and Conservatism while the Liberals were at best a distracting irrelevance. At worst, their inconstancy of purpose was a perversion of the wishes of their supporters which threatened to destabilise British politics.

Against this background, no one expected the Liberals to do well in 1924, but few predicted the cataclysmic disaster which engulfed them, nor the complete absence of any sign of future hope. Polling just 2,928,737 votes (17.8 per cent), the Liberals received 40 MPs – gaining only nine seats (all from Labour as a result of pacts) but losing 123 (105 to the Conservatives). In London, the South East and East Anglia, not a single seat defended was retained and in the English counties they lost all but four of the 67 won in 1923. In the English boroughs it was a similar picture of near-total annihilation. Nationally, they won only seven seats in three-cornered contests, while only perhaps fifteen seats were won completely unaided by either of the other parties and eleven of these were in Wales or Scotland. Among the fallen were almost all the Liberal leadership except Lloyd George, Simon and Mond.

8.6 The foundations of Conservative electoral hegemony

The Conservatives dominated interwar politics as they had under Lord Salisbury. They were in office alone or in partnership for all but three of these twenty interwar years and won most votes in all seven general elections. Yet perhaps because it is the 'Conservative century', this ascendancy is often treated as so natural that it scarcely warrants special explanation – particularly given the party's famous powers of adaptability and its traditional alignment with the dominant ideology and values of independence, self-reliance, nation, patriotism, Empire and stability.[61] Conservatives certainly exploited these themes for all they were worth at all interwar elections except that of 1923. Blood-curdling warnings about 'socialism' and the ultimate extinction of all wealth undoubtedly consolidated the support of even the most modest petit-bourgeois property owner behind a party whose centre of gravity was now thoroughly urban, commercial and industrialised. Yet closer examination suggests that this dominance was accompanied by a deep sense of foreboding and unease at all levels of the party engendered by collective apprehensions about the security of their ascendancy as a party of property in a mass electorate of the unpropertied. As Baldwin confessed to a friend in 1927 when looking back at events since the General Strike in the previous year: 'Democracy has arrived at a gallop in England, and I fear all the time that it is a race for life: can we educate them before the crash comes?'[62]

At one level, the 'franchise factor' provides a useful insight into the foundations of Conservative hegemony during the interwar years. Although the debate is often dominated by the impact of the 1918 'Fourth' Reform Act on Labour and Liberal fortunes, it is important to note that the Conservatives enjoyed a 'franchise factor' of their own. First, when mass democracy became unavoidable, the Conservatives successfully maximised the party advantage to be derived from it. A well-orchestrated campaign of parliamentary amendments thus preserved both the university seats and the plural business vote which after 1918 gave them between 9–11 and 5–9 extra seats respectively. Secondly, they benefited from the substantial reduction in Irish representation. In 1918 Ireland elected 105 MPs of whom only 26 were Unionists. The refusal of Sinn Fein to take their seats, however, removed a substantial anti-Conservative bloc from the Commons which the Irish Treaty of 1921 confirmed, by excluding the South altogether and reducing Northern Ireland to only thirteen seats, of which ten were normally held by Unionists. The result was thus a net Conservative gain of sixty-two seats – almost sufficient in itself to provide Bonar Law's majority in 1922. Whatever the damage inflicted upon Unionist doctrine by the Irish Treaty, therefore, it undoubtedly contributed to Conservative electoral hegemony in the interwar period. Third, it is generally agreed that active Conservative efforts to attract women voters 'by supporting an enhanced version of their traditional gender roles and by offering stability, protection, and assistance to women and their families', enabled the party to benefit disproportionately from female enfranchisement and created a favourable 'gender gap' in electoral loyalties and activism which persisted into the 1970s.[63] Finally, given the substantial rise in turnout and the reduction in uncontested seats in 1922, the Conservatives may even have benefited marginally from the fact that many new electors voted for the first time at an election when various factors favoured the Conservatives, thereby possibly conferring a long-term advantage among those with no prior habit of loyalty.[64]

An equally important Conservative 'franchise factor' derived from the effects of redistribution in 1918. First, as Conservative constituencies were typically larger than those of the Liberals, they were the principal beneficiaries of the Speaker's Conference recommendation in favour of the numerical equalisation of constituencies. Their net gain from redistribution was somewhere in the region of twenty to thirty seats as numerous Liberal strongholds in rapidly depopulating areas of Scotland and Wales disappeared and many new Conservative suburban seats were created.[65] Second, the Conservatives gained from a judicious amendment to ensure that redistribution acknowledged 'economic interests', thereby protecting up to seventeen declining agricultural seats.[66] Finally, like Labour, the Conservatives benefited from an increase in the size of their bedrock of safe seats. In 1910 Blewett calculates there were forty-eight 'predominantly middle class' seats. By 1921 there were at least seventy-five and probably nearer ninety. More generally, there were perhaps 200 largely suburban seats with a substantial middle class electorate. Add to this the solidly agricultural seats with strong Conservative loyalties and the outcome was to provide the party with 200–300 seats upon which they could rely in most circumstances throughout the interwar years from a total of 615 MPs.[67] The net effect of the mass democracy which Conservatives had viewed so suspiciously, was thus to deliver the party from the beleaguered minority position it occupied before 1914 and to establish the structural foundations for its sustained interwar electoral hegemony.[68]

Of all the parties, the Conservatives were perhaps also the most effective at responding to the organisational implications of the franchise factor after 1918. After the shock of a third defeat in December 1910, a Unionist Organisation Committee had been established to remedy the massive deficiencies in the Edwardian party machine and by 1914 many of its recommendations were beginning to bear fruit. Central Office acquired better accommodation and staff, an experienced Principal Agent was appointed in 1912 to take charge of the extra-parliamentary party and specialists were brought in to assist with press relations. In 1912 the Conservative and Liberal Unionist organisations were also finally merged, while ancillary bodies like the Anti-Socialist and Primrose Leagues were more directly harnessed to party needs. At the same time, the calibre of local party agents and candidates was improved through the judicious use of central funds. Although in virtual abeyance as a party machine during the war, its role in support of patriotic national causes ensured that Conservative local and national structures emerged weakened but still in 'reasonably good shape' in 1918, although postwar Coalition retarded recovery, particularly in seats with couponed Liberal MPs.[69] After 1922, however, the party machine rapidly recovered its morale and fighting vitality as it successfully adapted itself to the challenge of universal suffrage and the rise of Labour. Thereafter, as Stuart Ball notes, the interwar period – and particularly the 1920s – was 'an era of innovation and success' as a more professional mass organisation was built upon the foundations of sound finances and electoral success.[70] This was particularly so during J.C.C. Davidson's tenure as Party Chairman from 1926 to 1930. Central Office was reformed, rationalised and expanded from a handful of staff in 1911 to a total central and regional complement of 296 by 1928. Central finances were also increased and diverted to assist constituency parties in return for marginally greater control over their activities. Party managers were even more successful in their exploitation of new methods of propaganda and campaigning. To improve political education, the first party college opened in 1923 to train agents and local activists. With more staff, money and expertise devoted to publicity, there was an explosion in the output of material after 1924 and an advertising agency was employed for the first time in 1929. Perhaps most notable, the Conservatives led the way in the innovative use of radio, film and newsreel as propaganda tools during this period, reaching audiences of 15–20 million; a success which prompted the establishment of a fleet of twenty-two mobile cinema and radio vans by 1931.[71]

In the constituencies, organisational development was even more impressive. Although in many areas a wealthy candidate still obviated the need for active mass membership, the leadership was at least partly successful in encouraging an influx of middle class members into more democratic local parties, of which up to a third were financially self-supporting by the 1930s. On this basis, the Conservatives created a truly nationwide party structure with a full-time professional agent in virtually every constituency, although central efforts to direct the most skilled to marginal seats where they were most needed were obstructed by strong local autonomy. One key source of constituency strength was the ability to recruit female activists into their own branches within local associations under female organisers – albeit that despite a well-deserved reputation for vigour and hard work on behalf of the party, the intrusion of this 'feminine side' into the essentially masculine world of politics often generated considerable local tension, resentment and even outright hostility. Nevertheless, between 1923 and 1925 the number of constituencies with a women's branch rose from 303 to 401 and by 1928 the Women's Unionist organisation claimed a membership of over a million, rising to one and a half million by 1939. Similarly, the Junior Imperial League (established 1906) rapidly expanded to cover 473 of the 507 divisions in England and Wales during the 1920s, while half a million under-14s were enrolled in Young Britons (established 1925) to counter the Socialist Sunday Schools. As before the war, however, the Unionist Labour movement and local Labour Committees proved far less successful in enlisting working class trade union supporters.[72]

This combination of the franchise factor, redistribution and organisational developments played an important contributory role in establishing the Conservative electoral dominance between the wars. Together they assisted in the consolidation and mobilisation of a broader socio-regional base than their opponents. Even more than in 1900, by the 1920s this was rooted in the bedrock of middle class suburbia around London, the Home Counties, the county towns of south and central England and farming districts.[73] Yet Conservatives still won seats in medium-sized industrial towns in the West Midlands and Lancashire and captured significant working class support on the basis of Protestant sectarianism in Liverpool and West Scotland and elsewhere through a broader identification with stability, patriotism, tradition and Empire. Moreover, as Stuart Ball perceptively argues, organisational strength played an important role not just in mobilising voters, but also in projecting a positive face of Conservatism as the embodiment of the sort of stability, endurance and vitality expected of the 'natural' party of government.[74]

Yet despite the contribution of such factors, Conservative dominance did not simply fall into the party's lap. When Lloyd George resigned on 19 October 1922, he was followed into the political wilderness by the bulk of the Conservative party's most experienced leaders. As these rejected Coalitionists warned, it was now up to new men to find an electorally attractive and distinctively Conservative response to pressing national problems. Should they fail, the independent Conservative party would fail with them, as a prelude to the triumphant restoration of a permanent anti-socialist coalition under its former leadership. In the interim, these latter-day Peelites were content to stand aloof and pour derision upon the 'second class brains' who had succeeded them, in the confident belief that an incompetent 'second eleven' would swiftly engineer their own downfall. The result of the Carlton Club revolt was thus a formidable challenge as well as an opportunity for its Conservative victors. Moreover, during the next year, everything appeared to substantiate the optimism of the Coalitionists. Alarm at the paucity of experienced ministerial talent was gravely exacerbated by Bonar Law's sudden resignation in May 1923, suffering from terminal throat cancer. Lack of any improvement in Anglo-French relations thwarted early hopes of domestic economic recovery, while the persistence of over 1,200,000 unemployed aroused grave concerns about social stability on the eve of a third winter of slump. Problems of this sort were compounded by the even more fundamental absence of any distinctively Conservative rhetoric or programme with which to assert their differences of approach from the Coalition. As official Conservative responses to socialism and mass democracy had been framed within the parameters defined by their association with Lloyd George until October 1922, a distinct Conservative programme was not only unnecessary but positively antithetical to the notion of national unity espoused by Coalition leaders. Having justified their breach with the Coalition on grounds of political principle, however, it was incumbent upon Law and Baldwin to promulgate a substantive foundation for such claims.

Perhaps predictably for a party which has traditionally celebrated the non-ideological basis of its creed, Conservatives initially responded to this challenge not with abstract philosophical principles but rather by elevating style over substance to construct a public identity capable of transcending class divisions and aggregating support. Between October 1922 and Baldwin's adoption of tariff reform a year later, the Carlton Club rebels responded to the problem of independence by projecting themselves as the conscious antithesis of everything the Coalition had come to represent. In contrast to the unstable brilliance of an allegedly aggressive and politically corrupt Coalition, with its sectionalist policy at home and bellicose bluster abroad, Law and Baldwin portrayed themselves as decent, honest, principled men trying to fulfil the national desire for unity, peace and stability. Given the record and reputation of the Coalition and its principal architects, Conservatives believed that to be different from their predecessors was in itself a prescriptive claim to electoral popularity. Such logic underpinned the decision to fight the 1922 election with the promise of 'tranquillity and stability both at home and abroad'. Although dismissed by Lloyd George as a 'yawn', Conservatives believed it conformed well with an electoral desire not to be 'buggered about'.[75] Thereafter, the entire tone of the Law–Baldwin government was determined by the belief that it was more profitable for Conservatives to say *how* they proposed to approach the nation's problems, than *what* they actually intended to do about them. The enduring achievement of post-Coalition Conservatism was thus to create and maintain an atmosphere in which tone and style became central to the evaluation of policy. Perhaps nowhere was this more deliberately or persistently emphasised after 1922 than in the preoccupation of Conservative politicians with 'character'; a concern engendered both by tactical necessity and moral repugnance.

Tactically, the derision heaped upon the personnel of the Law–Baldwin Cabinets by rejected Coalitionists obliged them to change the focus for ministerial credibility. After 1922 'character' became central to the assessment of political virtuosity. Far from being denied, Birkenhead's jibe against the 'second class brains' became the badge of Conservative respectability: better to be a second class brain with a first class character than the other way around. In this context, the position Lloyd George commanded in Tory demonology was probably the most important negative influence upon the character of post-Coalition Conservatism. For Baldwin, Lloyd George was 'the real corrupter of public life'. In later years he talked freely about how he had sat in the Coalition Cabinet and had seen 'one decent fellow after another go to pieces under the influence of the Lloyd George group ... the morality ... "sucked out of them"'.[76] As Conservative leader and Prime Minister from May 1923, Stanley Baldwin became the living embodiment of this seductive ascendancy of personal style over policy substance. Although his famous denunciation of Lloyd George at the Carlton Club probably made no difference to the outcome of the meeting,[77] between 10 and 19 October Baldwin rose to prominence as the articulator of Conservative grievances. After the revolt, he became symbolic of the spirit of Conservative independence and the revolt against Lloyd George.

By nature and self-conscious design, Baldwin projected himself as the quintessential Englishman: a stolid, good-natured, phlegmatic, anti-intellectual rustic with an idealised nostalgic vision of the English character and countryside. In short, he appeared the plain, simple, decent Englishman writ large. Through his speeches, broadcasts and sheer presence, Baldwin made a major contribution to the popular appeal of interwar Conservatism. According to Philip Williamson, Baldwin offers 'an unusually refined instance of a politician as lay preacher and public moralist' articulating 'not so much a party programme as a public doctrine'.[78] He did so in order to restore some of the certainties and landmarks destroyed by the Great War and challenged in the 1930s by totalitarian ideologies. His political method was to channel party and nation away from class polarisation into paths of more measured progress based on the promotion of social improvement, industrial harmony and national cohesion wrapped in the semi-spiritual language of idealism, Christian duty and the spirit of service to country. Such a formula enabled him to transcend class, party and material interests to appeal directly to the shared decent instincts of his fellow countrymen. Even self-proclaimed 'academic Socialists' like Harold Laski could assure Baldwin in 1930 of his 'quite special place in our affections' as the foremost representative of 'the forces of sheer decency in public life': a respect prompted by 'the quality of human directness' which 'made the peaceful evolution of English politics much more certain than it would otherwise have been'.[79] Baldwin's broadly ecumenical Christian message may even have assisted the transition of Nonconformist Liberals to Conservatism, at a time when old confessional divisions were being superseded by the convergence of all organised Protestantism in resistance to the greater threat of secularism and religious indifference.[80] More certainly, his exposition of liberal values and decencies appealed to many of those appalled and alienated by the cynicism and unprincipled opportunism of Lloyd George.

In this context, perhaps the Conservatives' greatest and most enduring achievement after 1922 was that they consciously changed the measure of electoral credibility from intellectual brilliance to a sort of simple, homely trustworthiness. Yet this should not obscure the fact that in the immediate aftermath of the Carlton Club revolt, 'character' and 'principle' were emphasised for short-term party ends to fill the void created by independence in the absence of any consensus about more positive Conservative principles. By the summer of 1923, however, it was apparent that setting the tone of politics was not enough when confronted by an economic depression unamenable solely to the charms of this new political style. Baldwin initially attempted to fill the policy and doctrinal void by resurrecting tariff reform in October 1923. There were a variety of compelling motives for this decision, but the desire to reunite the party by separating the Chamberlainite Coalitionists from Lloyd George was not one of them.[81] Instead, tariffs appeared to offer a definite policy response to unemployment capable of silencing critics who claimed the much-vaunted Conservative principles rescued from putrefaction under the Coalition amounted to nothing more than good intentions. Moreover, it did so in a manner which not only sharply differentiated the Conservatives from their two free trade opponents, but also appealed to the ideological sensibilities of both the moderate Tory centre and the Diehard right.[82] In short, therefore, the appeal of tariff reform for the Conservative leadership in 1923 rested upon the fact that it appeared uniquely capable of resolving two key problems by combining a programme of economic radicalism with a guarantee that Conservatism would be based on the sort of positive political principle so conspicuously absent from the Coalition. As such, it was the programmatic corollary of the politics of 'character' and the refutation of the alliance with Lloyd George.

When Baldwin announced his conversion to protectionism at the Conservative party conference in October 1923, he intended merely to alert the country to the long-term possibility. At this juncture, he planned a protracted education campaign before holding the election necessary to release him from Bonar Law's pledge against any radical fiscal departure without a new mandate. In the event, the opposition parties immediately rallied to defend free trade and the election campaign began at once. Two weeks later the Cabinet recognised they had lost the initiative and that the policy and government could only be saved by snatching a victory before the free trade parties could mobilise fully. In the event, although they still held the largest share of the vote and 258 seats to 191 Labour and 158 Liberals, a net loss of 88 seats deprived them both of an overall majority and a mandate for fiscal change. Beyond defeat, this outcome had two important consequences for the Conservative party. First, although defeat almost cost Baldwin the leadership, the revelation of a plot by former Tory Coalitionists to displace him and form an anti-socialist coalition, forced most Conservatives to rally – albeit sometimes reluctantly – in defence of Baldwin as the embodiment of the spirit of the Carlton Club revolt against a resurgent coalitionism. After the failure of their plot, the Chamberlainites finally abandoned their aloof Peelite separation and accepted reunion on Baldwin's terms. Secondly, with the abandonment of tariff reform as official policy, in February 1924, the party began its search for new aims and principles which were electorally attractive, relevant to contemporary problems and capable of inspiring the sort of vitality and moral zeal possessed by Labour.

Although the quest for a new statement of Conservative faith was initiated outside the party machine almost immediately after defeat, the new statement of 'Aims and Principles' which finally emerged was master-minded by Neville Chamberlain and unmistakably reflected his preoccupation with social reform.[83] Published as *Looking Ahead* on 20 June, the document was as comprehensive as it was deliberately unspectacular. Abroad, it committed the party to 'strengthen and develop the Empire', defend British interests and support the League of Nations. At home, there were references to co-partnership in industry, abolition of the political levy, Lords reform, assistance for agriculture, temperance without compulsion, housing, pensions and social reform. While the document was being prepared for publication, Baldwin paved the way with three keynote speeches along similar lines in early May, intended to inject into equally well-meaning platitudes the requisite air of portent as befitted the birth of the 'New Conservatism'. Yet in practice, *Looking Ahead* was not designed to excite political histrionics, but rather to be a working restatement of the foundations of popular Conservatism for the second half of the decade. Like the post-1945 'New Conservatism' of Butler and the Industrial Charter, the primary intention was to be sweeping and emblematic, its significance lying less in the detail of what it said than the general tone and temper in which it said it.[84] With its publication, the age of modified 'tranquillity' had dawned. Having abandoned the potentially divisive and disruptive commitment to full-blooded tariff reform for the rest of the decade, Conservative leaders found it more advantageous to present themselves as a 'party of the nation' seeking to fulfil the palpable desire for peace, stability, moderation and ordered progress through a combination of social reform, a 'property-owning democracy' (a phrase first used in 1924) and sound finance.

Armed with the biggest Conservative majority since 1832, between 1924 and 1929 Baldwin's second ministry set out to implement this 'New Conservatism'. At their victory rally, Baldwin had movingly declared that a government had come to office committed to 'ordered progress', class accord and the 'redemption of the people' by 'help[ing] them to help themselves'. The 'spirit of service to the whole nation' was proclaimed 'the birthright of every member of the Unionist Party'.[85] According to John Ramsden, Baldwin's brand of Conservatism can be analysed under five broad headings; as something self-consciously ordinary, guided by an unsleeping moral purpose and characterised by its unprovocative conciliatory tone, its Englishness and its professionalism.[86] Insofar as his image, presence and moral values dominated the period via the mass media, it was truly the 'Baldwin age'. Yet if Baldwin provided the public image which shaped subconscious attitudes and sentiments, Neville Chamberlain was the dynamic force behind the policy content of this 'New Conservatism'. Convinced that 'unless we leave our mark as social reformers the country will take it out of us hereafter', Chamberlain rejected the Treasury in the hope of becoming a 'great Minister of Health'.[87] Entering office with a list of twenty-five reform proposals, by 1929 some twenty-one had been enacted covering widows, orphans and old age pensions, improved dental, hospital, midwifery and maternity care, rural housing, slum clearance and radical reform of the Poor Law.[88]

Although it is easy to be seduced by this positive face of Baldwinian Conservatism, it is important to remember that many Conservatives were profoundly unhappy at the 'semi-socialist' tone of this accommodation with mass democracy. Thus, although Baldwin consistently employed conciliatory language as the 'healer' of class antagonisms, this co-existed alongside another less unifying foundation for Conservative dominance. In part, this stemmed from a consistent preference for low taxation and deflationary monetary policy after 1920, which operated to the advantage of the suburban middle classes, rentiers and taxpayers earning over £500 a year, at the direct expense of industrial workers. Yet equally important, contrary to the views of Ramsden and Williamson about the essentially positive consensual basis of Baldwinian dominance, Ross McKibbin suggests that the broader Conservative electoral alliance was united by its normative hostility to a series of stereotypes and 'conventional wisdoms' about the organised working class and the unemployed as groups outside the dominant value system. Depicted as either aggressively greedy sectionalists or unemployed 'scroungers', these groups were presented as a challenge to the economic interests and social status of the rest of the community, among whom the commonsense precepts of not living beyond your means, paying your way and not keeping coal in the bath all flourished. This cleavage between the status categories of 'labour' and 'the public' thus enabled the Conservatives to rally a broad electoral alliance among the middle classes, much of the non-unionised working class, and perhaps particularly female voters who stood outside the masculine value-system of organised labour and to whom the Labour party was presented as anti-family and anti-woman. By identifying the Labour party with the union-ised and the unemployed rather than with the working class as a whole, the Conservatives thus successfully contained their opponents' electoral base and established their own ascendancy as a party of the nation and 'the public', of which the employed but non-unionised working class were a substantial part.[89]

Certainly after the General Strike in May 1926 these less positive aspects of the Conservative appeal became increasingly prominent as the Tory right asserted their hostility to the government's brand of 'semi-socialist' policy at home and 'softness' abroad. Until this stage, Baldwin's moral authority had effectively kept such challengers in check. In March 1925 he had defeated the efforts of his own backbenchers to use the MacQuisten Bill to attack Labour and the unions over the political levy with a moving personal appeal not to 'fire the first shot' in an industrial war.[90] After the General Strike, however, the party mood became substantially more aggressive, determined and reactionary as the Trade Disputes Act (1927) and the end of diplomatic relations with Russia demonstrated. Despite the Baldwinian gloss, as political circumstances became more favourable for fundamentalist Tory class warriors than liberal class healers like Baldwin, the government increasingly lost its sense of certainty, optimism and direction – particularly as its failure to satisfy party demands for tariffs and Lords reform further alienated those on the right who most enthusiastically championed such causes. Against this background, it seems reasonable to assume that if the Conservatives had won the 1929 election, the rightward drift would have continued as the depression deepened. In the event, defeat in 1929 and then National Government from 1931 to 1940 rescued Baldwin and his brand of doctrinal politics from his own atavistic and unreconstructed fundamentalists.

8.7 The 1929 election: the end of the three-party era

As the first general election for a generation to be free from xenophobic hysteria, red scares and acute political crisis, the 1929 contest was a remarkably dull affair. After four and a half years of solid but unspectacular achievement, the Baldwin government simply fizzled out. With an ageing and exhausted Cabinet, little new or attractive in policy and a worthy but unexciting record to fall back on, the electorate were asked to return a Conservative government to power for the simple reason that Baldwin requested it. Although 'Safety First' and trust in Baldwin reflected a positive decision to exploit his popularity in contrast to Lloyd George's 'Rashness First', the electorate agreed with MacDonald that the Tories were offering the opposite of 'Courage First'.[91] They thus turned towards Labour in the hope of a positive policy to address unemployment, leaving the Conservatives more dependent on middle class and agricultural seats than at any other interwar election.[92] Although polling 285,888 more votes than Labour, the Conservatives won twenty-seven fewer seats, largely because of the dis-proportionate impact of Liberal revival on Tory fortunes. Yet, in retrospect, for the Conservatives this was just an election defeat of no broader significance – and in view of the economic crisis which destroyed the Labour government only two years later, perhaps not such a bad one to lose. For its opponents the 1929 election also simply confirmed the pattern established five years earlier. By 1929 the long process of realignment into a Conservative–Labour duopoly had become an established fact.

Despite Lloyd George's money, dynamism and multicoloured policy documents, crushing Liberal defeat came as a devastating blow after a series of by-election gains since March 1927 and the most expensive campaign in real terms ever waged in Britain. At the general election, 513 Liberal candidates polled 5,308,738 votes (23.6 per cent), but this compared poorly with Labour's 8,656,225 (38.1 per cent). Worse still, they received a meagre 59 MPs to Labour's haul of 287. Although they had won most of their seats for the first time in three-cornered contests, this was little comfort to Liberals now fatally trapped as a third party in an electoral system designed to accommodate only two. While it required an average of around 30,000 votes for each Labour (29,165) and Conservative (33,293) MP elected, the Liberals required around three times this number (89,979): a fact which gave substance to the damaging allegation, first mobilised by the Conservatives in 1929, that a vote for the Liberals was a wasted vote. Moreover, the electoral geography of Liberal victories confirmed the depressing extent to which it had retreated from its former industrial heartlands into a rural and Celtic fringe. After 1929 the Liberals were consigned to the sidelines as a repository for by-election protest votes during periods of unpopular Conservative government, as in the early-1960s culminating in Orpington in March 1962, in the early 1970s where Heath's 'U-turns' led to sensational victories in Ripon and Ely and in the early 1980s where the failure of the Thatcherite monetarist experiment provided fertile ground for the illusion that the Alliance might again 'break the mould' of British politics. As in 1927–9, in each of these cases, the mid-term illusion tended to vaporise when the chips were down at a general election.

In contrast, Labour's progress during the 1920s can best be characterised as a steady advance assisted by some peculiarly good fortune rather than an explosive surge to second-party status. Undeniably Labour still had areas of massive weakness in organisational and electoral terms, most notably in rural areas where even in the Labour landslide of 1945 it still won only a handful of agricultural seats. Yet despite its poor showing, at least it showed the flag in well over half of these seats in 1929 and in so doing did achieve success of a kind, insofar as Labour's intervention often attracted sufficient votes to deny victory to their Liberal rival for the anti-Conservative vote. Yet as a party predominantly of unionised industrial Britain, the importance of 1929 was the degree to which it showed that Labour had consolidated its hold over this core heartland, capturing virtually all of the remaining mining and industrial seats held by the Liberals in the early 1920s. Many inner city seats also fell. Yet even more significant was the fact that it won seventy-three seats for the first time, including a number in Tory strongholds like Birmingham and London. Such progress in 1929 suggests that Labour was perhaps rather less dependent on its traditional 'core' support, as it advanced into 'new' working class or more socially mixed areas without massive trade union strength, at a time when union membership was declining after the General Strike. In such areas, Labour may also have benefited from an image as a practical party of reform championing a broader agenda of welfare, housing and public services to establish a new grassroots credibility in a way which it had not before. In this context, perhaps Labour learned important lessons in the late 1920s which enabled it to convince a broader audience than the trade unions that it could be 'their' party by learning to represent other needs.[93] Such a development pointed the way to Labour's success in 1945.

In seeking to explain the emergence of this new party alignment during the 1920s, the sheer weight of conflicting interpretation and evidence suggests there are precious few incontrovertible verities and absolutely no mono-causal explanations. Although some factors were undoubtedly more important than others, the processes of electoral and party realignment involved a complex interaction of forces, each of which assumed varying degrees of significance at different phases of the cycle within a socially and regionally fragmented environment. To explain these processes thus requires a more balanced approach towards causality than has sometimes been demonstrated in the past. A crucial background to these events in the 1920s is provided by that greatest of all unforeseen accidents, the First World War. This does not necessarily imply that without a war Labour would not have eventually displaced the Liberals, but as Trevor Wilson concludes, 'it would hardly seem to be in doubt that, on the most modest appraisal, the events of 1914–18 markedly influenced the time-scale (whether or not it influenced the ultimate course) of events.'[94] Already on his knees in 1918, during the next decade Wilson's 'Liberal pedestrian' was engaged in a hopeless struggle to escape the engulfing quicksand into which the 'rampant omnibus' of war had knocked him – and with at least one hand tied behind his back. In this sense at least, perhaps ultimately the Liberals were the victims of just 'one damned thing after another'. Whether heading towards the rocks before 1914 or as a result of the experience of war, after 1918 the Liberals were so divided and demoralised that they lost the will to fight and to adapt both locally and nationally. Without the expectation of power, there was a further haemorrhaging of finance, morale and votes as they increasingly appeared to be an irrelevant force locked in a vicious spiral of decline, while the same factors often placed Labour in a virtuous spiral in which nothing succeeded quite like success itself. By the same token, the Liberal failure to produce something akin to Baldwin's 'New Conservatism' was both a cause and consequence of more profound forces, but its impact upon Liberal fortunes was devastating for all that when voters were increasingly uncertain as to where the party stood on the political spectrum and what, if anything, it actually represented.

Notes and references ───────────────────────────────────

The place of publication is London unless otherwise stated.

1 See Keith Laybourn, 'The rise of Labour and the decline of Liberalism: the state of the debate', *History* 80 (1995), pp. 207–26.

2 Michael Kinnear, *The Fall of Lloyd George: The Political Crisis of 1922* (1973), pp. 152–3.

3 G.R. Searle, *The Liberal Party: Triumph and Disintegration 1886–1929* (1992), p. 157.

4 Ross McKibbin, *The Evolution of the Labour Party 1910–1924* (Oxford, 1974), p. 243.

5 H.C.G. Matthew, R.I. McKibbin and J.A. Kay, 'The franchise factor in the rise of the Labour Party', *English Historical Review* 91 (1976), pp. 723–52. See also Chris Cook, *The Age of Alignment: Electoral Politics in Britain 1922–1929* (1975), pp. 321–8; David Butler and Donald Stokes, *Political Change in Britain: The Evolution of Electoral Choice* 2nd edn (1974), pp. 168–70.

6 Duncan Tanner, *Political Change and the Labour Party, 1900–1918* (Cambridge, 1990), p. 412.

7 John Turner, *British Politics and the Great War: Coalition and Conflict 1915–1918* (New Haven, 1992), pp. 412–17, 435; Michael Hart, 'The Liberals, the War and the franchise', *English Historical Review* 97 (1982), pp. 820–32; Martin Pugh, *The Making of Modern British Politics 1867–1939* 2nd edn (Oxford, 1993), pp. 197–9, 254–5.

8 Duncan Tanner, 'The Parliamentary electoral system, the "Fourth" Reform Act and the rise of Labour in England and Wales', *Bulletin of the Institute of Historical Research* 56 (1983), pp. 205–19.

9 J. Davis, 'Slums and the vote, 1867–90', *Historical Research* 64 (1991), pp. 375–88; J. Davis and D. Tanner, 'The borough franchise after 1867', *Historical Research* 69 (1996).

10 Duncan Tanner, 'Class voting and radical politics: the Liberal and Labour parties, 1910–31', in J. Lawrence and M. Taylor, eds, *Party, State and Society: Electoral Behaviour in Britain since 1920* (Aldershot, 1997), p. 114.

11 Michael Childs, 'Labour grows up: the electoral system, political generations and British politics, 1890–1929', *Twentieth Century British Politics* 6 (1995), pp. 123–44.

12 Kenneth Wald, *Crosses on the Ballot: Patterns of British Voter Alignment since 1885* (Princeton, New Jersey, 1983), p. 251; Butler and Stokes, *Political Change in Britain*, pp. 174–9.

13 Childs, 'Labour grows up', p. 143.

14 Michael Kinnear, *The British Voter: An Atlas and Survey since 1885* 2nd edn (1981), pp. 71, 84, 116–18.

15 Exceptions are Searle, *The Liberal Party*, pp. 161–4 and Pugh, *The Making of Modern British Politics*, pp. 238–9.

16 David Butler, *The Electoral System in Britain 1918–1951* (Oxford, 1953), pp. 189–94.

17 Kinnear, *The Fall of Lloyd George*, pp. 30–5; Searle, *The Liberal Party*, p. 144.

18 Chris Cook, 'A stranger death of Liberal England', in A.J.P. Taylor, ed., *Lloyd George: Twelve Essays* (1971), pp. 287, 307–8; Tanner, *Political Change and the Labour Party*, pp. 430–1.

19 McKibbin, *Evolution of the Labour Party*, pp. 33–8, 124–5, 137–43.

20 Ibid., p. 161; Martin Pugh, *Women and the Women's Movement in Britain, 1914–1959* (1992), pp. 65–6; Michael Pinto-Duschinsky, *British Political Finance, 1830–1980* (Washington, 1981), pp. 73–82.

21 McKibbin, *Evolution of the Labour Party*, pp. 112–62, 243.

22 C. Howard, 'Expectations born to death: local Labour party expansion in the 1920s', in J. Winter, ed., *The Working Class in Modern British History* (Cambridge, 1983), p. 81.

23 McKibbin, *Evolution of the Labour Party*, p. 144.

24 Birmingham Conservative and Unionist Association: Minutes of Management Committee, 29 December 1922, vol. II, p. 245 (Birmingham Central Library). For anti-socialist alliances see Cook, *The Age of Alignment*, pp. 56–63, 131–6, 160, 287–94, 311–12.

25 Matthew, McKibbin and Kay, 'The franchise factor', pp. 742–50. See also M. Baines, 'The survival of the British Liberal party, 1933–1959', in Anthony Gorst, Lewis Johnman and W. Scott Lewis, eds, *Contemporary British History, 1931–1961* (1991), pp. 28–9.

26 Cook, 'A stranger death', p. 288.

27 Cook, *The Age of Alignment*, ch. 3 and 'Liberals, Labour and local elections', in Gillian Peele and Chris Cook, eds, *The Politics of Reappraisal 1918–1939* (1975), pp. 167–71.

28 Kinnear, *The British Voter*, pp. 84–5.

29 Cook, *The Age of Alignment*, ch. 10; Trevor Wilson, *The Downfall of the Liberal Party, 1914–1935* (Fontana edn, 1968), pp. 257–9, 275–84.

30 Cook, *Age of Alignment*, p. 79: J. Bulpitt, *Party Politics in English Local Government* (1967), pp. 6–9; Tanner, *Political Change and the Labour Party*, pp. 379–81, 404, 408, 430.

31 Michael Freeden, *Liberalism Divided: A Study in British Political Thought, 1914–1939* (Oxford, 1986), p. 78; John Campbell, 'The renewal of Liberalism: Liberalism without Liberals', in Peele and Cook, eds, *The Politics of Reappraisal*, pp. 88–113.

32 Freeden, *Liberalism Divided*, pp. 11, 101, 172.

33 Peter Clarke, 'Liberals and Social Democrats in historical perspective', in Vernon Bogdanor, ed., *Liberal Party Politics* (Oxford, 1983), pp. 39–42.

34 Cook, *Age of Alignment*, pp. 131–4, 147.

35 Michael Bentley, *The Liberal Mind, 1914–1929* (Cambridge, 1977), p. 127.

36 Cook, 'A stranger death', p. 301; Wilson, *The Downfall of the Liberal Party*, p. 233.

37 Liberal Industrial Inquiry, *Britain's Industrial Future* (1928), pp. xix, 63.

38 Kenneth O. Morgan, *Consensus and Disunity: The Lloyd George Coalition, 1918–1922* (Oxford, 1979), pp. 217–35. Also Geoffrey Foote, *The Labour Party's Political Thought: A History* 2nd edn (1986), ch. 3.

39 R.C. Whiting, 'The Labour Party, capitalism and the National Debt, 1918–24', in P.J. Waller, ed., *Politics and Social Change in Modern Britain* (Oxford, 1987).

40 Maurice Cowling, *The Impact of Labour, 1920–1924: The Beginning of Modern British Politics* (Cambridge, 1971), p. 28.

41 Morgan, *Consensus and Disunity*, pp. 228, 230, 235; Tanner, *Political Change and the Labour Party*, pp. 435, 438–41.

42 Trevor Wilson, *The Myriad Faces of War: Britain and the Great War, 1914–1918* (Oxford, 1986), p. 663.

43 Catherine Ann Cline, *Recruits to Labour: The British Labour Party 1914–1931* (Syracuse, 1963), p. 129. Also William L. Miller, *Electoral Dynamics in Britain since 1918* (1977), pp. 21, 24–5, 226.

44 John Ramsden, *The Age of Balfour and Baldwin, 1902–1940* (1978), p. 209.

45 See Rodney Barker, 'Socialism and progressivism in the political thought of Ramsay MacDonald', in A.J.A. Morris, ed., *Edwardian Radicalism* (1974). Also Bernard Barker, ed., *Ramsay MacDonald's Political Writings* (1972).

46 Rodney Barker, 'Political myth: Ramsay MacDonald and the Labour Party', *History* 61 (1976), pp. 51–6.

47 Butler and Stokes, *Political Change in Britain*, chs 4–5, 8.

48 See Lawrence and Taylor, eds, *Party, State and Society*, Introduction; M. Savage, 'Urban politics and the rise of Labour, 1919–39', in L. Jamieson and H. Corr, eds, *State, Private Life and Political Change* (1990), pp. 204–23.

49 M. Savage, *The Dynamics of Working Class Politics: The Labour Movement in Preston, 1880–1940* (Cambridge, 1987), pp. 165–74.

50 Cook, 'A stranger death', pp. 278–313.

51 Roy Douglas, *A History of the Liberal Party 1895–1970* (1971), p. 175.

52 K.O. Morgan, ed., *Lloyd George Family Letters 1885–1936* (1973), p. 202.

53 Robert C. Self, *Tories and Tariffs: The Conservative Party and the Politics of Tariff Reform, 1922–1932* (New York and London, 1986), pp. 333–46; Cook, *Age of Alignment*, ch. 14.

54 Lord Birkenhead, *Contemporary Personalities* (1924), p. 50.

55 Self, *Tories and Tariffs*, pp. 380–1.

56 Waterhouse memorandum, reporting MacDonald's view to Stamfordham (the King's secretary), 7 October 1924, MacDonald MSS 30/69/5/35 (Public Record Office).

57 L. Chester, H. Young and S. Fry, *The Zinoviev Letter* (1967).

58 Kinnear, *The British Voter*, p. 46.

59 Savage, *Dynamics of Working Class Politics*, pp. 175–6. Cook, *Age of Alignment*, pp. 280, 293–4, 314.

60 P.F. Clarke, *Lancashire and the New Liberalism* (Cambridge, 1971), p. 397; Cowling, *The Impact of Labour*, pp. 357–8.

61 See Stuart Ball, *The Conservative Party and British Politics 1902–1951* (1995), pp. 117–22 and '1916–29' in Anthony Seldon, ed., *How Tory Governments Fall* (1996), p. 260. See also David Jarvis, 'The road to 1931: the Conservative Party and political realignment in early twentieth-century Britain', *Historical Journal* 36 (1993), p. 473.

62 David Jarvis, 'The shaping of Conservative electoral hegemony, 1918–39', in Lawrence and Taylor, eds, *Party, State and Society*, pp. 121–52; Baldwin to Lord Irwin, 26 June 1927, Halifax MSS 14.2 (Borthwick Institute of Historical Research, York).

63 Neal R. McCrillis, *The British Conservative Party in the Age of Universal Suffrage: Popular Conservatism, 1918–1929* (Columbus, Ohio, 1998), pp. 81–2; David Jarvis, 'Mrs Maggs and Betty: the Conservative appeal to women voters in the 1920s', *Twentieth Century British History* 5 (1994), pp. 129–52 and 'The Conservative Party and the politics of gender, 1900–1939', in Martin Francis and Ina Zweiniger-Bargielowska, eds, *The Conservatives and British Society, 1880–1990* (Cardiff, 1996), pp. 172–93. In 1928 the Representation of the People (Equal Franchise) Act entitled women to vote at 21 as men had since 1918.

64 Kinnear, *The Fall of Lloyd George*, p. 154.

65 Kinnear, *The British Voter*, pp. 70–2; Cook, *Age of Alignment*, p. 4.

66 Tanner, *Political Change and the Labour Party*, p. 391.

67 Kinnear, *The British Voter*, pp. 122–4.

68 For a contrary view see David Jarvis, 'The shaping of Conservative electoral hegemony, 1918–39', in Lawrence and Taylor, eds, *Party, State and Society*, p. 133. Also McCrillis, *The British Conservative Party*, pp. 3–4.

69 Ramsden, *The Age of Balfour and Baldwin*, pp. 57–72, 124–6.

70 Ibid., pp. 218–62; Stuart Ball, 'Local Conservatism and the evolution of the Party organisation', p. 298. See also 'The national and regional party structure', in Anthony Seldon and Stuart Ball, eds, *Conservative Century: The Conservative Party since 1900* (Oxford, 1994), pp. 169–220, 261–313.

71 John Ramsden, 'Baldwin and film', in N. Pronay and D.W. Spring, eds, *Politics, Propaganda and Film, 1918–45* (1982), pp. 218–45; H.J. Hollins, 'The Conservative Party and film propaganda between the Wars', *English Historical Review* 96 (1981), pp. 359–74. Also McCrillis, *The British Conservative Party*, pp. 145–78.

72 Jarvis, 'The Conservative Party and the politics of gender', pp. 176–88; Joni Lovenduski, Pippa Norris and Catriona Burness, 'The Party and women', in Seldon and Ball, eds, *Conservative Century*, pp. 623–4; McCrillis, *The British Conservative Party*, chs 2–4.

73 J.P.D. Dunbabin, 'British elections in the nineteenth and twentieth centuries; a regional approach', *English Historical Review* 95 (1980), pp. 244–5.

74 Ball, 'Local Conservatism', p. 305.

75 Lord Swinton, *Sixty Years of Power* (1966), pp. 67–8.

76 Self, *Tories and Tariffs*, pp. 21–4.

77 Kinnear, *The Fall of Lloyd George*, pp. 120, 132.

78 Philip Williamson, 'The doctrinal politics of Stanley Baldwin', in Michael Bentley, ed., *Public and Private Doctrine* (Cambridge, 1993), pp. 181–208 and *Stanley Baldwin: Conservative Leadership and National Values* (Cambridge, 1999). See also Sian Nicholas, 'The construction of a national identity: Stanley Baldwin, "Englishness" and the mass media in interwar Britain', in Francis and Zweiniger-Bargielowska, eds, *The Conservatives and British Society*, pp. 127–46.

79 Harold Laski to Baldwin, 21 June and 30 October 1930, Baldwin MSS 165/202–3 (Cambridge University Library). Also Keith Middlemas, *The Clydesiders* (1965), pp. 281–2.

80 Williamson, 'Doctrinal politics', pp. 205–7.

81 Robert Self, 'Conservative reunion and the general election of 1923: a reassessment', *Twentieth Century British History* 3 (1992), pp. 249–73 and 'Baldwin's Blunder: a rejoinder to Smart on 1923', *Twentieth Century British History* 7 (1996), pp. 140–55.

82 Self, *Tories and Tariffs*, pp. 55–77.

83 Ibid., pp. 369–80 for these events.

84 R.A. Butler, *The Art of the Possible* (1971), pp. 146–8.

85 Self, *Tories and Tariffs*, pp. 385–6.

86 Ramsden, *The Age of Balfour and Baldwin*, pp. 208–24.

87 Neville Chamberlain to Ida Chamberlain, 26 October and 1 November 1924, Neville Chamberlain MSS NC18/1/457–8 (Birmingham University Library).

88 PRO. CAB24/168, CP499(24) 'Ministry of Health: Provisional Programme of Legislation', 19 November 1924. Reprinted in Keith Feiling, *The Life of Neville Chamberlain* (1946), pp. 459–62.

89 Ross McKibbin, 'Class and conventional wisdom: the Conservative Party and the "public" in interwar Britain', in *Ideologies of Class: Social Relations in Britain 1880–1950* (Oxford, 1990), pp. 259–93; McCrillis, *The British Conservative Party*, pp. 227–8.

90 Alan Beattie, ed., *English Party Politics* 2 vols (1970), II, p. 389.
91 Self, *Tories and Tariffs*, pp. 497–8. Also Philip Williamson, ' "Safety First":
Baldwin, the Conservative Party and the 1929 General Election', *Historical Journal*
25 (1982), pp. 385–409.
92 Kinnear, *The British Voter*, p. 48.
93 Kinnear, *The British Voter*, p. 48; Tanner, 'Class voting', pp. 120–2.
94 Wilson, *Myriad Faces of War*, p. 663. See also his *Downfall of the Liberal Party*, pp.
17–21.

Chapter nine

The National Governments

9.1 The party crisis, 1929–1931

During the second Labour government the political sky rapidly blackened as economic and ideological chickens came home to roost. The Wall Street Crash in November 1929 gravely exacerbated the problems of an already beleaguered British economy struggling with an over-valued currency bequeathed by the return to the gold standard in 1925 at the prewar parity of $4.86. Unemployment levels, which since 1921 had never fallen below 10 per cent of the insured workforce, rose dramatically after 1929 to 22 per cent by 1931. This placed an intolerable burden upon the chronically overstretched unemployment insurance fund, whose expenditure exceeded income by £36,420,000 in 1931 and whose indebtedness rose accordingly from £39,042,000 in March 1930 to £75,472,000 a year later.[1] Inevitably this massive increase in expenditure made it difficult to balance the budget at a time when government revenues were stagnant. When the May Committee exposed the full gravity of the economic situation in July 1931, investor confidence collapsed. The ensuing political crisis during August destroyed the second Labour government and installed a National Government which ruled until May 1940.

The 1929–31 Labour government proved a period of political as well as economic reckoning. According to its critics, the emerging economic crisis rapidly demonstrated the intellectual bankruptcy of Labour's traditional faith in a vaguely millenarian ethic. Labour's 'unqualified pledge' in its 1929 manifesto 'to deal immediately and practically' with unemployment was swiftly revealed as hollow cant. Although MacDonald always protested that it was the capitalist system rather than the Labour government which was on trial, his nebulous brand of socialism offered an indictment of the capitalist present and the promise of a better socialist future, without specifying the means to achieve the transition. Under Snowden's rigid Gladstonian orthodoxy at the Treasury, consideration of public works and protectionism was vehemently obstructed despite increasing pressure for both, while J. H. Thomas, as the minister responsible for unemployment, was manifestly out of his depth. Although Oswald Mosley's famous memorandum of February 1930 offered some constructive radical ideas about expanding purchasing power, import controls, massive public works and public control of banking to fund infrastructural developments, these efforts soon ran aground on the rocks of Cabinet and PLP scepticism and ended in narrow defeat at the party conference in October. Thereafter, the inexorable tide of events supposedly drew the Labour government to destruction with few opportunities for salvation. From this perspective, Robert Skidelsky argues that the 1931 crisis represented a failure of a party and a doctrine as much as of men, imagination and nerve. According to this interpretation, while the international experience suggests that the absence of a developed Keynesian theory was not a decisive barrier to what might loosely be termed Keynesian economics, in Britain these alternative policy options were wilfully (or cravenly) ignored by both the Labour government and its successors.[2]

Although this neo-Keynesian interpretation has been extremely influential, it has not gone uncontested. Some sceptics argue rightly that Labour was more innovative and more pragmatic than Skidelsky concedes, both in increasing public works and avoiding rigid deflation until overwhelmed by the 'economic blizzard'. According to McKibbin, not only were there no alternative solutions abroad, but in relation to almost universal deflation, British policy was 'generous and almost unorthodox'. Moreover, the sort of domestic economic action necessary for success depended upon policies it was 'scarcely conceivable that a Labour government would have been permitted to introduce … while the existing structure of power remained intact'.[3] At a different level, the neo-Keynesians can be criticised for their undue concern with the evaluation of the economic merits (or otherwise) of competing policy options, while ignoring the fact that much of the opposition to expansionist policies was based not on a myopic 'Treasury view', but on the practical problems of implementation in such a short time.[4] Whatever the retrospective verdict, however, the appearance of government stupefaction and incompetence in dealing with unemployment ensured the electoral tide had already begun to turn against Labour as early as the winter of 1929–30 – albeit as perhaps part of a more general disillusionment with all parties.[5]

Certainly Labour was not the only party in severe difficulties between 1929 and 1931. This period also witnessed the 'failure of an opposition', as the Conservatives engaged in some of the most ferocious and damaging internecine strife of the twentieth century, which by March 1931 had brought Baldwin to the verge of resignation.[6] Electoral defeat in 1929 dragged the party's centre of gravity markedly to the right. While many young liberal Tory MPs elected for northern industrial seats in the 1924 landslide were defeated in 1929, right-wing Diehards in generally secure southern constituencies accounted for at least 50 of the 261 MPs elected in 1929, compared with only 60 of the 400 elected in the 1924 parliament.[7] In opposition, their many pent-up frustrations with the excessive liberalism of the Baldwin government soon boiled to the surface. Moreover, party cohesion was scarcely assisted by Baldwin's apparent lethargy, indolence and lack of enthusiasm for the sort of combative leadership demanded from the opposition front bench. Always too constructive to be a good leader of opposition, between 1929 and 1931 Baldwin showed himself at his worst in terms of apathy, inertia and moderation. Unfortunately, when he did offer a positive lead, he often did so in the 'wrong' direction in support of policies to which the bulk of the party objected. In particular, Imperialist Diehards were infuriated in October 1929 by his support for the Irwin Declaration, to the effect that dominion status was 'the natural issue of India's constitutional progress'. This stance plunged Baldwin into a conflict with his own right wing from which the party would not emerge until the passage of the Government of India Act in 1935.

A far more immediately damaging crisis for the Conservatives emerged over tariff reform. Protectionist frustration at Churchill's free trade obstructionism and Baldwinian equivocation about the extension of 'Safeguarding' legislation, had been a source of increasing tension during the 1924–9 ministry.[8] In opposition, this rift became far more damaging through the intervention of the press lords, Beaverbrook and Rothermere. Beaverbrook launched his nominally non-party Empire Crusade at the end of June 1929 in support of 'Empire Free Trade'; a deliberately ambiguous slogan designed to attract free trade Liberal and Labour voters to a protectionist policy which unashamedly embraced food taxes. His main objective, however, was to convert the Tory party by using the popular press to appeal over the heads of the leadership direct to the rank-and-file. By mid-February 1930 the Crusade was transformed into the United Empire Party which boasted 173,000 members. Designed to carry the fight to the constituencies, UEP candidates appeared in a succession of by-elections where they succeeded in humiliating official Conservative candidates either by winning the seat, as in South Paddington in October, or by pushing the Tory into third place, as at Islington East in February 1931. To make matters worse, Baldwin refused to be galvanised into sustained activity to oppose this challenge. As new crises developed in June and October 1930, he was goaded and cajoled into some great effort to save himself, but on each occasion he swiftly relapsed into passivity and inertia to the despair of colleagues. In February–March 1931 the Conservative crisis reached a climax with the by-election at St George's, Westminster; a contest which provided Beaverbrook with a golden opportunity to challenge the leadership and force his policy upon the party after a trial of strength in the safest Conservative seat in Britain. Moreover, the menace of this challenge was further intensified by the fact that many Conservatives were now also convinced that, as Baldwin could neither unite the party nor save himself, he should resign sooner rather than later.[9] Against this background, Baldwin came within an ace of resignation before being persuaded that he should 'go down fighting'. After Duff Cooper secured victory by a majority of almost 6,000 on Baldwin's behalf, Beaverbrook's Crusade for Empire Free Trade collapsed. By the end of the month the so-called Stornoway House Pact with the Conservatives represented his total and unconditional surrender.

In retrospect, this was a farcical episode. The Empire Crusade was always essentially a one-man movement for the self-aggrandisement of its incorrigibly romantic architect in pursuit of an ill-considered and impracticable chimera. Moreover, the threat from the press lords themselves was always more apparent than real. Beaverbrook's contumacious challenge did not create the discontent which almost drove Baldwin from the leadership so much as painfully highlight his well-established inadequacies. Yet ironically, despite these deep discontents, perhaps the single most important factor in Baldwin's retention of the leadership was the fact that he was under attack from men who, in Baldwin's memorable phrase, were seeking 'power without responsibility – the prerogative of the harlot throughout the ages'.[10] Although galvanised into a more active lead during the spring of 1931, by the autumn Baldwin found himself in a far more congenial situation within a National Government in which the party remained for the rest of the decade.

For the Liberals, the second Labour government represented just another painful stage in their now inexorable long-term collapse.[11] After mid-1930 Lloyd George moved into closer cooperation with Labour in the hope of promoting his own radical economic policy to save the nation and some measure of electoral reform to save his party. In the event, MacDonald was unwilling to accept either, although by the spring of 1931 he appeared to be considering Cabinet places for Lloyd George and other Liberals. Whether genuine or not, such negotiations kept Lloyd George out of mischief and in the Labour lobby. On the other hand, however, this apparent drift to the left provoked a further damaging exit from the Liberal right. Conservative overtures to sympathetic Liberals had begun in November 1930 after Sir John Simon led four other Liberals in symbolic support for the Conservative amendment to the King's Speech. After much coaxing and cajoling from Neville Chamberlain urging them to form a separate 'Liberal Unionist' wing, in June 1931 Simon finally resigned the Liberal whip and established a 'Liberal National' group. Although the sudden onset of the political crisis two months later rendered such manoeuvres irrelevant, within a few months this formalised schism heralded the final dissolution of the Liberal alliance.

9.2 The political crisis and the National Government

The collapse of the Austrian Kredit-Anstalt bank in May 1931 instigated a panic-stricken struggle to maintain banking liquidity throughout Europe. By mid-July the international liquidity crisis had arrived in Britain. With gold flooding out of London at the rate of £4 million a day, loans were obtained from America and France to restore foreign confidence. The publication of the May Committee Report on National Expenditure on 31 July turned foreign nervousness into panic when it predicted a £120 million budget deficit for the coming year and called for drastic retrenchment of £96 million in public expenditure (including £67 million from unemployment assistance). This event radically transformed the nature of the crisis from a purely technical financial crisis into a political crisis, based on a lack of confidence both in sterling and the underlying ability of the Labour government to run the economy responsibly. Without corrective action to restore confidence, it would not be possible either to halt the flood of gold or to obtain loans to cover short-term indebtedness given the insistence of the American and French bankers that further financial aid was conditional upon the restoration of budgetary equilibrium and the support of the other parties for any economy package; a condition which decisively transferred the initiative to the Conservative opposition.

The debate over levels of unemployment assistance lay at the heart of the crisis and determined its outcome. Although the May Committee had specifically proposed a 20 per cent cut in unemployment insurance as part of a broader package of economies, the Cabinet's five-man Economy Committee initially planned cuts of £78,500,000, including a 10 per cent reduction in unemployment insurance, before these were shelved on 19 August when the Cabinet as a whole refused to impose them. Next day, leaders of both the opposition parties and the TUC rejected the Cabinet's more modest proposals. The former did so because they insisted that any credible economy package needed to include a cut in the standard rate of benefit and this condition became a central feature of all future negotiations. Conversely, under Bevin's guidance, the TUC rejected both the diagnosis and prescriptions proposed by the May Committee, believing that they would serve only to depress demand and erode wages still further, thereby intensifying the slump. Instead, they proposed a radical alternative of tariffs, tax increases and devaluation. In the event, a majority of the Cabinet led by Henderson also refused to go beyond £56 million until a further flight from sterling led them to consider a 10 per cent cut in benefit on 22 August. By the evening of the next day, however, the Cabinet remained split down the middle over the issue and at 10 p.m. MacDonald left for the Palace to resign and recommended a tripartite conference for the following day. During this Buckingham Palace conference MacDonald was prevailed upon to remain at the head of an emergency three-party National Government intended to last only a few weeks to balance the budget, restore confidence and then (by the terms of the Buckingham Palace agreement) be dissolved to fight an election on a normal party basis.[12]

For the Labour party and its leaders, the crisis and its outcome was a disaster beyond measure. Underlying debates about different economy packages were alternative conceptions of the Labour party's fundamental purpose and the 'national interest' they were there to serve.[13] For Henderson and Bevin, the May Committee's proposals were unacceptable because they imposed the greatest burden upon those least able to bear it, particularly the unemployed. While Henderson and his Cabinet allies were prepared to countenance cuts in unemployment assistance if it could be done covertly, they were not prepared to be seen to advocate such measures at the expense of the working class and the unemployed given vigorous union opposition. As such, it was far better to accept the opprobrium of resignation, than commit the ultimate sin of splitting the movement. When MacDonald and his small group of supporters did so, they were expelled from the party and denounced for joining a 'Wall Street government'. As MacDonald's biographer notes, the decision was perfectly understandable: 'to many Labour activists, he was now a kind of political blackleg, who deserved to be treated accordingly.'[14] Yet MacDonald adopted a diametrically opposing view. His entire leadership had been devoted to the transformation of Labour from a sectional class-based pressure group into a credible party of government – with all that implied in terms of the need to make unpalatable decisions. From MacDonald's perspective, therefore, the crisis of 1931 represented a choice between either placing national duty over personal, sectional and party interests or surrendering Labour's credibility as a responsible party of government for a generation.[15]

The principal controversy about these events concerns the degree to which the Conservatives deliberately exploited the financial crisis in order to destroy the Labour government and prepare the way for a National Government under Conservative control. Although some historians detect the 'workings of a subcutaneous Conservative plan, all through 1931, to use and indeed aggravate, the financial situation for the purpose of displacing and discrediting Labour',[16] such allegations have been subjected to vigorous rebuttal, principally on the grounds that the formation of the National Government was 'neither sought nor desired' by the Conservatives. Rather it was something into which they were 'stampeded' by the panic atmosphere of August 1931, and then accepted out of national duty and an ardent desire for economy. As a result, the notion that 'any Conservatives were principally concerned ... with cunning notions of wrecking the Labour party' is dismissed as 'patently absurd'.[17] Yet although this latter view now commands wide support, the problem with rebuttals based upon close examination of the events of August 1931 is that they often obscure the partisan dimension underlying Neville Chamberlain's longer-term strategy. In this context, although the creation of a National Government may not have been the outcome Chamberlain initially anticipated or consistently desired, in a crucial sense it was the logical outcome of the strategy he had pursued throughout the preceding year. In opposition, the Conservatives had condemned the Labour government's allegedly irresponsible finance and demanded economy, particularly in relation to borrowing for the unemployment insurance fund. By February 1931 Chamberlain confidently predicted that the government would soon fall because 'their policy of spending will have its effect in the money market and public opinion would make itself felt in condemnation'. As the crisis developed in August, Chamberlain had borne the full burden of negotiation and strategic leadership happily free from interference, for although Baldwin made it clear before the recess that he would assist in government economies but never join a coalition, he abdicated any influence he might have held early in the negotiations by appearing 'not ... to have a strong view one way or the other' and by leaving London on 13 August with the promise to support Chamberlain to the end.[18]

What Chamberlain wanted from the developing crisis was an opportunity to split the Labour government on the economy question. By making a 10 per cent cut in unemployment insurance the measure of economic responsibility and the government's willingness to face up to the crisis, Chamberlain sought to detach those Labour ministers committed to responsible government and balanced budgets from the rest of the Cabinet committed primarily to notions of class and party unity and assistance for the most deprived members of the community. In pursuit of this goal, Chamberlain was guided by two central convictions. First, his short-term horizon was defined by the belief that 'from the party point of view the chance of getting "economy" out of the way before a General Election and of destroying the enemy's most dangerous weapon by identifying the present Government with "economy" is so important that it would be worth much to obtain it.' Secondly, if successful, in the longer term he anticipated either 'a new alignment of parties' or 'an appeal to the country in conditions offering the utmost advantage, seeing that we could no longer be saddled with the unpopularity of economy, but could concentrate on tariffs and Imp[erial] Preference as the restorer of prosperity'. Although initially the intention was to force a Labour government to take the blame, when a National Government proved the more likely vehicle to obtain the same goal, Chamberlain found little difficulty in accepting it as equally advantageous – particularly as the Buckingham Palace concordat had specified that the government would deal only with the financial emergency before its dissolution and a party election.[19] In the event, the National Government proved to be anything but a temporary arrangement. Despite further credits and an emergency budget on 8 September, the Invergordon 'mutiny' over mishandled naval pay cuts delivered a final devastating blow to foreign confidence and the gold standard was suspended on 21 September. Expectations of a party election fought on tariffs were swiftly destroyed when the bankers warned that such a course would have disastrous external repercussions unless fought on an agreed programme to restore the trade balance. On 5 October it was eventually decided to hold an election as a National Government calling for a 'Doctor's Mandate' to resolve these outstanding problems.

After a bitter and acrimonious campaign, the election results proved a resounding endorsement of the National Government. The Conservatives were the principal beneficiaries of national fears, emerging with 55 per cent of the vote and 470 MPs – a total of 202 gains and not a single loss. Supported by thirty-five National Liberals, four Nationals, thirteen National Labour and thirty-two Samuelite Liberals, the National Government commanded a majority of over 500. In contrast, when confronted by 409 straight fights against the combined forces of anti-socialism, Labour was virtually annihilated at the polls. Reduced to a pathetic vestige of forty-six MPs (plus six ILP members elected without official endorsement), Labour had only ten more MPs than in December 1910 and nine fewer than in 1918. It had also lost almost all of its experienced leadership, with only Lansbury surviving from the former Cabinet, supported by Attlee and Cripps from the junior ranks. Although Labour's popular vote plummeted from 8,370,417 to 6,649,630, some consolation could be derived from the fact that its 30.7 per cent of the poll was still fractionally above that achieved in 1923 when Labour formed its first ministry. Yet despite the apparent solidity of its bedrock support in the slums of Glasgow and London, areas of high unemployment and those more solidaristic proletarian communities with strong trade union affiliations such as in the coalfields, even Labour's core working class vote was subject to substantial defection as a result of disillusion with its failure to deal adequately with unemployment since the winter of 1929–30.[20] Little wonder that Henderson's inquest into the disaster concluded that 'the work of rebuilding must cover policy, organisation, education and propaganda'.[21]

9.3 The character of the National Government

Although arguably eclipsed by the fall of the Lloyd George Coalition in October 1922, many would agree with Reginald Bassett's classic verdict that the political crisis of August 1931 'probably had an influence upon the course of British politics greater even than that of 1846, with which it has sometimes been compared'.[22] Yet while there is a consensus about the general importance of these events, the precise contours of this party watershed have been much less clearly defined. Skidelsky's *Politicians and the Slump* provided one influential attempt to fill this void. The novelty of this interpretation stems from the central contention that the real cleavage of opinion in interwar politics was not the struggle between socialism and capitalism but rather one between heterodox 'economic radicals' and orthodox 'economic conservatives': a division which centred around unemployment and cut across party lines. In these terms, the 1931 crisis represented the decisive defeat of the 'bold men' of the 1929 Parliament like Lloyd George, Mosley, Macmillan and the ILP who called despairingly for a radical policy of budgetary expansion, and the victory of complacent, economic conservatives of all parties whose failure of imagination and nerve left them clinging to an outworn and ineffectual faith in balanced budgets and the 'Treasury view'. From this 'neo-Keynesian' perspective, 1931 thus represented 'a turning point when Britain failed to turn'.[23] Despite the more general influence of this interpretation, however, the underlying proposition with regard to the party system is extremely questionable – particularly given the dubious centrality of a cleavage which separated the overwhelming majority of the political community from a few disparate individuals who by 1931 were almost wholly lacking in credibility and united only by their political isolation, lack of effectiveness and adhesion (to a greater or lesser extent) to some species of 'expansionist' economic strategy. The contention that this was the principal cleavage in interwar politics would thus appear to exaggerate the coherence and significance of both the so-called 'economic radicals' and their creed. It throws even less light on what actually did happen to party alignments after 1931.

A less dramatic, but far more pervasive approach to the party significance of 1931, has been to treat it as the final act in the long-term drama of Liberal decline and anti-socialist consolidation. In this context, 1931 marked a watershed only insofar as it finally restored the classical two-party system on the basis of a simple contest between two groupings – 'the purged Labour Party on the one hand, and its opponents on the other'.[24] In this popular contemporary version, Labour was weakened but not fundamentally damaged by the defection of MacDonald and thereafter rebuilt itself upon the foundations of a rediscovered faith in the fundamentals of 'socialism'. On the

other side, the dominant characterisation of the National Government was
that after the 1931 general election and the departure of Snowden and the
Samuelite Liberals eleven months later the sheer weight of Tory parliamentary
strength ensured that it swiftly degenerated into little more than a façade for
'Conservative Dictatorship': a coalition held together by little more than
opportunism and an austere lack of alternatives for the helpless .dupes and
knaves who lent credence to the Conservatives' cynical appropriation of the
'National' label.[25] On the basis of hostile contemporary testimony and a
simple head count, historians have been remarkably willing to adopt such a
view of both the nature of the central cleavage between the parties in the
1930s and the balance of power, influence and control within the National
Government itself.[26]

Yet despite the apparent numerical basis for allegations of 'Tory
dictatorship', such an interpretation offers an excessively simplistic and
misleading view of the complex dynamics and power relationships operating
within the National Government. Undeniably, many Conservatives in the
country and on the backbenches believed that they were now the undisputed
masters of the situation and free to do as they wished. Equally clearly,
Conservative ministers were united in their undisguised detestation of the
Samuelites and were determined to jettison them if they could, although
Neville Chamberlain was far more anxious to retain Snowden despite his
fanatical commitment to free trade. Ultimately, it is also true that the
Conservatives did prevail over the introduction of tariffs in February 1932, in
spite of MacDonald's anxious equivocation and the outright opposition of
Snowden and the Samuelite Liberals. Yet what is often overlooked is that, in a
world of devalued currencies, rampant 'dumping' and high tariff barriers, there
were no practicable alternatives open to a government seeking an immediate
solution to the adverse balance of trade and the more enduring problems of
industrial reconstruction. Nor is it sufficiently recognised that this was neither
an exclusively Conservative policy nor one imposed upon entirely reluctant or
helpless allies. By 1931 the entire Simonite *raison d'être* rested upon support
for the National Government as a means to obtain retrenchment, if necessary
at the expense of free trade. Similarly, within the National Labour group,
Thomas had been a vociferous protectionist during the 1929 government and
Sankey was open-minded about tariffs but hostile towards Snowden's bigoted
free trade obstructionism. Most important, despite the emphasis in the
literature upon MacDonald's doubts and prevarications over tariffs, the fact
remains that throughout the 1929 government he had been far more willing
to countenance pragmatic protectionism than has often been conceded and
that in 1931–2 his principal reservation was not that it was the wrong policy
but rather that its adoption would split the government and leave him the
prisoner of the Tories.[27]

Against this background, the most striking feature of the tariff debate
within the National Government during 1931–2 was not the brutality with
which Conservatives imposed their policy upon reluctant allies, but rather
their recognition of the constraints imposed upon them by the need to

conciliate these allies in order to sustain the credibility of the 'National' label – with all the advantages that went with it. This sensitivity explains the influential positions given to Simon, Samuel and Runciman in the Cabinet and anxious Conservative handling of MacDonald's fears about becoming a Tory prisoner. It also underpinned their acceptance of the 'agreement to differ' over tariff legislation, despite a heartfelt personal loathing for Samuel. Moreover, when Snowden and the Samuelite Liberals did resign in September 1932, to bolster 'National' representation it was necessary to make concessions to the non-Conservative contingent. Far from sustaining the contention of naked 'Tory Take-Over',[28] therefore, the battle over tariffs demonstrated the degree to which Conservative leaders valued the 'National' label and the lengths to which they were prepared to go in order to sustain it. Nor was this an early atypical example of power relationships. Cabinet discussions were not conducted on party lines and on several key questions (like unemployment), there were no obvious party divisions at all. Moreover, the inner Cabinet of MacDonald, Baldwin, Chamberlain, Thomas, Simon and Runciman 'operated as a team of colleagues rather than a meeting of party representatives', and the same was true of the committee preparing for the 1935 election. As such, John Ramsden rightly concludes that the National Government 'continued to operate unlike a party government until at least 1934–35'.[29] Arguably, it was not until Neville Chamberlain's succession to the premiership in 1937 that the 'National' composition and tenor of the government were completely undermined by a provocative style of leadership which introduced a new tone of sectional animosity into politics so studiously avoided by MacDonald and Baldwin.

If examination of the dynamics of policy-making does not sustain the 'Tory dictatorship' thesis, then consideration of the personal positions of the non-Conservative contingent suggests that diversity of symbolic personal representation was of far greater importance than any crude head count of ministers, backbenchers or votes polled. In 1931 the Conservatives held just over half the Cabinet places, and even after the withdrawal of the free traders in September 1932, they still held only thirteen of nineteen Cabinet posts despite their massive numerical superiority on the backbenches. Although his failing eyesight and health were the subject of grave anxiety from the outset, MacDonald enjoyed sustained influence long after the initial crisis had passed. Although prey to regular bouts of neurotic self-pity about being ridiculed as a 'Tory slave', ironically such allegations created an immensely strong bargaining position given Conservative fears that his resignation would torpedo the credibility of the 'National' label and undermine its appeal to moderate and progressive opinion. Thus, despite the assertion that after September 1932, 'it was a Conservative Government which happened to have a non-Conservative at its head and a number of other non-Conservatives attached to it', even David Marquand is compelled to concede that MacDonald was not a Tory dupe to be dismissed at will and that he made full use of his Prime Ministerial powers to prevent them from doing so. Marquand is undoubtedly correct in the view that National Labour 'had no distinctive policies, no identifiable grass roots support, and, apart from personal loyalty to MacDonald, no obvious *raison d'être.'*[30] Yet the reality was that even as a party of chiefs without Indians, it still enjoyed an influence out of all proportion to its size, simply because of the critical importance of symbolic representation. As Harold Nicolson wryly observed in 1936, 'a party which has a meeting of all its members and can only fill one dinner-table with seven, six of whom have Government jobs, cannot be called an ill-used party.'[31]

Similarly, Sir John Simon retained the Foreign Office long after his diplomatic usefulness and credibility had passed, while his transfer to the Home Office, the Exchequer and then the Lord Chancellorship reflected the continued symbolic significance of a non-Conservative party leader in a National Government. Moreover, in contrast with National Labour, Simon's small group of thirty-five Liberal Nationalist MPs were more secure, more independent and exerted far more leverage than is often recognised. Keenly aware that 'the P.M. needs all the Liberal help he can get and deeply appreciates anything we can do to stand by him and prevent submergence in the Tory flood', after the resignation of the Cabinet free traders in September 1932 the Simonite leaders rightly recognised that autonomy offered some prospect of influence and advancement, 'partly for the look of the thing – preserving the broad base – and partly to keep alive loyalty to the Government in circles which had Liberal antecedents'.[32] Contrary to expectations that the creation of an all-party National Coordinating Committee in November 1932 would lead to fusion with the Conservatives on 1886 lines, the Simonites remained robustly independent and (unlike National Labour and the Samuelites) they had funds from Lords Nuffield and Inchcape to make this a reality. By March 1933 a separate party headquarters had thus been established at Westminster because in a world in which bargaining power and influence depended on the maintenance of a separate identity, the Simonites had much to lose and absolutely nothing to gain by premature fusion into any sort of 'National Party'. Moreover, although inevitably regarded as a junior partner by the Conservatives, the Liberal Nationals did at least have the satisfaction of knowing that their continued presence in the National Government provided their brand of Liberalism with a far more effective voice in shaping government policy than that enjoyed by their independent Samuelite counterparts impotently carping from the opposition benches. Significantly, the Liberal Nationals retained this tenacious commitment to their independent identity well into the postwar years. Not until the Woolton–Teviot agreement of May 1947 did they formally fuse with the Conservatives and even then they retained a separate whip until 1966.[33]

The response of many Conservative backbenchers and activists towards the National Government casts further doubt upon the idea of unbridled 'Conservative dictatorship'. Although at least seventy Tory MPs elected for the first time in 1931 depended on the perpetuation of 'National' cooperation for their ability to retain their seats,[34] many Conservatives on the backbenches and in the country resented the compromises necessitated by the National Government. Having won an unprecedented victory, many Conservatives expected to exploit it for party purposes and voiced their frustration and irritation with their leaders when they did not – particularly as confusion over whether to promote specifically Conservative or 'National' causes prevented constituency activists from driving traditional adversaries from the field. As a result, intra-party tensions between leadership and rank-and-file were never far from the surface over issues like economies, India and later defence. It was predictable that a veteran Diehard like Lord Lloyd should have confessed in 1934 to right-wing alarm at 'the general slide and swing to the left of "Conservative" thought as directed by S.B. and we are trying to do what we can to counter these tendencies by throwing out some strong anchors to the right'.[35] Yet it was indicative of a more general concern at the disconcertingly 'National' tone of the government that in the same year the party conference lamented the apparent lack of difference between socialist and Conservative economic policy, while the Central Committee overwhelmingly passed a comprehensive resolution demanding a 'reaffirmation of the major principles of the Conservative faith' from their own leadership: a request all too reminiscent of the sort of rank-and-file anxiety which had undermined the Lloyd George Coalition a decade earlier.[36]

Fundamentalist sentiments of this sort were scarcely surprising given the attitude of their leader. Despite his well-known aversion to coalitions, Baldwin embraced the National Government because it offered a uniquely favourable environment in which to promote his own brand of consensual liberal Toryism, insulated from the Diehard right wing whose reactionary influence had blighted the second half of his 1924–9 ministry. In this respect, the National Government unquestionably represented 'the natural culmination of Baldwin's New Conservative phase of 1924–25'.[37] As he told the 1932 party conference, in language reminiscent of November 1924, they had a duty 'to carry our share in the letter and spirit of the National Government; our aims must be national and not party; our ideals must be national and not party'.[38] Nowhere were these bipartisan advantages more important to Baldwin than over India. According to his biographers, after 1930 Baldwin's last 'great mission' was to prevent India becoming another Ireland in British politics.[39] Yet from the outset he also recognised that the depth and bitterness of the divisions within his own party over India meant that only a consensual approach capable of mobilising cross-party support stood any chance of success. Although Churchill and the reactionary Diehard Imperialists of the India Defence League were eventually marginalised and decisively defeated in 1935, at times this was an uncomfortably close-run thing. At the same time, on the other wing of the party, young radicals like Macmillan were moving rapidly towards corporatist interventionism and State planning within the 'Next Five Years Group'. Indeed, it was indicative of the fluidity of the prevailing party situation that despite the centre-right composition of the group, during 1936 Macmillan briefly dallied with the idea of turning it into 'some kind of Popular Front', to capture the support of the centre-left under the leadership of someone like Herbert Morrison![40] Confronted by such a polarisation between left and right in his own party, it is scarcely surprising that Baldwin should have considered the National Government to be an ideal vehicle to steer his own version of a 'middle way' between the extreme conflicting passions of his nominal supporters.[41]

9.4 The collapse of independent Liberalism

After 1931 independent Liberalism was almost completely extinguished as a parliamentary and electoral force. Without any residual sense of unity or cohesion and devoid of a distinctive identity, the historic Liberal party finally fragmented into three separate factions. On the government side of the Commons, the Simonite National Liberals converged with the Tories, while on the other side Lloyd George's family party of four MPs opted wholeheartedly to move to the left and to revive the Lib–Lab alliance. Between them stood Herbert Samuel and the remnants of the official party machine championing a form of independent centrism. Despite an increasingly humiliating position, the Samuelites did not resign from the National Government until September 1932 and initially remained on the government benches, largely from fear of unleashing Tory electoral retribution if they actively opposed the government. Increasingly carping about irrelevant details, the Samuelites eventually moved into formal opposition in November 1933 simply because they had no other strategy and a demoralised rank-and-file demanded it. Alas, even this decision led to the defection of four of their tiny parliamentary group, although they got one Simonite defector in return. The move to opposition also brought about the total collapse of their by-election vote in 1933–4, before poverty forced them to withdraw from seven of the next twelve contests altogether after the death of their principal benefactor in October 1933. As Ramsay Muir conceded privately in 1934, 'as an effective political force, the Liberal Party is all-but extinct'.[42]

The party was also doctrinally bankrupt. The Liberal Summer School had now degenerated into a pointless talking shop and in May 1933 even the NLF was compelled to recognise that free trade was no longer a viable option.[43] Without free trade as a defining article of faith, the party ceased to possess any distinctive identity whatsoever. During 1932 Ramsay Muir and the NLF did attempt to re-establish a doctrinal *raison d'être* as a 'new Radical party', but such efforts depended upon a rapprochement with Lloyd George and he would neither forget nor forgive Samuel's treachery in 1931.[44] By the same token, although Lloyd George eventually found a new issue to re-establish his own position, with his 'New Deal' proposals in January 1935 and his plans for Councils of Action for Peace and Reconstruction, their momentum soon petered out when confronted by Neville Chamberlain's implacable hatred. Sir Archibald Sinclair's succession to the defeated Samuel after the 1935 election witnessed an attempt to adopt a more aggressive radicalism capable of differentiating the Liberals as the party of 'freedom' (rather than free trade), but it had balefully little effect. Faced with deep doctrinal divisions within even these desperately depleted ranks, in 1936 Sinclair confessed that, 'To throw all our weight on one side or the other would create another split.' He thus settled back to stress those traditional Gladstonian slogans which united them, while hoping the electorate would eventually tire of the National Government.[45] It was a desperate hope. With 1,443,093 votes (6.7 per cent) and twenty-one seats, the Liberals reached their interwar nadir in 1935. After polling a humiliating 4 per cent in the Ross and Cromerty by-election in February 1936, in a seat formerly with strong Highland Liberal traditions, they withdrew from by-elections almost completely. Similarly, increasing reliance upon anti-socialist pacts meant their municipal vote fell from an already meagre 12.5 per cent in 1929 to 5.6 per cent by 1938. Yet despite all of this, in the absence of any other options, the Liberals clung to their strategy of presenting themselves as a 'party in being', and struggled to maintain the semblance and privileges of a full-blooded parliamentary party despite 'National' hostility, demoralisation and chronic absenteeism.[46] After the failure of reconciliation talks with the National Liberals in January 1938, the party appeared to be irrevocably doomed.

9.5 Labour responses to 1931: leadership, power and organisation

Most of the key developments in Labour doctrine, leadership and internal power relationships during the 1930s were a direct response to the trauma of 1931 and a reaction against the evils of 'MacDonaldism'. This is certainly true of attitudes towards the question of the party's future leadership. Central to all Labour explanations of 1931 was the omnipresent spectre of 'betrayal' by a leader so corrupted by the aristocratic embrace that he abandoned the movement to which he owed everything. MacDonald's fondness for high society and his remoteness from the party's rank-and-file had become increasingly suspect during the 1920s. 'He is an egotist, a poseur and snob, and worst of all he does not believe in the creed we have always preached', Beatrice Webb noted acidly in 1925. 'He is not a Socialist and he has not been one for twenty years: he is a mild radical with individualistic leanings and aristocratic tastes.' In the aftermath of disaster, it was thus scarcely surprising either that MacDonald should be presented as 'its author, producer and principal actor' or that other centres of power within the movement sought to curb the autonomy of the parliamentary leadership to prevent any repetition of this state of affairs.[47] To this end, the 1933 party conference compelled the next Labour Prime Minister to consult the membership over ministerial appointments and to be bound by majority decisions in Cabinet. Equally indicative of this new mood of subordination was Lansbury's confession to conference the following year that he regarded himself more as a 'spokesman' of the party than its 'leader': a theme periodically echoed by Attlee.[48] Although this consultative deference to the movement still prevailed in May 1940 when Attlee and Greenwood joined Churchill's wartime coalition, by 1945 such constraints had been conveniently dropped.

After Henderson's defeat at the 1931 election, George Lansbury succeeded to the leadership for the simple reason that he was the only Cabinet minister to survive the rout, although his advanced age, failing health and physical decrepitude ensured he was always more of an inspirational figurehead than an active leader of parliamentary opposition. From the outset, this task fell on the shoulders of Clement Attlee, who as Deputy Leader bore an enormous burden on a depleted front bench. The circumstances of Attlee's own succession in 1935 provide eloquent testimony to the persistence of party suspicions towards the idea of leadership in the 1930s. After Lansbury's effective dismissal for his failure to be bound by majority decisions, Attlee was appointed as a transitional stop-gap leader until a more senior figure was returned after the impending election. Yet in the event, he defeated both Greenwood and Morrison for the post because his tireless leadership in thankless conditions after 1931 had earned him the respect and loyalty of the PLP, while his low key approach, loyalty and deference to majority decisions won him many supporters in the unions and the broader movement. Above all, after the trauma of leadership betrayal, his self-effacing modesty was precisely what the party wanted. Critics like Hugh Dalton could sneer that he was 'a small person with no personality', but Attlee understood that after the searing bitterness of 1931 any leader needed to present themselves as the antithesis of MacDonald and a humble servant of the movement, 'prepared to submit to their will'.[49]

This reaction against leadership took place in circumstances of astonishing parliamentary weakness. The small size and mediocrity of a PLP composed overwhelmingly of inarticulate union men robbed it of the predominant influence it had enjoyed since 1910 and shifted the locus of power back into the hands of the trade unions. Although the potential for union domination had existed since the introduction of the 1918 constitution, MacDonald's 'betrayal' turned this into a reality. Between 1918 and 1931 an average of sixteen of the twenty-three NEC members were MPs. After 1931, only three were members of the PLP.[50] On this basis, Pelling describes Labour in the 1930s as 'the General Council's party'.[51] The principal vehicle for this control was through the National Joint Council, renamed the National Council of Labour in 1934. Established in 1921, the NJC was virtually moribund by 1931.[52] Yet, at a joint TUC–NEC meeting on 19 November 1931 it was agreed that the NJC should meet regularly to 'enable Labour to speak with one voice on all questions of national importance, and to pursue a policy in support of its common ends'.[53] Although formally a forum for the TUC, NEC and PLP, in practice it was dominated by a very strong union contingent which grew in authority throughout the decade under the leadership of Ernest Bevin (TGWU) and Walter Citrine (TUC General Secretary).

This shift in the locus of power ensured that throughout the 1930s the Labour left won precious few battles against the bureaucratic control, defensive 'realism' and anti-intellectual suspicion of the unions. The disaffiliation of the ILP in 1932 was both a cause and consequence of this shift in the distribution of power. Although a founding partner in the party and an important source of socialist ideas, after 1924 the ILP had become an increasingly critical and disruptive force. By the summer of 1931 it was less a radical wing of Labour than a fully-fledged opposition 'party within a party', deeply critical of the leadership, its blind faith in the 'inevitability of gradualness' and its efforts to preserve a failing capitalist system. Despite the ideological foundations of this intra-party conflict, however, it soon resolved itself into an essentially procedural battle as the PLP applied mounting pressure for obedience to its Standing Orders, while after the 1931 election the ILP retaliated by forming a separate parliamentary group officially recognised by the Speaker. Increasingly dominated by the Marxist analysis of Maxton, Brockway and the Revolutionary Policy Committee, in July 1932 the ILP voted to disaffiliate from the Labour party by 241 to 142.

Disaffiliation proved an unmitigated disaster. Between July and November 1932 the ILP lost 203 of its 653 branches, with a consequent collapse in members, finance, local vigour and electoral support. After a fierce battle for control between Communists and Trotskyists, by 1935 membership had plummeted to 4,392. Despite talks about possible reaffiliation in early 1938, acceptance of the PLP's Standing Orders remained a major obstacle at a time when the ILP still opposed Labour's support for rearmament. With the outbreak of war, this once influential force was finally extinguished.[54] In many respects, the fate of the ILP was the logical culmination of efforts since 1918 to use bureaucratic managerial controls to transform Labour into a more monolithic mass party with less room for troublesome mavericks like the ILP, and its disaffiliation undoubtedly served to intensify official hostility towards all organised factions which threatened to develop into 'a party within a party'.[55] A similar fate thus befell the Socialist League which had been formed in October 1932 from a fusion of Cole's Society for Socialist Inquiry and Propaganda (established June 1931) and ILP opponents of disaffiliation. Although from the outset the explicit intention had been to offer a focus for socialist ideas free from any taint of factional disloyalty, it soon confronted precisely the same dilemmas about primary loyalties which had destroyed the ILP in a climate far less tolerant of such diversity. In practice, Labour's new managerial regime did not prevent a successful challenge to union ascendancy from the Constituency Parties Movement, whose campaign for a fairer distribution of power overcame union resistance at the 1937 conference by a narrow margin.[56] Yet this was not a movement instigated by the left and it enjoyed the support of Dalton. Conversely, in 1937 the dismissal of claims by both the Socialist League and the Labour League of Youth to an independent voice represented further defeats for the left and a decisive movement away from the tolerant pluralism which had prevailed during the party's first two decades (see section 9.7 below).

9.6 Labour's ideological response to 1931

In the aftermath of 1931, the reaction against 'MacDonaldism' extended beyond matters of leadership to encompass a broader indictment of his tantalisingly vague vision of 'socialism' which had failed to equip the party with a programme capable of carrying them forward from a capitalist present to the future socialist utopia. As a result, it became a central article of faith that the party needed to reaffirm its fundamental 'socialist' ideology in order to restore its sense of mission and purpose. To give substance to that promise, it also needed a detailed and practical programme for a future Labour government. Although the degree to which Labour ideology, ideas and policy were actually transformed during the 1930s is contested by historians, contemporaries undoubtedly believed that this was their objective and achievement.[57]

The prevailing mythology that Labour had fallen victim to a 'Banker's Ramp' in 1931 had a major impact upon its perceptions of the problems confronting a future Labour government. For a few on the left, like Laski, Cripps and Strachey, it also raised doubts about whether vested capitalist interests would ever allow the achievement of socialism under a parliamentary system. Often employing explicitly Marxist–Leninist language, this analysis led to the conviction that only an Enabling Act with 'drastic emergency measures' would be sufficient to overcome the capitalist obstacles to the necessary socialist transformation.[58] In retrospect, what is most significant about the Laski–Cripps analysis is not that it was articulated at all, but rather that it received so little sustained support given the circumstances of Labour's fall from office. Despite occasional naïve rhetoric about the failure of democracy and the glories of the Soviet command economy, for the vast majority of its activists, Labour's objective was never to subvert a hostile political system but rather to ensure greater control through parliamentary means. Similarly, with regard to the economic structure, the purpose was not to replace capitalism but to make it more efficient in delivering 'socialist' goals. Once the dust had settled, therefore, the lessons learned from 1931 for the majority within the party took a very specific form. While concluding that 'socialism' was still the only answer to economic crisis, mass unemployment and social injustice, there was to be an end to MacDonaldite vagueness. In 1932 the Leicester conference thus resolved that the next Labour government should introduce 'definite Socialist legislation ... immediately' it got into office and this would require detailed preparation while in opposition.

As it turned out, under the auspices of the NEC's eight-man Policy Committee (established in December 1931), Labour's doctrinal renaissance produced a technocratic vision of socialism defined almost exclusively in terms of public ownership and planning. From the outset, the principal priority was to compile a list of suitable industries to be brought under public control. In contrast, many crucial details were left unresolved, as over the vexed question of worker representation on these new public boards. Obsessed by the need to transfer ownership from the private to the public sector, there was an equally important failure to give much consideration to the precise structure for control. Herbert Morrison's public corporation thus became the model for advance after 1945 simply because no other options had been considered, rather than because it represented the best means of socialist planning and control.[59] Similarly, although Labour's enthusiasm for 'planning' had a variety of roots and a long history, beneath the surface ambiguity and ambivalence remained as to whether the objective was to promote socialist transformation or merely enhance industrial and economic efficiency.

The search for detailed policy commitments culminated in July 1934 with the publication of *For Socialism and Peace*. As the title implies, this successor to *Labour and the Nation* (1928) dealt with both domestic and international policy. While vigorously reaffirming Labour's commitment to parliamentary democracy, it declared boldly that 'what the nation now requires is not mere social reform, but socialism'.

> The choice before the nation is either a vain attempt to patch up the superstructure of a capitalist society in decay at its very foundations, or a rapid advance to a Socialist reconstruction of the national life. There is no half-way house.

To overcome the 'fatal restrictions' upon productive capacity, centrally controlled economic planning and reorganisation were declared to be the only solutions. In deliberate contrast to *Labour and the Nation*, the document was far more specific in its pledges. Transport, power, land, water, banking, coal, iron and steel, shipping, ship-building and engineering were all identified as industries in which 'the time has come for drastic reorganisation, and for the most part, nothing short of public ownership and control will be effective'. For those initially outside public control, government would assume powers to enforce reorganisation and the regulation of prices, profits, wages and conditions.[60] *For Socialism and Peace* represented the principal exposition of Labour policy and the high-water mark of its radicalism for the rest of the decade. Yet despite its importance, its significance should not be misunderstood or exaggerated. In one sense, *For Socialism and Peace* did represent an end to the vague generalities of MacDonald's vision of 'socialism'. Yet for all that, in many ways it was also simply a restatement of the commitments of *Labour and the New Social Order* and a reassertion of the lines of party cleavage that it had established after 1918 – particularly with regard to nationalisation and Labour's unbridled faith in the benign power of the State as an agency for economic and social change.[61]

From a policy perspective, the radicalism of *For Socialism and Peace* was confined to its unapologetically socialist language and pledges, without any sign of a real revolution in Labour's broader economic thinking. In particular, despite some interest in notions of deficit financing and demand stimulation within the ILP, the New Fabian Research Bureau and the discreet XYZ Club, Labour's response to 1931 did not entail an official acceptance of quasi-Keynesian economics as it did in Sweden.[62] Why this was so is a fascinating question. The association with Lloyd George 'stunts' in 1929, the mistaken belief that this was merely a variant of the unproductive municipal public works before the Great War and the suspicion that these were merely palliatives to prop up a crumbling capitalist system, while delaying the advent of full socialism, all played their part. In some quarters there was also the fear that by offering full employment under an unreformed capitalism, Keynesian theories undermined the socialist claim that only fundamental economic transformation could deliver social justice and jobs: a logic which inhibited the adoption of such ideas well into the 1940s.[63] Whatever the reason, the fact remains that neither Keynes nor Roosevelt's New Deal prompted Labour to rethink its ideas. Labour was 'interested ... but not receptive' because, as Barbara Malamet argues, the timing was wrong, coinciding as it did with Labour's decision to reaffirm and redefine its faith in 'socialism' in terms of structural transformation.[64]

Labour's decision to equate 'socialism' with its traditional commitment to public ownership and planning had fundamental implications for the nature of party competition and ideological cleavage during the 1930s and beyond. After 1931 the party divide was not between Labour's socialism and a modest revision of classical economic liberalism, but rather between different species of intervention, planning and pre-Keynesian economic management. Contrary to the assertions of many historians who dismiss the Import Duties Act of February 1932 as simply the emotional fulfilment of a backward-looking crusade for full-blooded Tory tariff reform, pragmatic protectionists within the National Government regarded the general tariff less as a political end in itself than as a crucial permissive foundation for the achievement of a far broader set of economic policy objectives. Above all, for Neville Chamberlain, the long-awaited 'scientific' tariff structure in the hands of the Import Duties Advisory Council (IDAC) offered a mechanism through which to 'manage' the economy and resolve the industrial and unemployment problems of the interwar era through the active promotion of rationalisation and wholesale structural reorganisation. At the heart of Chamberlain's long-term industrial strategy was the ability of the IDAC to inform ailing staple trades that further tariff protection was contingent upon active measures of reconstruction to restore competitiveness. The Import Duties Act and IDAC were thus consciously designed to provide 'such a lever as has never been possessed before by any Government, for inducing or, if you like, forcing industry to set its house in order'. As Chamberlain wrote to Snowden in January 1932, 'my belief in the advantages of Protection is not so fanatical as to close my eyes to the vital importance of a thorough reorganisation of such industries as [cotton, iron and steel], if they were ever to keep their heads above the water in the future.'[65]

Despite the tendency to emphasise the emergence of a 'middle opinion' favourable to planning in the 1930s,[66] however, the degree of party consensus is often exaggerated with regard to ends as well as means. Even among non-socialists, the rhetoric of 'planning' concealed a deeply fragmented movement characterised less by consensus than a vague policy overlap. The divergence between these groups and Labour over planning represented a far sharper ideological polarisation between Conservatives seeking to reorganise industry, control competition and reform capitalism and Labour intent upon paving the way to a classless 'Socialist Commonwealth'.[67] Moreover, even if it were true that differences between Conservative and socialist planners were 'mainly ... of degree, ideological overtone and language',[68] this conscious return to the language and rhetoric of 1918 mattered far more than is often appreciated, insofar as it was not only what Labour said about nationalisation and planning that was similar to 1918, but also its reasons for saying it. Just as Clause IV and the 'socialist' commitment had fulfilled a unifying 'umbrella function' in

1918, the reassertion of an ostensibly more detailed commitment to public ownership and planning in the 1930s served precisely the same role, by reaffirming a distinctive sense of common direction, identity and purpose after the disorientating traumas that had befallen them in 1931. The only difference was that while in 1918 vagueness was essential to unity, by the early 1930s the belief that this ambiguity was in itself a central cause of Labour's failure now prompted the deliberate pursuit of detail – even if this was confined to the compilation of a list of industries to be nationalised.

After 1934 Labour began its rightward drift under the influence of Bevin and Dalton. During the late 1930s inconvenient commitments acquired during the initial radical spasm were unobtrusively abandoned. This process was completed in a short policy statement entitled *Labour's Immediate Programme* in March 1937. Designed to outline 'four vital measures of reconstruction' for a majority Labour government in its first five-year term, the Bank of England, coal, power and transport were all identified for nationalisation, but the joint stock banks, cotton and iron and steel were all conspicuously absent as were any references to worker directors, emergency powers and Enabling Acts. The document also enshrined commitments to a non-Keynesian National Investment Board, State control of industrial location, a forty-hour week and paid holidays. In contrast, despite references to pensions, health reform and abolition of the hated Means Test, the low profile of social policy conformed with the dominant technocratic assumption that economic transformation should precede social amelioration. Although this was Labour's last major statement of policy before the war, and shortage of finance prevented the preparation of the detailed blueprints necessary to translate manifesto promises into legislative reality, the ideological recovery was complete. Left-wing notions about the crisis of capitalism and emergency powers had been replaced by a return to traditional assumptions that socialism would evolve gradually from a successful, if more efficient, capitalism. Yet at the same time, the old ethical imperatives underlying Labour's socialism before 1931 were replaced by a new structural approach which equated socialism with planning and public ownership and which emphasised control and efficiency over economic and productive relations.

9.7 Party politics and the 'impact of Hitler'

Although it is beyond the scope of this work to consider the foreign policy of the National Government, as Maurice Cowling has argued, the 'impact of Hitler' had a direct bearing upon party politics in the 1930s.

> In these years foreign policy became central not only because it was but because politicians could fit it into the political battle which had begun in the twenties ... In the late thirties, foreign policy was the form that party conflict took.

Thus, for Conservative appeasers, the perpetuation of a National Government became essential, not just to resist European fascism but also because they recognised that 'Hitler must be obstructed because Labour could not otherwise be resisted'.[69] Equally clearly, the 'impact of Hitler' implied a fundamental challenge to Labour's traditional philosophy and Gladstonian past. By the end of the decade, under the leadership of Bevin, Dalton and Attlee, Labour had jettisoned these sentimental attachments and moved towards a *Realpolitik* position which enabled it to join the Churchill Coalition in May 1940 on terms of equality with the stigma of 1931 permanently expunged. Yet this transition during the 1930s involved a far more painful and protracted process than anything which occurred in domestic policy because while the latter involved the exaltation of existing sacred cows, in foreign affairs they were expected to slaughter them.

Mussolini's invasion of Abyssinia precipitated the first major clash. Before the 1935 annual conference, the TUC statement supporting 'any action consistent with the principles and status of the League' prompted the resignation of Cripps from the NEC and Ponsonby as Leader in the Lords. When Lansbury echoed their criticisms, his actions conflicted not just with Bevin's policy preferences but also his priority upon majority decisions over personal conscience. At the Brighton conference in September 1935, Bevin's fierce personal attack upon Lansbury prompted his resignation as leader and represented the first step towards the defeat of the anti-militarist wing of the party, although it was not until 1937 that Dalton finally persuaded the PLP grudgingly to abstain rather than vote against the Defence Estimates. The Spanish Civil War exacerbated these intra-party tensions. Although for many on the left this was nothing less than a moral clash between good and evil, leadership concerns about electoral indifference and Catholic hostility to this radical crusade tended to dampen official enthusiasm for anything more than humanitarian gestures and a call for an end to the arms embargo. These tensions over foreign policy were further intensified after February 1933 by Communist proposals for a United Front with Labour and the unions against fascism. These overtures were easily rebuffed in 1933–4 when united action with the CPGB was deemed incompatible with Labour party membership and similar hostility greeted the Comintern's call for a Popular Front to unite all opponents of fascism in 1936. Thus, when the Socialist League issued its 'Unity Campaign' manifesto, signed jointly with the ILP and CPGB in January 1937, the NEC acted decisively. Confronted by a choice between expulsion and voluntary dissolution, the Socialist League chose the latter. Efforts to launch an all-party Popular Front of anti-appeasers the following year provoked an equally draconian response and where constituency parties did cooperate (as in Oxford) the threat of severe sanctions soon followed.[70] This process of managerial control culminated in the expulsion of Cripps in January 1939 after he attempted to relaunch the Popular Front by appealing directly to the rank-and-file in defiance of the NEC. When other notable left-wingers like Bevan, Strauss and Trevelyan launched a National Petition Campaign in support of Cripps they were also expelled, as much for their persistent dissent throughout the decade as for this specific act of defiance.[71]

The defeat of various plans for a United or Popular Front says less about Labour's attitudes towards fascism than its instinctive antipathy towards the

CPGB stretching back to the early 1920s. Yet Labour also saw few advantages and very real dangers in any cooperation with the Communist party – particularly given the failed experience of Popular Front in France and Spain and the beginning of the Moscow show trials in August 1936. Moreover, while Labour's first victory in the London County Council elections in 1934 suggested the advantages of moderation rather than alliance with communist extremism, in broader terms Labour was also rightly sceptical about the benefits likely to accrue from any alliance with anti-appeasement Conservatives and Liberals – particularly as Churchill was mistrusted as a maverick pariah while Eden, although more liberal and acceptable, was remarkably reluctant to appear disloyal to the Conservative party. For all these reasons, Labour's internal battles over foreign policy confirmed the trend away from the relaxed intra-party pluralism which prevailed before 1918 towards a very different managerial orthodoxy of unity, obedience and central control, deeply rooted in a trade union tradition of solidarity, disciplined collective action and unquestioning loyalty to class, movement and majority decisions. For men like Ernest Bevin, the claims of the ILP, Lansbury and Cripps to independent freedom of conscience and action were a treacherous affront to the entire ethos of the movement and the common class experience from which it had grown. This unbridgeable gulf between these two views of intra-party democracy came to a head at the 1939 party conference. Cripps defended his actions over the Popular Front memorandum with the principled argument that it was 'the vigour and struggle of contending views that preserves the warmth of life within a democracy'. Replying for the NEC, Dalton declared that 'without some measure of healthy discipline and the submission of the individual to the collective will, there can be no democracy, but only egotism and anarchy'.[72] The triumph of such a view was the direct product of the experience of 1929–31. The consolidation of this new 'managerial regime' during the 1930s represented a watershed in Labour's organisational transition from adolescence to maturity almost as significant as its acceptance of rearmament and the need to resist fascism with force. Nevertheless, when war finally came in September 1939 a united party was able to accept the need for intervention with very little difficulty and it benefited substantially from that fact.

9.8 The failure of political extremism in the 1930s

During the 1930s the British political system was not immune to the sort of extremist challenge which rapidly gained ground throughout much of Europe. The combination of paralysing economic crisis and mass unemployment appeared ostensibly to offer fertile ground in which extremism could flourish. Certainly this was the expectation on both political fringes at the time. The British Communist party thus rejoiced at the 'final crisis of capitalism', while Oswald Mosley proclaimed that only fascism could save capitalism and the middle class from collapse and communist takeover. Yet in reality, such hopes were always illusory. Membership of Mosley's British Union of Fascists never exceeded 40–50,000 at its peak in July 1934 and some authorities put the figure much lower.[73] Despite a well-established tradition of working class anti-Semitism in London's East End, elsewhere the BUF made few real inroads into the ranks of the working class, trade unions or the unemployed and gained most support among the lower middle class and *petit bourgeoisie*.[74] In contrast, the Communist party only achieved a membership of around 9,000 in January 1932 and even this had fallen to 5,600 by November. Ironically, mass unemployment did not rally the working class to Communism. Although in a few isolated mining communities 'Little Moscows' did flourish, it has been calculated that only 3,140 unemployed actually joined the CPGB during the 1930s from the several millions who experienced unemployment.[75] Communist front organisations fared little better in exploiting the issue. Although the National Unemployed Workers' Movement (NUWM, established 1921) was most successful, it failed to become a mass movement as the Comintern planned and despite three million unemployed, its maximum paid-up membership was only 50,000 at the depth of the depression in 1932 and this fell away sharply as the economy recovered.[76] Only after 1936, with Communist leadership against fascism in Spain, did the CPGB experience a dramatic rise in recruitment among young middle class intellectuals. From 7,700 in 1935, CPGB membership rose to almost 18,000 on the eve of war before peaking at 56,000 in 1942.

By any standard, such statistics suggest that the most striking fact about the 1930s was not the challenge posed to the party system by extremism as despairing voters defected wholesale into revolutionary mass movements, but rather the immobility of the electorate and the robust stability of established party allegiances. The explanation for this remarkable phenomenon is complex and multi-faceted.[77] Economic factors undoubtedly played a crucial part. Although the scale of unemployment was no less severe than in Germany, the British experience of the Great Depression was significantly different in several key respects. Unlike Germany, unemployment in Britain had been a persistent feature of the decade after 1921; the Great Depression simply represented an intensification of an existing trend. It was also confined to specific regions and industries, particularly the old staple trades of coal, cotton, shipbuilding and iron and steel. Often this meant the geographical isolation of the long-term unemployed, hidden away in closed communities like pit villages or towns like Jarrow, where the prevalence of unemployment as a uniform way of life engendered an apathy and fatalism which ensured that its victims were depoliticised rather than radicalised by the experience. In a variety of ways, the 'dole' also acted as an agent of social control. First, although scarcely above subsistence level, it did at least prevent the unemployed from becoming a separate class with interests distinct from the rest of the working class and thus more receptive to new parties offering revolutionary solutions. Secondly, as the administration of unemployment assistance became a primary focus for political activity in its own right, this deflected attention away from more fundamental questions about the deficiencies of capitalism. Even the NUWM found itself increasingly drawn into day-to-day casework on behalf of the unemployed at the expense of the longer-term revolutionary objectives dictated by the CPGB and the Comintern.[78] Finally, the fact that throughout the worst of the depression the dole and the Means Test were administered as humanely as possible by Public Assistance Committees, composed of working class community leaders, exerted a powerful degree of social control upon the unemployed and reinforced their established party affiliations.

Some historians also emphasise the impact of political culture in reducing the scope for extremism. Although both communism and fascism were perhaps handicapped by being alien creeds and profoundly 'un-English', such arguments have more explanatory value with regard to public repugnance towards the political violence with which these movements were associated. This was particularly damaging to the BUF after the Olympia meeting in June 1934 when the shift from the 'respectable' to the 'disreputable' violence of the anti-Semitic phase of BUF strategy imposed a heavy cost upon its support-base.[79] Yet ultimately, the most important constraint imposed by the political culture upon extremist movements was its profound attachment to established class-based parties. Unlike those states in which extremism flourished, economic crisis did not undermine the credibility and authority of British democracy or its party system. On the contrary, the existence of a truly 'National' Government, endorsed by a massive vote from almost all sections of the community, obviated the need for the middle class to embrace fascism as an effective bulwark against economic disaster and communist takeover. Similarly, despite the trauma of 1931, Labour remained indisputably the party of the working class (whether in employment or out of it), while its uncompromising commitment to parliamentary democracy was matched only by its hostility to any prospect of cooperation with communists. Despite superficial appearances to the contrary, therefore, there simply was no real opportunity for revolutionary extremism to flourish in Britain during the 1930s.

9.9 Electoral competition and the onset of war

For most of the 1930s the National Government faced few real challenges. Fascists and communists were easily contained, Labour had been decimated and the Liberals had ceased to count for anything. If there was an enemy on the horizon it was likely to be the passage of time. Certainly the trend after 1931 appeared to suggest a gradual subterranean shift in support away from the National Government which culminated in a string of severe by-election defeats between East Fulham in October 1933 and West Toxteth in July 1935. Although partially a consequence of the Samuelite defection which deprived the government of at least some Liberal votes, this adverse trend was undoubtedly exacerbated by the use of by-elections to register 'protest votes' over specific government policies, such as at Liverpool Wavertree in February 1935 where the intervention of Churchill's son in opposition to official policy on India handed the seat to Labour. Whatever the cause of the electoral slump in 1934–5, however, the effect was to create a state of near-panic in Conservative ranks. By the same token, Labour optimism rose as the pendulum began to swing in its direction. Between 1931 and 1935 Labour made ten gains (nine from the National Government) and achieved large swings in other classical Conservative seats. Its apparent revival was even more impressive at municipal level. Yet in reality, Labour's electoral recovery was less robust than it appeared and was certainly well below the 20 per cent swing needed to win a bare majority at the next election.[80] As a result, against a background of economic recovery and solid government performance, the outcome of the 1935 general election was a foregone conclusion – particularly as the loss of Wavertree to Labour in February because of Churchillian intervention had a chastening effect upon rebellious Tory voters who were more anxious to prevent a Labour government than to register a protest vote about India or anything else. The inevitable result was the return of a National Government with 53.3 per cent of the vote and a smaller but still overwhelming majority. In contrast, Labour obtained 38 per cent of the vote but won only 154 seats. Although among their number were twenty-four returning former ministers to strengthen the front bench, the depressing reality was that even in its traditional heartlands Labour had still not regained all of the ground lost in 1931.[81]

Ironically, although the National Government lost more by-elections after 1935 than before it, these defeats never had the same impact – not least because the average swing was a mere 3.9 per cent, compared with the 15.8 per cent in the early 1930s. Moreover, although the government lost Bridgwater and almost lost Oxford to Independent anti-Munich candidates in October–November 1938 in the immediate aftermath of Chamberlain's return from his meetings with Hitler, the unpopularity of appeasement should not be exaggerated. In the three conventional party contests at the same time as Oxford and Bridgwater, the swing against the government was far more modest and in only three of its thirteen defeats between 1935 and 1939 was the swing sufficient to provide Labour with an overall majority. As an issue, therefore, appeasement may have increased interest and turnout on both sides, but there is little reason to suppose that foreign policy would have automatically lost the election for Chamberlain – particular as the swing against the government actually decreased slightly after Hitler's invasion of Prague in March 1939 compared with the period around Munich.[82] Even more remarkable were the findings of the ten Gallup polls during the last year of peace, which showed an average of 58 per cent satisfied with the Prime Minister's performance compared with 42 per cent who were critical.[83] While the National Government is unlikely to have won an overwhelming majority in 1940, therefore, there is little evidence to suggest that Labour would have displaced it completely.

Nor did the British declaration of war on 3 September 1939 immediately transform the party or electoral situation. Although Labour accepted an electoral truce on 8 September, it declined to join any government in which Chamberlain and Simon remained prominent members. 'Constructive opposition' thus enabled it to appear patriotic while leaving it free to criticise the government where necessary. As Dalton noted, the intention was for Labour to exercise what he called 'influence from without', while leaving Chamberlain with direct responsibility for a situation which many believed would destroy him.[84] On the other side, Chamberlain was equally glad that Labour had refused to join the government. Anticipating that a limited war of conquest in Poland would soon peter out, he may even have expected that another approach from Hitler would enable him to win a general election as the restorer of peace.[85] Although this proved to be a disastrous gamble, by the end of 1939 Chamberlain's stock had risen to a new peak of popularity in the opinion polls and the government still retained a narrow lead.[86]

The final crisis of the Chamberlain government arrived swiftly in May 1940. On 4 April the Prime Minister complacently assured the Conservative Central Committee that Hitler had 'missed the bus'. Four days later German troops invaded Denmark and Norway, leading the *Manchester Guardian* to lament that Chamberlain's 'capacity for self-delusion is a national danger'.[87] Yet although the ignominious withdrawal of British forces from the ill-conceived Norwegian campaign fuelled backbench discontents, there was little inevitable about Chamberlain's defeat. Ironically, like his own half-brother's loss of the Conservative leadership eighteen years earlier, with more sensitive handling and judicious promises of reform the crisis may have been delayed, if not entirely averted.[88] With his Conservative critics divided and leaderless since Churchill and Eden had joined the government in September 1939, Chamberlain was relatively sanguine – particularly as Churchill was heavily implicated in the Norwegian military fiasco. The Norway debate on 7–8 May 1940 is famous for the appearance of Admiral Sir Roger Keyes in full dress uniform denouncing the government and Amery's Cromwellian injunction to 'Depart, I say, and let us have done with you. In the name of God, go.'[89] Yet Chamberlain's fate was sealed largely by the PLP's last minute decision to divide the House (despite front bench fears of rallying Conservatives behind their leader), and by the Prime Minister's ill-judged efforts to turn this into a personal vote of confidence in his war leadership. Although the vote on 8 May gave Chamberlain a numerical victory of 281 votes to 200, the massive fall from its usual majority of well over 200 was a devastating slap in the face. The simmering but fragmented backbench discontents over foreign policy which had been suppressed in peacetime, bubbled to the surface under the pressure of war in a more cohesive form.[90] Despite strong pressure from the whips, some forty government backbenchers voted against Chamberlain and between thirty-six and forty-three attended the debate but abstained.[91] Despite last minute efforts to obtain the support of Labour in a reconstituted ministry, their refusal to serve under Chamberlain compelled him to resign. The decision of Halifax to exclude himself from the succession, and Labour's decisive support for Churchill, sealed the question of war leadership.

Churchill's emergence as Prime Minister in May 1940 represented the true end of the interwar era and a major watershed in the history of British politics. The scars left by Chamberlain's dismissal created lingering resentments among querulous Tory backbenchers which continued to fester and to debilitate effectiveness and morale long after the initial trauma of May 1940 had passed. In contrast, Labour did well out of the May crisis. When judged in terms of their initial share in office, there was no sudden shift in power. Despite receiving two of the five seats in the War Cabinet, Labour received less than a third of all government posts. Yet as Attlee told the annual conference sitting at Bournemouth in May 1940, the entire party was joining the Coalition 'as partners and not as hostages'.[92] By 1943, Labour dominated the Home Front, with Attlee, Bevin and Morrison in the War Cabinet and Dalton, Johnston and Jowitt playing key roles in reconstruction planning. Participation in the wartime Coalition restored the respect and credibility Labour had so dramatically forfeited in August 1931 and which it had fought so hard but so vainly to retrieve over the next decade. As Labour's deputy leader reassured party delegates at Bournemouth, 'when we have played our part fully, we shall have won in this country an even greater respect than we have today. We shall have greater power than we have today.'[93] Although at times participation in the wartime Coalition imposed a high cost upon Labour cohesion and unity, this proved to be a remarkably prescient judgement. The experience of Total War fundamentally transformed electoral attitudes and expectations and, in so doing, it radically enhanced the standing and popularity of Labour and its brand of socialism.[94] In the immediate aftermath of victory in Europe, Labour's landslide election victory in July 1945 ushered into power a confident and restored party intent upon building the promised 'Socialist Commonwealth' on the ruins of an old and discredited social order.

Notes and references

The place of publication is London unless otherwise stated.
1 Bentley B. Gilbert, *British Social Policy 1914–1939* (1970), p. 163.
2 Robert Skidelsky, *Politicians and the Slump: The Labour Government of 1929–1931* (1967), pp. 426, 433–4.
3 Ross McKibbin, 'The economic policy of the second Labour Government, 1929–1931', *Past and Present* 86 (1975), pp. 95–123. See also Peter Gourevitch, *Politics in Hard Times: Comparative Responses to Economic Crises* (Ithaca, 1986), ch. 2.
4 Jim Tomlinson, *Problems of British Economic Policy, 1870–1945* (1981), p. 88.
5 D.H. Close, 'The realignment of the British electorate in 1931', *History* 67 (1982), p. 395.
6 Stuart Ball, 'Failure of an opposition? The Conservative Party in Parliament, 1929–1931', *Parliamentary History* 5 (1986), pp. 83–98 and *Baldwin and the Conservative Party: The Crisis of 1929–31* (New Haven and London, 1988); Andrew Thorpe, *The British General Election of 1931* (Oxford, 1991), ch. 2.
7 John Ramsden, *The Age of Balfour and Baldwin, 1902–1940* (1978), p. 298.
8 Robert C. Self, *Tories and Tariffs: The Conservative Party and the Politics of Tariff Reform, 1922–1932* (New York and London, 1986), chs 7–8.
9 Gillian Peele, 'St George's and the Empire Crusade', in Chris Cook and John Ramsden, *By-Elections in British Politics* (1973), pp. 79–108.

10 Self, *Tories and Tariffs*, p. 582.

11 Thorpe, *The British General Election of 1931*, ch. 3.

12 For the development of the crisis see: ibid., ch. 4; Ball, *Baldwin and the Conservative Party*, ch. 9; Skidelsky, *Politicians and the Slump*, ch. 13; Philip Williamson, *National Crisis and National Government: British Politics, the Economy and the Empire, 1926–1932* (Cambridge, 1992).

13 R. Dare, 'British Labour, the National Government and the "National Interest": 1931', *Historical Journal* 18 (1978–9), pp. 345–64.

14 David Marquand, *Ramsay MacDonald* (1977), p. 663.

15 MacDonald to Lord Parmoor, 29 August 1931, MacDonald MSS 30/9/5/180 Public Record Office; Reginald Bassett, *Nineteen Thirty-One: Political Crisis* (1958), p. 347.

16 L.C.B. Seaman, *Post-Victorian Britain, 1902–1951* (1966), p. 233. The principal advocate of this view is J.D. Fair, 'The Conservative basis for the formation of the National Government of 1931', *Journal of British Studies* 19 (1980), pp. 142–64.

17 J.D. Wrench, '"Cashing in": the parties and the National Government, August 1931–September 1932', *Journal of British Studies* 23 (1984); Stuart Ball, 'The Conservative Party and the formation of the National Government, August 1931', *Historical Journal* 29 (1986), pp. 159–82 and *Baldwin and the Conservative Party*, pp. 151–97. Also Andrew Thorpe, *Britain in the 1930s: The Deceptive Decade* (Oxford, 1992), p. 10.

18 'The First National Government', memorandum by Samuel Hoare, n.d. Templewood MSS VII.I (Cambridge University Library); Neville Chamberlain to Hilda Chamberlain, 16 August 1931, Neville Chamberlain MSS NC18/1/752 (Birmingham University Library).

19 Chamberlain to H.A. Gwynne, 13 August 1931, Gwynne MSS Box 17 (Bodleian Library, Oxford); Neville Chamberlain to Hilda Chamberlain, 16 August 1931, NC18/1/752. For this strategy see Self, *Tories and Tariffs*, pp. 597–600.

20 Close, 'The realignment of the British electorate', p. 397; Michael Kinnear, *The British Voter: An Atlas and Survey since 1885* 2nd edn (1981), pp. 50–1; Keith Laybourn, *The Rise of Labour 1890–1979* (1988), pp. 88–91. But see John Stevenson and Chris Cook, *The Slump: Society and Politics During the Depression* (1977), pp. 107–12.

21 Tom Stannage, *Baldwin Thwarts the Opposition: The British General Election of 1935* (1980), pp. 62–3.

22 Bassett, *Political Crisis*, p. xi.

23 Dennis Kavanagh, 'Crisis management and incremental adaptation in British politics: the 1931 crisis of the British party system', in G.A. Almond *et al.*, eds, *Crisis, Choice and Change: Historical Studies of Political Development* (Boston, 1973), pp. 153–4.

24 Ball, *Baldwin and the Conservative Party*, pp. 197–8. Also Brendan Evans and Andrew Taylor, *From Salisbury to Major: Continuity and Change in Conservative Politics* (Manchester, 1996), p. 50.

25 C.R. Attlee, *The Labour Party in Perspective* (1937), p. 58; Ramsay Muir, *The Record of National Government* (1936), p. 49; Philip Snowden, *Autobiography* 2 vols (1934), II, pp. 919, 1029–30; Mary Agnes Hamilton, *Arthur Henderson: A Biography* (1938), p. 392; Viscount Samuel, *Memoirs* (1945), p. 209.

26 See, for example, Ivor Bulmer-Thomas, *The Growth of the British Party System* 2 vols (1965), II, p. 68; Martin Pugh, *The Making of Modern British Politics 1867–1939* 2nd edn (1993), p. 273; Bruce P. Lenman, *The Eclipse of Parliament:*

Appearance and Reality in British Politics since 1914 (1992), p. 139; Seaman, *Post-Victorian Britain*, p. 221; C.L. Mowat, *Britain Between the Wars 1918–1940* (1956), p. 399; Roy Douglas, *The History of the Liberal Party, 1895–1970* (1971), pp. 233–4; Trevor Wilson, *The Downfall of the Liberal Party, 1914–1935* (1966), pp. 380–1.

27 Self, *Tories and Tariffs*, pp. 608–13, 648–50, 662–6, 708–13.

28 Seaman, *Post-Victorian Britain*, p. 221.

29 Ramsden, *The Age of Balfour and Baldwin*, pp. 325–6; Stannage, *Baldwin Thwarts the Opposition*, pp. 12–13; Williamson, *National Crisis*, pp. 484–7.

30 Marquand, *Ramsay MacDonald*, p. 677.

31 Nigel Nicolson, ed., *Harold Nicolson Diaries and Letters, 1930–39* (1966), p. 246. Entry for 24 February 1936.

32 Sir John Simon to Walter Runciman, 21 September 1932, Runciman MSS 254 (Newcastle University Library). See also Graham D. Goodlad, 'The Liberal Nationals, 1931–1940: the problems of a party in "partnership government"', *Historical Journal* 38 (1995), pp. 137–8.

33 Goodlad, 'The Liberal Nationals', pp. 138–43; David Dutton, 'John Simon and the post-war National Liberal party: a historical postscript', *Historical Journal* 32 (1989), p. 357.

34 Stannage, *Baldwin Thwarts the Opposition*, pp. 13, 24, 47; G.R. Searle, *Country Before Party: Coalition and the Idea of 'National Government' in Modern Britain, 1885–1987* (1995), p. 183.

35 Stannage, *Baldwin Thwarts the Opposition*, pp. 40–1; Ramsden, *The Age of Balfour and Baldwin*, p. 336.

36 Evans and Taylor, *From Salisbury to Major*, pp. 51–2. Stannage, *Baldwin Thwarts the Opposition*, p. 46.

37 Ramsden, *The Age of Balfour and Baldwin*, pp. 326–7; Nick Smart, *The National Government 1931–40* (1999), pp. 59–62.

38 Stannage, *Baldwin Thwarts the Opposition*, pp. 42–3.

39 Keith Middlemas and John Barnes, *Baldwin: A Biography* (1969), pp. 584–5, 698.

40 Ben Pimlott, *Labour and the Left in the 1930s* (Cambridge, 1977), p. 147; Harold Macmillan, *Winds of Change, 1914–39* (1966), p. 487.

41 Lord Butler, *The Art of the Possible* (1971), p. 30.

42 Stannage, *Baldwin Thwarts the Opposition*, ch. 3; Smart, *The National Government*, pp. 90–2, 104–13; Michael Freeden, *Liberalism Divided: A Study in British Political Thought, 1914–1939* (Oxford, 1986), p. 350.

43 Stannage, *Baldwin Thwarts the Opposition*, pp. 94–5.

44 Self, *Tories and Tariffs*, pp. 691, 728, 751–3.

45 Malcolm Baines, 'The survival of the British Liberal party, 1933–59', in Anthony Gorst, Lewis Johnman and W. Scott Lucas, eds, *Contemporary British History 1931–1961* (1991), pp. 19–20.

46 Chris Cook, 'Liberals, Labour and local elections', in Gillian Peele and Chris Cook, eds, *The Politics of Reappraisal, 1918–1939* (1975), pp. 178–87; Baines, 'Survival', pp. 19–21.

47 Margaret Cole, ed., *Beatrice Webb's Diaries* 2 vols (1952 and 1956), II, p. 65. Entry for 22 June 1925; Sidney Webb, 'What happened in 1931: a record', *Political Quarterly* (January–March 1932), pp. 1–17.

48 Henry Pelling, *A Short History of the Labour Party* 8th edn (1985), p. 77; Stannage, *Baldwin Thwarts the Opposition*, p. 171.

49 Ben Pimlott, ed., *The Political Diary of Hugh Dalton, 1918–40, 1945–60* (1986),

p. 169, entry for 8 October 1932; C.R. Attlee, *The Labour Party in Perspective* (1937), p. 136. Also W. Golant, 'The emergence of C.R. Attlee as leader of the Parliamentary Labour Party in 1935', *Historical Journal* 13 (1970), pp. 318–32.

50 Pugh, *The Making of Modern British Politics*, p. 278.

51 Pelling, *Short History*, p. 71.

52 J.H. Brookshire, 'The National Council of Labour, 1921–1940', *Albion* 18 (1986), pp. 43–69.

53 Stannage, *Baldwin Thwarts the Opposition*, p. 64.

54 Robert E. Dowse, *Left in the Centre: The Independent Labour Party, 1893–1940* (Evanston, 1966), pp. 185, 198–200.

55 Eric Shaw, *Discipline and Discord in the Labour Party: The Politics of Managerial Control in the Labour Party, 1951–87* (Manchester, 1988), pp. 4–19.

56 Pimlott, *Labour and the Left*, pp. 118–24, 134–40.

57 Compare Ralph Miliband, *Parliamentary Socialism: A Study in the Politics of Labour* (1961), p. 193 with R. Eatwell and A. Wright, 'Labour and the lessons of 1931', *History* 63 (1978), p. 40.

58 Stafford Cripps, *Can Socialism Come by Parliamentary Methods?* (1934), p. 4; Harold Laski, *The State in Theory and Practice* (1935).

59 Kenneth Morgan, *Labour in Power, 1945–51* (Oxford, 1984), pp. 94–9; Emanuel Shinwell, *I've Lived Through it All* (1973), p. 192.

60 Labour Party, *For Socialism and Peace* (1934), pp. 12, 15, 20.

61 Adrian Oldfield, 'The Labour Party and planning – 1931, or 1918?' *Bulletin of the Society of Labour History* 25 (1972), pp. 41–55.

62 See Elizabeth Durbin, *New Jerusalems: The Labour Party and the Economics of Democratic Socialism* (1985); Noel Thompson, *Political Economy and the Labour Party* (1996), ch. 10; D.I. MacKay, I. Forsyth and D.M. Kelly, 'The discussion of public works programmes, 1917–35: some remarks on the Labour movement's contribution', *International Review of Social History* 11 (1961), pp. 8–17.

63 Stephen Brooke, *Labour's War: The Labour Party During the Second World War* (Oxford, 1992), pp. 245–66.

64 Barbara C. Malamet, 'British Labour and Roosevelt's New Deal: the response of the Left and the unions', *Journal of British Studies* 17 (1978), pp. 85–123.

65 Neville Chamberlain to P. Snowden, 15 January 1932, NC7/11/25/41. See also Self, *Tories and Tariffs*, pp. 775–81 for a broader discussion of this theme. For the 'managed economy' in the 1930s see S.H. Beer, *Modern British Politics: A Study of Parties and Pressure Groups* (1965), ch. 10. For a broader discussion see A. Booth, 'Britain in the 1930s: a managed economy?' *Economic History Review* 40 (1987), pp. 499–522.

66 Arthur Marwick, 'Middle opinion in the thirties: planning, progress and political "agreement" ', *English Historical Review* 64 (1964), pp. 285–98.

67 D. Ritschel, *The Politics of Planning: The Debate on Economic Planning in the 1930s* (Oxford, 1997); Freeden, *Liberalism Divided*, pp. 356–62.

68 Donald Winch, *Economics and Policy: A Historical Survey* (Fontana edn, 1972), p. 225.

69 Maurice Cowling, *The Impact of Hitler: British Politics and British Policy 1933–1940* (Cambridge, 1977), pp. 1, 5, 9.

70 Iain McLean, 'Oxford and Bridgwater', in Cook and Ramsden, *By-Elections in British Politics*, p. 145.

71 Shaw, *Discipline and Discord*, p. 26.

72 Ibid., pp. 27–8.

73 G.C. Webber, *The Ideology of the British Right 1918–1938* (1986), pp. 43–5; and 'Patterns of membership and support for the British Union of Fascists', *Journal of Contemporary History* 19 (1984), pp. 575–606; Robert Skidelsky, *Oswald Mosley* (1975), p. 332.

74 Stuart Rawnsley, 'The membership of the British Union of Fascists', in Kenneth Lunn and Richard Thurlow, *British Fascism* (1980), pp. 150–66; J.D. Brewer, *Mosley's Men: The British Union of Fascists in the West Midlands* (Aldershot, 1984), pp. 28–44.

75 K. Newton, *The Sociology of British Communism* (1969), p. 34.

76 H. Harmer, 'The failure of the Communists, the National Unemployed Workers' Movement, 1921–1939: a disappointing success', in Andrew Thorpe, ed., *The Failure of Political Extremism in Inter-War Britain* (Exeter, 1989), pp. 29–47.

77 For an excellent discussion see Stevenson and Cook, *The Slump*, ch. XIV.

78 Harmer, 'The failure of the Communists', pp. 46–7; Henry Pelling, *The British Communist Party: A Historical Profile* (1958), p. 64.

79 Skidelsky, *Oswald Mosley*, pp. 322–3; Richard Thurlow, *Fascism in Britain: A History, 1918–1985* (Oxford, 1987), pp. 104–11. The short-term effects were not all negative, however; see Martin Pugh, 'The British Union of Fascists and the Olympia debate', *Historical Journal* 41 (1998), pp. 529–42.

80 Thorpe, *The British General Election of 1931*, pp. 270–1.

81 Close, 'The realignment of the British electorate', pp. 400–4; Stannage, *Baldwin Thwarts the Opposition*, pp. 234–6.

82 McLean, 'Oxford and Bridgwater', pp. 154–5, 159–62.

83 Steven Fielding, Peter Thompson and Nick Tiratsoo, *'England Arise!': The Labour Party and Popular Politics in 1940s Britain* (Manchester, 1995), p. 14.

84 Pimlott, *The Political Diary of Hugh Dalton*, p. 297. Entry for 6 September 1939. See also Brooke, *Labour's War*, pp. 37–9; Kevin Jeffreys, *The Churchill Coalition and Wartime Politics, 1940–45* (Manchester, 1991), pp. 64–6.

85 Paul Addison, *The Road to 1945: British Politics and the Second World War* (Quartet edn, 1977), p. 63.

86 Jeffreys, *The Churchill Coalition*, p. 18; Brooke, *Labour's War*, p. 29.

87 Arthur Marwick, *Britain in the Century of Total War: War, Peace and Social Change 1900–1967* (1968), p. 272.

88 Jeffreys, *The Churchill Coalition*, p. 28.

89 For the parliamentary debate see Addison, *The Road to 1945*, pp. 94–8.

90 See Nick Crowson, 'Conservative parliamentary dissent over foreign policy during the premiership of Neville Chamberlain: myth or reality?', *Parliamentary History* 14 (1995), pp. 315–36 and *Facing Fascism: The Conservative Party and the European Dictators, 1935–40* (1997). Also Neville Thompson, *The Anti-Appeasers: Conservative Opposition to Appeasement in the 1930s* (Oxford, 1971), ch. 13; Jorgen S. Rasmussen, 'Government and intra-party opposition: dissent within the Conservative Parliamentary Party in the 1930s', *Political Studies* 19 (1971), pp. 172–83.

91 Jorgen S. Rasmussen, 'Party discipline in wartime: the downfall of the Chamberlain government', *Journal of Politics* 32 (1970), pp. 379–406; Kevin Jeffreys, 'May 1940: the downfall of Neville Chamberlain', *Parliamentary History* 10 (1991), pp. 363–78; Nick Smart, 'Four days in May: the Norway debate and the downfall of Neville Chamberlain', *Parliamentary History* 17 (1998).

92 Kenneth Harris, *Attlee* (1982), p. 178.

93 Brooke, *Labour's War*, p. 53.

94 Addison, *The Road to 1945*, pp. 126–7.

Select bibliography

Throughout this volume the Notes and References supporting the text have been designed to direct the reader to further detailed specialist sources for each of the issues discussed. The purpose of this brief note is thus not to repeat this information, but to provide some guidance about key readings on specific themes. The place of publication is London unless otherwise specified.

General background histories

For the broader background to this period, an excellent introduction can be found in John Davis, *A History of Britain, 1885–1939* (1999) and Martin Pugh, *The Making of Modern British Politics, 1867–1939* 2nd edn (Oxford, 1993). Other useful works covering the early part of the period are Michael Bentley, *Politics Without Democracy, 1815–1914: Perception and Preoccupation in British Government* (1985), E.J Feuchtwanger, *Democracy and Empire: Britain, 1865–1914* (1985) and Richard Shannon, *The Crisis of Imperialism, 1865–1915* (1976). For the later period, despite its considerable age, there is still much information and interest in C.L. Mowat, *Britain Between the Wars, 1918–1940* (1956). Also Max Beloff, *Wars and Welfare, 1914–1945* (1984).

The electoral system

A useful brief introduction to these developments can be found in H.J. Hanham, *The Reformed Electoral System in Great Britain, 1832–1918* (1968) and Martin Pugh, *The Evolution of the British Electoral System, 1832–1987* (1988). More detail is to be found in Charles Seymour, *Electoral Reform in England and Wales 1832–1885* (New Haven and Oxford, 1915) and David Butler, *The Electoral System in Britain 1918–1951* (Oxford, 1953). Another work on this subject scheduled for late 2000 is Ian Machin, *The Rise of Democracy in Britain, 1830–1918* (forthcoming).

Party development and management

The classical works on nineteenth century development are Norman Gash, *Politics in the Age of Peel* 2nd edn (Hassocks, 1977) and H.J. Hanham, *Elections and Party Management: Politics in the Time of Disraeli and Gladstone*

2nd edn (Hassocks, 1978). For the development of Labour organisation during its critical formative period see Ross McKibbin, *The Evolution of the Labour Party 1910–1924* (Oxford, 1974) while John Ramsden, *The Age of Balfour and Baldwin 1902–1940* (1978) is particularly strong on Conservative organisation. There are also impressive accounts of central, regional and local organisation by Stuart Ball in Anthony Seldon and Stuart Ball, eds, *Conservative Century: The Conservative Party since 1900* (Oxford, 1994). Neal R. McCrillis, *The British Conservative Party in the Age of Universal Suffrage: Popular Conservatism, 1918–1929* (Columbus, Ohio, 1998) is very useful on Conservative women's, youth and labour organisation.

Elections and electoral behaviour

A useful introduction to the study of elections during this period is Michael Kinnear, *The British Voter: An Atlas and Survey since 1885* 2nd edn (1981). On specific elections see Trevor Lloyd, *The General Election of 1880* (1968), A.K. Russell, *Liberal Landslide: The General Election of 1906* (Newton Abbot, 1973), Neal Blewett, *The Peers, the Parties and the People: The General Elections of 1910* (1972), John Turner, *British Politics and the Great War: Coalition and Conflict, 1915–18* (New Haven, 1992), Michael Kinnear, *The Fall of Lloyd George: The Political Crisis of 1922* (1973), Chris Cook, *The Age of Alignment: Electoral Politics in Britain, 1922–1929* (1975), Andrew Thorpe, *The British General Election of 1931* (Oxford, 1991) and Tom Stannage, *Baldwin Thwarts the Opposition: The British General Election of 1935* (1980). For by-elections see Chris Cook and John Ramsden, eds, *By-Elections in British Politics* (1973).

For a valuable collection on electoral behaviour see Jon Lawrence and Miles Taylor, eds, *Party, State and Society: Electoral Behaviour in Britain since 1820* (Aldershot, 1997). Also useful are Henry Pelling, *Social Geography of British Elections, 1885–1910* (1967), William L. Miller, *Electoral Dynamics in Britain since 1918* (1977) and Kenneth D. Wald, *Crosses on the Ballot: Patterns of British Voter Alignment since 1885* (Princeton, New Jersey, 1983). Among the many illuminating articles on this subject see Peter Clarke, 'Electoral sociology of modern Britain', *History* 57 (1972), J.P.D. Dunbabin, 'Parliamentary elections in Great Britain 1868–1900', *English Historical Review* 61 (1966) and 'British elections in the nineteenth and twentieth centuries: a regional approach', *English Historical Review* 95 (1980) and D.H. Close 'The realignment of the British electorate in 1931', *History* 76 (1982).

Party histories: the Conservatives

There is an abundance of excellent volumes detailing the histories of each of the individual parties during this period. A useful brief introduction to the Conservative party is provided by Stuart Ball, *The Conservative Party and British Politics, 1902–1951* (1995) and a fuller account is to be found in Brendan Evans and Andrew Taylor, *From Salisbury to Major: Continuities and Change in Conservative Politics* (Manchester, 1996) and John Charmley, *A*

History of Conservative Politics, 1900–1996. Indispensable detailed accounts are provided in Richard Shannon, *The Age of Salisbury, 1881–1902: Unionism and Empire* (1996) and John Ramsden, *The Age of Balfour and Baldwin, 1902–1940* (1978). Anthony Seldon and Stuart Ball, eds, *Conservative Century: The Conservative Party since 1900* (Oxford, 1994) also contains much of value on this period.

The Labour party

Although the standard 'short history' has for many years been Henry Pelling, *A Short History of the British Labour Party* (1st edn 1961, 11th edn 1996), a much more recent study which incorporates a large body of specialist work is Andrew Thorpe, *A History of the British Labour Party* (1997). On the early period of Labour development, Henry Pelling, *The Origins of the Labour Party 1880–1900* (Oxford, 1965) is still very useful. Among the various parties involved in Labour's formation see D. Howell, *British Workers and the Independent Labour Party, 1888–1906* (Manchester, 1983), Michael Crick, *The History of the Social Democratic Federation* (Keele, 1994) and A.M. McBriar, *Fabian Socialism and English Politics, 1884–1918* (Cambridge, 1962).

The Liberal party

Chris Cook, *A Short History of the Liberal Party 1900–1992* (1993) is the classic 'short history' for the twentieth century, but there is much of value in Alan Sykes, *The Rise and Fall of British Liberalism, 1776–1988* (1997), Roy Douglas, *History of the Liberal Party 1895–1970* (1971), G.R. Searle, *The Liberal Party: Triumph and Disintegration, 1886–1929* (1992) and Michael Bentley, *The Climax of Liberal Politics: British Liberalism in Theory and Practice, 1868–1918* (1987). Although each of these volumes is particularly strong on the earlier period, for the war and interwar years Trevor Wilson, *The Downfall of the Liberal Party, 1914–1935* (1966) remains a classic and is usefully complemented by Chris Cook, *The Age of Alignment: Electoral Politics in Britain 1922–1929* (1975).

Extremist parties

For a very useful collection on the parties of the political extremes see Andrew Thorpe, ed., *The Failure of Political Extremism in Interwar Britain* (Exeter, 1988). For the British Union of Fascists and its antecedents see Richard Thurlow, *Fascism in Britain: A History, 1918–1985* (Oxford, 1987) and the collection of essays in K. Lunn and R.C. Thurlow, eds, *British Fascism* (1980). For the far left see John Callaghan, *The Far Left in British Politics* (Oxford, 1987), Stuart Macintyre, *A Proletarian Science: Marxism in Britain 1917–33* (Cambridge, 1980), and R. Challinor, *The Origins of British Bolshevism* (1977). On the Communist party see Henry Pelling, *The British Communist*

Party: A Historical Profile (1958) and L.J. Macfarlane, *The British Communist Party: Its Origins and Development until 1929* (1966).

Coalition and 'National Government'

As a reminder that single-party majority government is less of a norm than is often assumed, see the excellent account in G.R. Searle, *Country Before Party: Coalition and the Idea of 'National Government' in Modern Britain, 1885–1989* (1995) and Brian Harrison, 'The centrist theme in modern British politics', in *Peaceable Kingdom: Stability and Change in Modern Britain* (Oxford, 1982). For histories of the various coalitions in this period see John Turner, *British Politics and the Great War: Coalition and Conflict 1915–1918* (New Haven, 1992), Kenneth O. Morgan, *Consensus and Disunity: The Lloyd George Coalition Government, 1918–1922* (Oxford, 1979) and Nick Smart, *The National Governments, 1931–40* (1999).

Party doctrine and thought

For introductions to the subject see Michael Bentley, 'Party doctrine and thought', in Michael Bentley and John Stevenson, eds, *High and Low Politics in Modern Britain: Ten Studies* (Oxford, 1983), Rodney Barker, *Political Ideas in Modern Britain* (1987) and W.H. Greenleaf, *The British Political Tradition, II, The Ideological Heritage* (1983). For Labour's political thought and socialism see John Callaghan, *Socialism in Britain since 1884* (Oxford, 1990), Geoffrey Foote, *The Labour Party's Political Thought: A History* 2nd edn (1986) and Noel Thompson, *Political Economy and the Labour Party: The Economics of Democratic Socialism, 1884–1995* (1996). For MacDonald's contribution see Rodney Barker's excellent 'Socialism and progressivism in the political thought of Ramsay MacDonald', in A.J.A. Morris, ed., *Edwardian Radicalism* (1974). Among the many works on Liberalism there is much of value for this period in Peter Clarke, *Liberals and Social Democrats* (Cambridge, 1978) and Michael Freeden, *The New Liberalism: An Ideology of Social Reform* (Oxford, 1978) and *Liberalism Divided: A Study in British Political Thought 1914–1939* (Oxford, 1986). On Conservative thought in this period there are particularly valuable insights in Paul Smith, ed., *Lord Salisbury on Politics: A selection from his articles in the Quarterly Review, 1860–1883* (Cambridge, 1972) and Philip Williamson's 'The doctrinal politics of Stanley Baldwin', in Michael Bentley, ed., *Public and Private Doctrine* (Cambridge, 1993) and Williamson's *Stanley Baldwin, Conservative Leadership and National Values* (Cambridge, 1999).

Index